Worship that Cares

Worship that Cares

An Introduction to Pastoral Liturgy

Mark Earey

scm press

© Mark Earey 2012

Published in 2012 by SCM Press
Editorial office
Invicta House
108-114 Golden Lane,
London, EC1Y 0TG, UK

SCM Press is an imprint of Hymns Ancient & Modern Ltd
(a registered charity)
13A Hellesdon Park Road
Norwich NR6 5DR, UK

www.scmpress.co.uk

British Library Cataloguing in Publication data

A catalogue record for this book is available
from the British Library

978-0-334-04411-6
Kindle 978-0-334-04475-8

Typeset by The Manila Typesetting Company
Printed and bound by
CPI Group (UK) Ltd, Croydon, CR0 4YY

Contents

Acknowledgements

The late Michael Vasey was my liturgy tutor during my training for ordination, and has shaped much of my thinking. I owe him more than I can say. In parish ministry I have been fortunate to work with wonderful colleagues who have taught me much, either deliberately or by osmosis. They include Canon Glynn Richerby, Canon Chris Collins, the Revd Margaret Dye, the Revd Anne Woods and the Revd Heather Woods. I would also like to thank the congregations and communities of South Wigston in Leicester, Princes Park in Chatham, and Morley in West Yorkshire, where I honed the practical skills in pastoral liturgy on which I draw in this book and began the pondering about the principles which has informed my thinking ever since. Where I have used examples from my own experiences in these places, I have changed the names of those involved in order to protect their privacy.

This book has developed out of a course I teach at the Queen's Foundation for Ecumenical Theological Education in Birmingham, and I would like to thank all those who have been part of the Pastoral Liturgy module, who may well spot elements of conversation and discussion in those classes which are reflected here. In particular, the Revds Wendy Biddington, David Ford, Nancy Goodrich and Alison Richards have given me valuable feedback on the draft text and made suggestions for improvement and for examples and case studies. None of them are, of course, responsible for any inadequacies which remain.

At Queen's we train Anglicans and Methodists for ordained ministry, so we are always conscious of the need not to make assumptions about how things are in all churches. Increasingly we also welcome leaders and members from Black-majority Pentecostal Churches and other Independent Churches to share in our learning. I would particularly like to thank the students from these churches, who have sat graciously through some of the minutiae of Anglican (and occasionally Methodist) requirements, and have consistently challenged me and other students to remember how broad is the range of perspectives in the Church in the UK today. If most of what follows in this book still tends to draw on Methodist and Anglican perspectives, I can only plead that these are the traditions I know best, and if I talk about them more it does not mean that I assume that they matter more, either to God or to me.

I would like to thank my colleagues at The Queen's Foundation for allowing me the privilege of a term's study leave in which to focus on the writing of this book. Those in the Centre for Ministerial Formation in particular took on a range of extra work to cover for me at a busy time of report writing. I count it a privilege to work with these colleagues, and it was a wonderful gift from them to be released to read and think and write. I hope they consider it was worth it.

Above all those mentioned above, however, I must thank Alison and Hannah, who accompany me on my own pastoral journey – liturgical or otherwise – and do so with much patience and wonderful love.

Mark Earey
The Queen's Foundation, Birmingham
The Feast of the Epiphany, 2012

Preface

This book is intended as an introduction to the principles and skills of 'pastoral liturgy', by which I mean primarily those services sometimes called pastoral rites or occasional offices – funerals, weddings, services surrounding childbirth and ministry to the sick.

It is primarily a work of reflective practice rather than a work of scholarship (though I hope that it is not unscholarly). In parish ministry, I found pastoral rites wonderfully fulfilling and enjoyed working to make what I offered better, adjusting and reviewing my practice over the course of 16 years. However, when I came to The Queen's Foundation, I found myself having to teach a module labelled Pastoral Liturgy, and it was at that point that I began to reflect more systematically on what those years of practice had taught me. Though my own ministry had included time as minister of an Anglican/Methodist Local Ecumenical Partnership Church, teaching at Queen's also caused me to reflect more ecumenically. Though I thought a lot about what I was doing when I was doing it, it was only when I stepped back and looked at the wide range of pastoral services that I began to see how the elements of developed practice and the instincts of the moment shared some common frameworks. It is these frameworks which I have tried to name and articulate here, and to reflect on further.

We begin with an overview of the ways that worship can be a means of pastoral care. This includes the ways that Sunday worship can extend care to those who attend, before moving on to those acts of worship which begin with a particular pastoral need. Although focusing on some of the pastoral services which are common in Christian churches, the book also aims to consider the principles which underlie these 'standard' rites, so that they can also be applied to what might be considered 'new' pastoral contexts or needs (such as rites to mark retirement, leaving home, etc.), and to those situations which are often not acknowledged in church circles (such as divorce, miscarriage, etc.). A final section discusses ways that the Church can move out into the community, offering what Ann Morisy has dubbed 'apt liturgy' to help community groups to mark crises and joys with non-churchy rituals which nonetheless help people to connect with a world beyond themselves, with the divine and with the Christian story.

The end result is, I hope, a toolkit of principles and skills which can be applied across different denominations and Christian traditions, in both formal and informal contexts, and to meet traditional and non-traditional pastoral needs.

Abbreviations

Introduction

Clarifying some terms

This is a book about 'worship that cares'. By that I mean acts of worship through which people experience the love of God and the pastoral care of the Church. The subtitle of this book uses the term 'pastoral liturgy', and I shall use this term regularly as a convenient shorthand for 'worship that cares'. I realize that this is a risk, because for some the word 'liturgy' carries with it particular baggage, some of it negative. However, there is no escaping the dangers of terminology, because for others the word 'worship' has become too closely associated with singing and music of a particular style. To be clear, then, in this book I will generally use *worship* and *liturgy* to mean public corporate worship of whatever form or style. Neither term should be taken to imply a particular level of formality (often associated with the use of the word 'liturgy') or informality (often associated with the use of the word 'worship'), and when I talk about them, I am not necessarily assuming the use of a particular service book.[1]

In the wider Church, 'pastoral liturgy' is a term that can be understood in different ways. It began to be used primarily in the Roman Catholic Church in the 1960s in the wake of the Second Vatican Council, and in its mould-breaking first public document, *The Constitution on the Sacred Liturgy (Sacrosanctum Concilium)*.[2]

---

1 For more on the terms 'worship' and 'liturgy', see Mark Earey, *Liturgical Worship: A Fresh Look – How It Works, Why It Matters*, London: Church House Publishing, 2002, pp. 13–26.

2 The text of *Sacrosanctum Concilium* is published in various places, including, Austin Flannery (ed.), *Vatican Council II: The Basic 16 Documents*.

This document shook up liturgy in the Catholic Church, and one of the resulting changes was the need to improve training in liturgical skills. 'Pastoral liturgy' became the common term for this new approach, stressing the skills needed to lead real worship, as opposed to knowledge of liturgical history or theology, or the detail of canon law. Pastoral liturgy became a synonym for 'practical liturgy' or worship at the local level. Many books, organizations, and programmes of study (and not just Roman Catholic ones) continue to use the term in this way.[3]

In this book we are going to use the term pastoral liturgy in a more restricted sense to refer to the ways that corporate worship pastors, or cares for, people. We shall consider what might be called 'regular Sunday worship', but we shall do so specifically from the point of view of how such worship cares for those who are part of it, rather than considering the practicalities of how that worship is planned, led or 'performed' more generally. Our primary focus, however, will be on those services which are sometimes called pastoral rites or occasional offices (that is, services, *occasioned* by a particular need). These sorts of service include funerals, weddings, infant dedications, and so on – the services which mark stages and moments on our journey through life, and which are therefore also referred to as rites of passage. There will be more to say about this latter terminology later in the book. In addition, we shall consider services of wholeness and healing. Corporate healing services are not usually rites of passage in the strict sense, though the rites of anointing and reconciliation when used with individuals can have that aspect. Services of wholeness and healing are, however, places where worship is often experienced or sought in a strongly pastoral

---

Constitutions, Decrees, Declarations, Northport, NY: Costello, 1996. It is also available online at www.vatican.va.

3 For instance, Harold Winstone (ed.), *Pastoral Liturgy: A Symposium*, London: Collins, 1975, and from a more recent Church of England angle, Michael Perham, *The New Handbook of Pastoral Liturgy*, London: SPCK, 2000. Though the latter book covers some of the services I shall term pastoral rites, its view is much broader, and it covers the practicalities of good Sunday liturgy as well as the more specific pastoral services.

mode, and so they too come under our umbrella of worship that cares.

I will use *pastoral rite* or *pastoral service* to refer to a particular act of worship which is pastorally focused (that is, not Sunday worship for a regular congregation, but an act of worship which comes out of a particular pastoral need or context for a specific individual or group). The word *rite* should not be heard to imply a particular style or form. I mean simply a combination of word and action, whether that is informal or formalized, spontaneous or meticulously planned.

Pastoral rites and the sacraments

One of the ways that Christians have approached pastoral rites is to consider them under the umbrella of the seven sacraments of Catholic tradition:

- Baptism.
- Confirmation.
- Eucharist (sometimes called Holy Communion, the Lord's Supper, or Mass).
- Marriage.
- Reconciliation (often called Penance or Sacramental Confession).
- Ordination.
- Anointing (sometimes called the Last Rites or Extreme Unction when used at the end of someone's life).

Books from a Catholic perspective (whether Roman or Anglican) often use this framework, and those wanting to read more on the topics covered in this book will find that some of them are covered in books which are about the seven sacraments.[4] Some,

---

4 See, for example, Joseph Martos, *Doors to the Sacred: A Historical Introduction to Sacraments in the Christian Church*, London: SCM Press, 1981, or Liam Kelly, *Sacraments Revisited: What Do They Mean Today?* London: Darton, Longman and Todd, 1998.

who do not necessarily hold rigidly to the model of seven sacraments, have taken the model and considered the seven as places
of connection with God's grace and as loci or foci of God's presence, and have applied the model by extrapolation to other life
experiences too.[5] Hence, the framework is often used as a way
of structuring thinking about pastoral rites. However, this approach also has some weaknesses.

Though at first glance the list of seven sacraments looks as
if it parallels the journey through life, a closer look reveals a
more complex situation. The first thing to notice is that not all
sacraments would be experienced by all people, not even by all
Christians. Ordination and marriage, for instance, are particular
callings which not all Christians share. More fundamentally, the
two key points on the human journey – birth and death – are not
explicitly included. Baptism can look like a birth rite, but only in
a cultural context in which infant baptism dominates. Similarly,
funerals do not feature in the list. The only sacramental rite in
the seven which relates to death is anointing (coupled with viati-
cum, the final receiving of the Eucharist), and then only if it is
skewed to become the 'last rites' – less about healing and more
about preparation for dying.

In addition, there is much disagreement among Christians
about exactly how to understand sacraments. We cannot even
agree about how many there are. For Catholic and Orthodox
Christians there are the seven listed above. However, this clear
categorization was only formalized in the West in the twelfth
century. Before that the list varied considerably and the term
sacrament could be used to refer to any object with sacred use
or symbolism. For most Christians of a Protestant tradition
there are only two sacraments; the dominical or gospel sacraments of Eucharist and baptism. For Protestant Christians these
two are 'safe' because they are clearly instituted by Christ in
the New Testament. The Roman Catholic Church also considers

---

5 See, for instance, Stephen Burns, *SCM Studyguide to Liturgy*, London, SCM
Press, 2006, pp. 142–5, for an outline of how Protestant traditions 'tend to focus the care of persons around the moments touched by the seven sacraments'
(p. 144).

sacraments to have been instituted by Christ, but the evidence in Scripture can be much more tentative or ambiguous, for Christ is also understood to institute a sacrament through the developing tradition of the Church. But the disagreements go further than that.

First, even if we could agree about how many sacraments there are, Christians have very different views about how they work and what they do. This often results in tangles and arguments about *which* objects, symbols and actions are required, and *who* may perform them.

Second, the sacramental model assumes that a sacrament is a covenanted way of receiving God's grace or encountering God's presence. That leaves a huge question about whether there are other ways of encountering God's presence in the events of our lives. What about those pastoral events which don't fit the seven sacraments grid, even when it is stretched and expanded? The model can be restrictive, as Roger Grainger reminds us:

> The Church tends to use its rites of passage as barriers rather than gateways: only such and such kinds of people can be baptized, married, buried, remembered in church. This happens, though, because the Church tends to underestimate ritual anyway; or rather it respects its theological meaning and its ecclesiastical significance while misunderstanding its psychological, and sociological, functions.[6]

I would rather work with what Adrian Thatcher has called 'a non-possessive approach to the dispensing of God's grace' which recognizes and rejoices in God's action beyond the mediating structures of the Church.[7]

Third, for Christians such as Quakers and the Salvation Army the sacramental model does not help because they do not have a regular use of sacraments (even the two dominical ones). They

---

6 Roger Grainger, *The Message of the Rite: The Significance of Christian Rites of Passage*, Cambridge: Lutterworth Press, 1988, p. 21.

7 Adrian Thatcher, *Marriage after Modernity: Christian Marriage in Postmodern Times*, Sheffield: Sheffield Academic Press, 1999, p. 243.

need a different way of forming theological principles and liturgical ideas which can help them care through their worship.

At times it can feel as if a terminological tail is wagging a theological dog: that is, we have inherited the term 'sacrament' and now spend much time and energy trying to make our understanding of God's action fit this particular grid. Perhaps the taxi driver giving directions to a confused and harassed traveller was right: 'If I were you, I wouldn't start from here'. I intend to start somewhere else.

TO THINK ABOUT – Christendom and the seven sacraments

One of the complications of the seven sacraments model is that it lumps together a range of rites which seem to fit well together in a Christendom context, but not necessarily beyond it. Hence, one of two things happens.

The first possibility is that all rites are conformed to the baptism and initiation model, and become seen as means of deepening a Christian commitment. In this way of thinking, a Christian wedding must somehow help me in my Christian discipleship, and becomes odd to imagine for someone whose discipleship has not yet begun. A Christian funeral, likewise, only makes sense as a rite to commend a Christian disciple into God's nearer presence.

The other possibility is for baptism (and confirmation) to be conformed to other rites, and become primarily markers on the human journey, so that baptism becomes a birth rite (associated with babies) rather than a rite of new birth (associated with faith in Christ) and confirmation becomes a rite of adolescence.

Once the seven sacrament package is placed to one side, baptism, confirmation and ordination are freed to operate as rites of passage connected with definite and decided Christian discipleship, and other pastoral rites are freed from carrying that weight. This will be very important when exploring the model of pastoral rites as a gift from the Church which I will be developing later.

However, though I will not be organizing my consideration of pastoral rites in a framework closely tied to the seven sacraments grid, I want to affirm two aspects of the sacramental approach which are important. The first is the basic idea that God uses physical objects, symbols and actions to work in our lives. I am taking this as fundamental. The second is an expectation that pastoral rites are used by God to actually 'do' something, and are not merely visual aids or testimony to something which has happened somewhere else and at some other time. The approach taken in this book is sacramental, but only in this broad and generous sense. I intend to approach pastoral rites by analysing some of the key theological and liturgical principles and tools of ritual which can be transferred and applied both to the traditional sacraments and also to new pastoral needs, arising from contexts not envisaged by the traditional pattern.

Some theological foundations

Though I am not relying on a traditional seven sacraments framework in thinking about pastoral services, there are some key theological foundations which connect with what sacramental theologies are seeking to protect and express. The three theological foundations which are essential for this are:

- **Creation** – the fundamental belief that God is the source of all creation, that the created order is created good, and that every human being, whether professing the Christian faith or not, is made in God's image, is valuable to God and can be helped to connect with that image within them.
- **Incarnation** – the further insight, that Christ's incarnation forces us to engage with the created order, and humanity in particular, as a place made holy, a place to encounter God in Christ, and not something to be escaped from or avoided in favour of something more 'spiritual'.
- **Salvation** – the recognition that there is, nonetheless, a call on us to follow Christ, to be changed by God to be more like Christ and to recover the image of God in us which is so often hidden or spoiled. This suggests that the metaphor of life as a journey will be a helpful one in recognizing that change is part of God's work in us.

These foundations are crucial to our later thinking about a key question for churches today: is it right (or even possible) to offer Christian rites for non-Christian persons? My contention is that the answer can be 'Yes'. The foundations which I have outlined above form the basis for this answer, and though they connect with a sacramental model, I think they are more clearly applied if they are separated from it and stand on their own.

Worship on life's journey

It has become a cliché to describe life as a journey, but that makes it neither untrue nor necessarily unhelpful. For every person the journey involves key moments (the sort of moments that, either at the time or in retrospect, mark key turning points) and more ordinary periods. For Christians (and, in different ways, those of other faiths) that journey will be interspersed with worship. There are two basic ways in which that worship may care for us.

First, we are cared for through the regular worship of the Church. For some, participation in this corporate worship may be daily, or several times a week. For others the worship may be weekly, or less frequent. However frequent or infrequent it may be, each of us brings to this corporate worship our own concerns and the pastoral needs and events which are current in our own lives.

Second, we are cared for through special acts of worship which take as their starting point an event or need in the journey of a particular individual or family. Typical examples include marriage or funerals.

In the first chapter we will focus on the first of these ways that worship pastors people, through regular corporate worship. The rest of the book will then consider in greater depth how particular acts of worship which are geared to the needs of a particular person or group can also care for people.

I

Worship that Cares on Sundays

One way of understanding liturgy – the public, corporate, worship of the Church – is that it helps to provide a map for the journey.[1] It prepares us 'on paper' as it were, for the actual journey of life, so that when we meet particular features for real, we recognize them from the map and are at least partly better equipped to negotiate them.

For instance, through regular preaching about the death and resurrection of Jesus Christ, and through the regular pattern of the Christian year, Good Friday, Easter and so on, the Christian's understanding of, and assumptions about, death are shaped, so that we have a 'map' to help us negotiate that difficult terrain when a loved one dies or we face our own mortality. This is pastoral care through worship – primarily of a preparatory or orientational nature. Corporate worship shapes us for living.

There may be other ways in which regular corporate worship can care for people. Leslie Virgo suggests that the very nature of worship itself is part of long-term pastoral care, giving us the bigger perspective of the One who is beyond us yet loves us, enabling us to see ourselves as loved and valued.[2] However, more than simply giving us a bigger vision, worship allows us to begin to live it, to act it out, through its 'dramatic' quality – it cares

---

1 For more on how Sunday worship can help people negotiate life, see Tim Stratford, 'Using Worship to Negotiate an Action Reflection Cycle', in Tim Stratford (ed.), Worship: Window of the Urban Church, London: SPCK, 2006, pp. 127–42.

2 'Worship and Pastoral Care', in Leslie Virgo (ed.), First Aid in Pastoral Care, Edinburgh: T&T Clark, 1987, pp. 253–63.

for us by allowing for imagined change in our lives.[3] This in turn releases us to love others: for some this may be a release from self-absorption; for others, a release from self-loathing.

One would hope that this would be true simply by virtue of following Christ, but the act of worship takes these truths and articulates them, inviting us to 'act them out' in the concrete world of words and actions, rather than merely in our own thoughts and feelings. Ritual makes these truths physical. In this sense we might agree with Elaine Ramshaw that 'the paradigmatic act of pastoral care is the act of presiding at the worship of the gathered community'.[4] Where the presiding is done well and with appropriate hospitality, people are helped to feel and discover God's love.

For Ramshaw, there is a further dimension, for the minister's role in regularly leading corporate worship means that she or he is also seen as a potential ritualizer in other more 'pastoral' contexts, 'holding out the possibility of access to a symbolic world large enough and powerful enough to embrace the most intractable events of life and death'.[5] In practice, this means that a pastoral conversation might naturally lead into 'a prayer, or a ritual touch, to heal or bless or absolve . . . a wordless kneeling together, a symbol of the community of beseeching . . .'.[6]

Regular corporate worship can also care in more direct, short-term ways, making a difference there and then. Here are some of the ways that Sunday worship can care:

- The sort of welcome we receive when we come to worship may reflect the welcome that God offers and help us to feel part of a loving community.
- The opportunity to hear and receive God's forgiveness through the regular corporate confession in worship may

---

3 For more, see Mark Earey, *Worship as Drama* (Grove Worship Series 140), Cambridge: Grove Books, 1997.

4 Elaine Ramshaw, *Ritual and Pastoral Care*, Philadelphia: Fortress Press, 1987, p. 13.

5 Ramshaw, *Ritual*, p. 57.

6 Ramshaw, *Ritual*, p. 57.

help us to be released from guilt and to learn to live with our weaknesses, knowing we are loved even with them.

- The prayers of intercession may touch on something which is pertinent in my life, or simply hearing myself prayed for may boost my morale or help me recognize my worth to God.

- The sermon may connect with life experiences which I share. The mere mention of them in a sermon can help, but the sermon may go on to give practical advice, comfort, reassurance, or challenge, all of which may help me to face the realities of my life through the week.

- The chance simply to be with other people may be 'caring', before and after the service, but also during the sharing of the Peace. There is anecdotal evidence that reminds us that for some people, that Sunday handshake and greeting is the only physical contact they might have had with other human beings all week.

IN PRACTICE – The power of touch

Here is one minister's recent experience: 'At the Christmas morning service, a single man spoke to me and said how rarely he had human contact. I turned and was approached by another man who was struggling for breath but had made it to church. His son asked if I would speak to him before I rushed to the next service. I knelt down beside him and held his hand, not knowing what to say, and let God do the rest.'

Some of this caring will happen subconsciously: we may not be aware that it is doing us good, but when we look back over years of experience of it, we recognize that it has strengthened us for all that life throws at us. Certainly we may often come to church with no particular agenda for the care we need, but leave conscious that God's care has been felt or God's finger placed on a particular need.

Sometimes it is different: the particular need in my own life is more obvious to me, and I am much more conscious of it. When I come to church, I may be hoping for some help with it. For example, I may bring with me the fact of my impending redundancy.

This is not necessarily shared by other worshippers, but the worship I experience may care for me by helping me to recognize God's love for me and God's desire to help me through this particular need and time. This might come through something said in the sermon or through something mentioned in prayers of intercession, or it could be something more personal which I hear in the words of a song or hymn.

When Sunday worship does not care

Sadly, worship can have the opposite effect. The welcome which I should have received at the door was lacking, and I had to push my way past a group of the congregation chatting happily but completely indifferent to my arrival. The confession, which was meant to leave me feeling cleansed and free, instead passes so quickly that I am not properly able to engage with it, and am left holding the burden of guilt instead of having let it go. When it comes to the sermon, a thoughtless joke leaves me feeling on the edge rather than included, and the prayers make assumptions about how I will feel about the global financial situation which do not ring true. The songs and hymns chosen this morning seem to suggest that all I need to do to be happy as a Christian is to keep trusting in God, but I have been trusting for weeks, and all that seems to happen is things get worse and I feel scared and helpless. Finally, I decide to go to the side chapel at the end of the service where prayer with laying on of hands is being offered. I explain the situation which I face and am told by the person offering prayer that 'all things work together for good' and that probably I just need a bit more faith and then things will start to look up.

TO THINK ABOUT – Confession and forgiveness

I had always understood confession to be a positive aspect of Sunday worship, setting us free at the start of a service, so that we could focus on God. Then I listened to someone who had come to our church for the first time. They shared their feeling that the

---

service had 'rubbed their nose' in their own sinfulness, and they had left church feeling worse about themselves than when they started. Within minutes of the service starting, they said, we were 'banging on' about how unworthy we all were and how much we needed mercy, and this had gone on throughout the service. I begged to disagree – the whole point of the confession was to get that out of the way, so that we could worship as forgiven people. But then I looked again at the order of service for our communion service, and there it was: a constant and repeated request for mercy, which, to my friend's ears, made it sound as if God's love was grudging and had to be dragged out of him.

From the newcomer's perspective, having confessed our sins and been told that we were forgiven, we promptly behaved as if we were not really sure it was true. The absolution had been followed by the *Gloria in Excelsis* ('Lord Jesus Christ, only Son of the Father . . . you take away the sin of the world: have mercy on us . . .'). Before long we were praying for the world in our intercessions ('Lord in your mercy / hear our prayer'). As we got near to communion the Lord's Prayer reminded us yet again of our sin ('Forgive us our trespasses, as we forgive those who trespass against us . . .') and then we sang *Agnus Dei* ('Jesus, Lamb of God, have mercy on us'). The invitation to communion made it clear that our natural state is unworthiness ('Jesus is the Lamb of God who takes away the sin of the world . . . Lord, I am not worthy to receive you, but only say the word . . .') and this was followed by the Prayer of Humble Access which further reinforced the theme, reminding us that 'we are not worthy so much as to gather up the crumbs from under your table . . .'. I began to see the point, and I never saw confession the same way again. Even what we call it can make a difference: 'Confession and Forgiveness' might enable us to emphasize the positive point of it all, in a way that just 'Confession' or 'Prayers of Penitence' does not.

There is also a deeper question, which is about whether confession (which assumes specific sin, and a sense of guilt) is itself enough to care for worshippers today. Without wanting to deny the reality of sin and the need to address it, some have suggested that the more pressing need for many people today is to deal with a sense of shame, unworthiness or lack of self-esteem, rather than guilt. As Fraser Watts has observed: '. . . the liturgical practice of forgiveness speaks to guilt rather than to shame.'[7] What is needed is a bigger framework which affirms the love of God for the individual, and helps each person to hear and receive the message that they are loved and worthy – something which many traditional patterns of worship are not well-placed to do, if they constantly interrupt every affirmation of God's love with a reminder that we are unworthy sinners.

Ways that Sunday worship can pastor people

To sum up, there are several ways that ordinary Sunday worship can care for people. Different persons may experience that care in different ways, to different extents and in different parts of the service, but for most people there are some key ways that we can make sure that worship cares for people. We have noted above the ways that different aspects of the service can provide some of that care, but there are other, more subtle, ways that Sunday worship can care, or might fail to care.

- The most obvious way that worship can care is when there is a clear and explicit mention of **particular needs**, either pro-actively when the need could be anticipated (for instance, someone praying about the impact of the global financial crisis, or a sermon about how to deal with debt) or responsively (for instance, prayer for a bereaved family in the prayers of intercession).

---

7 Fraser Watts, 'Concluding Reflections', in Fraser Watts and Liz Gulliford (eds), *Forgiveness in Context: Theology and Psychology in Creative Dialogue*, London: T&T Clark, 2004, p. 185. See also, Neil Pembroke, *Pastoral Care in Worship: Liturgy and Psychology in Dialogue*, London: T&T Clark, 2010, p. 40. Barbara Glasson reflects on similar issues in relation to the particular needs of those who are survivors of abuse in *A Spirituality of Survival*, London: Continuum, 2009, pp. 136–41. John Watson includes some reflections on the implications for preaching and worship in *Shame* (Grove Pastoral Series 101), Cambridge: Grove Books, 2005, pp. 23–5.

- More subtly, worship can care through ensuring basic **human contact and belonging** – simply being with others, listening and being listened to, sharing the peace, being touched, having a part to play. There are ways to encourage and foster this in worship, and ways in which it can be inhibited. It is essentially connected with the fundamental necessity for corporate participation and engagement in worship itself, so that I know that my presence in the act of worship is important and valued. It must not be relegated only to the coffee and chat after the service is over.[8]

- Equally subtle is the care that comes not so much from having a need acknowledged but simply from **your 'reality' being named** – that is, a recognition that you exist. At a very basic level, can everyone access the worship? For instance, is there level access for wheelchair users and those with prams or buggies? Is there a hearing loop for those who use hearing aids, and have you thought about provision for signing of services for those who are deaf or deafened? Are there large-print copies of orders of service and/or hymnbooks for those with visual impairment, and if your worship is all on-screen, have you considered the implications for those who cannot easily see the words? Then think about content. What about the notices, for instance? Who gets mentioned and which events get included, and who is not mentioned or whose concerns do not feature? Or what about those who take a visible 'up front' role? Do they reflect the congregation, or more importantly, the wider community? Do any women preach or lead worship? Are all the musicians of a certain age or ethnicity? Perhaps all the sermon illustrations are about family, and you are single. Are lay people's perspectives included, or are all the examples in sermons based on a particular idea of calling and service which assumes full-time ministry or ordination? Here we hit the crucial question: whose human story gets heard? It is hard enough to expand this from the church leaders to 'ordinary' church members, though it can happen through the giving of testimony,

---

8 Ramshaw, *Ritual*, pp. 29–30.

a variety of persons and approaches in preaching, and through a breadth of approach to prayers of intercession. But how do we hear the stranger's story? It can be hard to make room for the stories of those who are 'different' when we are trying to attract more people 'like us' into church.[9]

- To be 'included' is a key step forward in worship caring for you, but it is not always the same as **your reality being 'us'**. Many churches seek to include a whole range of different people, but it is still very clear who the assumed 'norm' is. Often the give-away is in the way that people are spoken of: some are 'we' and 'us' and some are 'they' and 'them'. Perhaps it is obvious from the jokes in the sermon or from the notices or prayers, that everyone here is assumed to be sighted or heterosexual, or well-educated. Who do we pray for? If we pray for 'the poor', for instance, there is a clear, if unintended, assumption that the poor are 'out there' and not in here with us, praying the same prayer and singing the same songs. Not only so, but by using labels like that we risk de-humanizing people by referring to them as a category ('the poor') or defining them in terms of just one aspect of their experience as humans. And it is not just about how words are used. Perhaps at communion you include gluten-free bread for those who need it? How different it feels for those who need that provision when *everyone* has gluten-free bread and they no longer feel 'special'.

CASE STUDY – Praying for the children

There are many churches which would consider themselves child-friendly and where children are seen as the church of today, not merely the potential church of tomorrow, and then when it is time for the sermon and children leave the main worship space to go to age-specific groups the prayer for 'them' gives it away. Very

---

9 There is helpful reflection on the importance of story and which stories get told in Sunday worship in Herbert Anderson and Edward Foley, *Mighty Stories, Dangerous Rituals: Weaving Together the Human and the Divine*, San Francisco: Jossey-Bass, 2001, pp. 149–66.

often the prayer goes something like this: 'Dear God, we thank you so much for our children and all they mean to us. Bless them as they leave us to go to their groups and guide those who lead them. Amen.' Notice the use of 'us' and 'our', 'them' and 'they' in this prayer. In this case the adults are 'us'. They are seen as the default church members (they are certainly not going to be leaving the worship area to go and sit in a cold church hall) and the children are 'them' whom 'we' pray for. It is not just that the children are the ones who leave the main space, it is the prayer itself which signals that adults are the norm. If the children prayed for the adults, or if someone prayed for all of us, of every age, as we take part in learning, then it would be clear that the children are 'us' too.

- Another key way of making Sunday worship pastoral is by making sure that the service includes room for a **range of emotional responses,** and not just a narrow range of praise or thankfulness. Many have recognized that one of the weaknesses of worship today is its lack of space for rage, protest or lament.[10] Some traditional hymns, while sometimes offering simplistic perspectives, do at least recognize that life is not always easy (for instance, 'What a friend we have in Jesus', with its, 'Have we trials and temptations?'). Many modern worship songs can be equally simplistic and take a much more relentlessly upbeat tone, which can make them hard to sing when life is not treating you well. However, some writers are recognizing this and working to give expression to the hard times in the Christian life as well as the good times. A notable recent example of this is Matt and Beth Redman's 'Blessed be your name', which includes lines about 'the road marked with suffering' and 'pain in the offering'.[11] Though this is not exactly rage or lament, it is a step away from naïve triumphalism. Perhaps one of the

---

10 See, among others, Paul Bradbury, *Sowing in Tears: How to Lament in a Church of Praise* (Grove Worship Series 193), Cambridge: Grove Books, 2007, and Pembroke, *Pastoral Care*, Chapters 3 and 4.

11 Matt and Beth Redman, 'Blessed be your name', ThankYou Music, 2002. See also www.resoundworship.org for other worship songs on themes such as

reasons why silence can be so important in worship is that it makes space for a range of responses and emotions, rather than putting words into the congregation's mouths which impute feelings they may not be experiencing.

- Finally, it is important to recognize that true pastoral care through worship may include our reality being **challenged** as well as recognized. 'The "sweet hour of prayer" can be used as an hour in which to reinforce our defenses, our denial, and to shore up our beliefs about ourselves and others, beliefs that sometimes need to be challenged.'[12] In other areas of pastoral care the true pastor has to ask hard and challenging questions, to suggest other possible ways of seeing things, to make room for growth and development. In worship which is pastoral we also need to address questions such as how can liturgy or songs move from simply reinforcing our assumptions, and comforting us in challenging circumstances. How can we move beyond the cosy, to make room for change, growth, and transformation?

Inclusive language as pastoral care

One of the key issues in inclusion is how we use language.[13] Though the term 'inclusive language' has come to be used primarily of language which avoids forms of speech that can be heard to exclude women (or to normalize the masculine), it can also be extended to other areas in which the use of language in

---

'Brokenness' and 'Lament', such as Judy Gresham's 'Lord, why does it seem you're so far away? When I need you most, don't cover your face.'

12 William H. Willimon, *Worship as Pastoral Care*, Nashville: Abingdon, 1979, p. 63.

13 For more on a broad range of issues of marginalization and inclusion in worship, see Stephen Burns, Nicola Slee and Michael N. Jagessar (eds), *The Edge of God: New Liturgical Texts and Contexts in Conversation*, London: Epworth, 2008. There is a brief but very clear summary of some of the issues mentioned here in Janet R. Walton, *Feminist Liturgy: A Matter of Justice*, Collegeville, MN: Liturgical Press, 2000, pp. 34–6. For inclusive language in songs and hymns see Mark Earey, *How to Choose Songs and Hymns for Worship* (Grove Worship Series 201), Cambridge: Grove Books, 2009, pp. 16–18.

worship can subconsciously reinforce or create negative associations which impact on particular people.

Race

Because the English language makes no clear distinction between darkness of colour (including darkness of skin colour) and darkness caused by the absence of light, the consistent use of 'darkness' in ways that associate it with evil, danger, and the unspiritual can be heard to reinforce racist stereotypes. The Bible regularly contrasts light and darkness, and in English usage it is a small step for this to sound like a contrast between *white* and darkness. Because this imagery pervades so many hymns and songs, and so much biblical and liturgical material, it is not easy to address, but one important step is to be aware of the impact when it is used relentlessly. Some have suggested that phrasing which contrasts light and *shadows* may be more helpful.[14]

Disability

There are other ways that the language of hymns and songs can marginalize the experience of people who have disabilities. For blind people who live with 'darkness' as a normal state, the constant equation of darkness with sin and evil (as mentioned above) can have a negative impact, and marginalizes their experience of darkness. In addition, John Hull has written about the way that many hymns use physical blindness as a metaphor for spiritual fault, and the way this can reinforce prejudice and a sense of marginalization. Examples include the hymn 'Thou whose almighty word', with its lines: 'health to the sick in mind,

---

14 See Michael Jagessar and Stephen Burns, 'Liturgical Studies and Christian Worship: The post-colonial challenge', *Black Theology*, 5, No. 1, 2007, and their Chapter 5 'Hymns Old and New: Towards a Postcolonial Gaze', in Burns, Slee and Jagessar, *The Edge of God*, for a fuller discussion of the issues. See also Michael N. Jagessar and Stephen Burns (eds), *Christian Worship: Postcolonial Perspectives*, London: Equinox, 2011.

sight to the inly blind.'[15] Blindness is not the only form of disability to which this applies.

Anti-Semitism

Some hymns may reinforce or support anti-Semitic sentiment, which has been such a deep and shameful element of Christian tradition. For instance, the hymn 'My song is love unknown' (Samuel Crossman, 1624–83) includes this verse:

> Sometimes they strew his way,
> and his sweet praises sing;
> resounding all the day
> hosannas to their King.
> Then 'Crucify!' is all their breath,
> and for his death they thirst and cry.

The 'they' in this verse is clearly those who encountered Jesus in his own day, including those who ultimately called for his crucifixion. This can easily become a projection of blame for the death of Jesus onto the Jews of Jesus' day, and thence to a projection onto Jewish people generally. The hymn and the singers may not intend that, but it can *reinforce* prejudice that is stirred up in other more explicit ways. This is particularly so when this verse is contrasted with other verses which speak so clearly of 'my dear Lord', so that 'we' are associated with Jesus, over against 'them', who are responsible for his death. This is not the only song or hymn to run this risk.[16]

---

15 John Marriott (1780–1825). Another example is from John Newton's 'Amazing Grace': 'I once was lost, but now am found, was blind, but now I see'. For more on this issue, see Burns, Slee and Jagessar, *The Edge of God*, Chapter 8, 'Songs without Words: Incorporating the linguistically marginalized' by Frances Young and Chapter 10, '"Lord, I was Deaf": Images of disability in the hymn books' by John Hull. Further writing by John Hull can be accessed at www. johnmhull.biz.

16 'Lo, he comes with clouds descending' (John Cennick, 1718–55, Charles Wesley, 1707–88, and others) includes the verse: 'Those who set at naught and sold him . . . shall the true Messiah see', which is a clear reference to the Jews of Jesus' day.

Us and them

What all of this reinforces is the need, already mentioned above, to question the implied 'us' in any prayer, or hymn, or song, and the consequentially implied 'they' and 'them'. Who are 'we' – does it mean the whole human race? Or perhaps it only means Christians (especially ones that share our views or are part of our nation or denomination)? Or does it just mean those who are sharing now in this act of worship? These are huge issues, and the more we explore, the more complex it gets. Many of the problems which are identified have long-term rather than short-term impacts, and it is therefore hard to show easily how they affect people. In all likelihood, as soon as we recognize and begin to address one potential problem, we will cause another. But that is no reason not to even make the attempt, and sometimes a basic awareness can save unintended damage being done. Whatever our reaction to the particular issues raised here, there can be no argument with the basic idea that the way we use words and symbols and images, the stories and jokes we tell, and the issues which make it onto the weekly church notice sheet will all play a part in shaping assumptions about who belongs and who is here, who matters and who is within God's love.

Beyond content to process

There is a further level to be aware of, which goes beyond the content of worship and reaches to the deeper levels of how worship is planned and led, who makes the decisions, how authority is exercised and so on. These too can have pastoral implications for those in our congregations. Feminist theologians have often been at the forefront of helping us to explore these issues, along with others who come from a clearly expressed contextual starting point, such as black theology, queer theology, womanist theology, or post-colonial perspectives.

Of course, all theology comes from a contextual starting point, and none is neutral, but those who recognize their starting point and are not afraid to state it can help those of us who tend to assume that our theology is just 'regular' theology. Because these perspectives are often from the margins, they can be particularly good at seeing how well-intentioned and carefully led worship can nonetheless perpetuate oppressive or marginalizing patterns in church life and in Christian worship. These are sometimes uncomfortable voices, but they need to be heard. The patterns of worship developed among groups which experience exclusion or marginalization have a lot to teach those of us who feel we are at the centre of things, particularly about how worship is led, the importance of listening and participation in planning, and how gesture and room layout and symbols all have an impact on what results.[17]

TO THINK ABOUT – Beyond the verbal

It is not just the words that we use in worship which can inhibit or contribute to feelings of being cared for by God and others. The buildings in which we meet for worship and the ways in which they are arranged can also make an impact.

Think about your own church building. Does it speak most powerfully of a God who is transcendent and ultimate, or of a God who is immanent and intimate? Does the seating suggest a community in which relationships are cool and distant, or in which they are close and but potentially intrusive? Is it possible to hide in the building, if that is what you need to do, or do you feel dwarfed by the space, or perhaps exposed and vulnerable? In recent decades there has been a move away from seating in straight rows and more exploration of seating in circles or arcs. Circular seating can feel including, as long as you are on the inside – from the outside it can look forbidding and exclusive, and once you are inside you can feel exposed to the gaze of other worshippers. It is impossible to predict with accuracy the impact of such things on each individual worshipper, because individual needs vary so greatly. It is possible, however, to be aware that there is an impact, and not to treat buildings and the use of space as neutral factors in the way that worship can care.

---

17 For a helpful way in to some of these insights, see Walton, *Feminist Liturgy*, pp. 3–47 and 81–93.

When Sunday is not enough

This chapter has explored the ways that ordinary regular 'Sunday' worship can pastor people. The regular pattern of the Christian year, or the needs of the corporate body of the Church (or indeed of the wider community) are the things which set the agenda. My need may be met, but it is not articulated as a key aspect of the worship, and other worshippers may not be aware of it or of the way I am receiving God's care through the service.

Sometimes, however, this is not enough. Sometimes I come to church so conscious of a particular pastoral situation that it completely fills my mind and heart. That could be a bereavement, or an illness, or it could be my impending marriage, or the birth of a child. It may be that I have been the victim of crime, or discovered that my teenage daughter is pregnant. Maybe my home is in danger of being repossessed, or I have made a decision to emigrate.

In these situations, the 'ordinary worship' may still care for me, and I may leave comforted or strengthened, but in reality much of it is likely to feel either banal or that it simply does not fit my own particular need or context. That is when Sunday worship is not enough, and we need a different sort of worship to pastor us, the sort of worship that begins much more clearly with a particular need, and works from that starting point. These are the services which I am calling pastoral services, and later chapters will give us the chance to consider some of them in detail.

Before we leave Sunday worship behind, it is good to remind ourselves that the individual pastoral services and the pastoring done by regular Sunday worship cannot be kept in separate airtight containers – often the two overlap. For example, the couple who are planning on getting married in your church later in the year may well be attending regular services during the preparation time. As well as the generic caring that the service extends, there may be a more direct connection made, such as praying for them and for other couples preparing to be married in the church.

Pastoral services and mission

Pastoral services can be places where the gospel connects with those who otherwise have little connection with the Christian Church, and they produce contacts which may bear later fruit. What that fruit may be can vary. In some cases the result may be that those who have been helped by a pastoral service start to attend worship and may become members of the church. Many churches claim that they have grown in numbers primarily through careful follow-up of funeral families or wedding couples. The Church of England's Weddings Project has been just one recent context in which churches have been encouraged to maximize the potential of contacts made through pastoral services, such as weddings. For other situations the fruit may be less tangible in terms of church growth, but nonetheless significant in terms of helping people to experience something of the kingdom of God. If our mission is to be God's mission (the *missio Dei*, as it is increasingly recognized to be), then we need to think more long term than simply getting visitors to come back next week.[18]

However, we also need to recognize that the connections we make with people through pastoral services are not unproblematic, when Sunday worship is also trying to care for a range of other people whose needs may be very different.

CASE STUDY – A clash of needs

At the all age service on Sunday you notice a couple in their twenties who are joining in the marriage preparation group which is running at present.[19] On the other side of church you spot the grandparents of Jade, who was baptized in last week's service, who have presumably decided to see if church is as much fun on a normal Sunday. Just

---

18 For more on this, see Mark Earey and Carolyn Headley, *Mission and Liturgical Worship* (Grove Worship Series 170), Cambridge: Grove Books, 2002, pp. 5–11.

19 I am grateful to Stephen Burns for the ideas which I have adapted in this case study.

behind them sit several people who seem to be from one family. You recognize them as the family of Bill, whose funeral you took earlier in the week. You mentioned to them that the bereaved are included in the prayers at church on Sunday for the first few weeks after a funeral, and you guess that they have come to hear Bill mentioned and to feel the prayerful concern of the church. Bill's widow looks very uncomfortable and looks quite out of place, dressed more formally than anyone else in church, wearing mainly black.

At the start of the service, the youth group band lead some worship songs, including a song with actions which many of the young children lead from the front. You notice that the bereaved family don't join in the actions.

At the end of the service you stand at the door, ready to greet those who are not staying for refreshments. As you look around you become conscious that members of the youth group are sitting sullenly on one side of church, one boy with his head in his hands. You turn away and see the bereaved family heading straight for you. They don't look happy. They had clearly shared their feelings with the teenagers before leaving. 'You call this a church?' says the widow, 'With that lot' (she indicates the youth group) 'dressed up like they're at a football match!' This seems to be a reference to the jeans, trainers, football shirts and baseball caps which many of the young people are wearing. However, most of their anger is directed at the woman and her grandson who led the prayers. 'How could they be so insensitive as to pray for half the blooming world before they remember my mum, sitting here with her heart nearly breaking?' asks one of the widow's grown up children. Before you have a chance to answer, they are gone. Perhaps it's just as well, as it isn't clear to you what you would say in response. And things seemed to have started out so well! Let's hope those associated with the wedding and the baptism felt more cared for . . .

Above all, Sunday worship cannot and should not be hijacked for the pastoral needs of any one group of people. If Sunday worship becomes dominated by the needs of the bereaved, or the needs of those shortly to be married, or the needs of those bringing young children for baptism or blessing, then it is failing to do its core job. Sunday worship needs to be the place where the whole of the gospel is celebrated and proclaimed, and while we need to be sensitive to the needs of those who are present, the worship of God cannot be determined by the uncertainties of who might be there each week.

Summary

In this chapter we have looked at the ways that ordinary regular Sunday worship can care for people – both our regular congregations and, to a certain extent, those who may join that worship because of an experience of a particular pastoral service. In later chapters we will begin to look at particular types of pastoral service and the different ways that they care for people. Before we get into the detail of those particular services, the next chapter will explore how these pastoral rites connect with particular events in our lives, and then in the following chapter we will consider some key principles which we can apply to pastoral rites.

2

Markers on Life's Journey

We have considered the ways that regular corporate worship can form part of the Church's pastoring and caring for people along life's journey and have suggested, by way of analogy, that such worship can provide a map to help us on the journey of life. Sometimes, however, a life event which someone brings to church is too 'big' to be held or carried by regular worship alone.

One possible response to such situations is to leave the corporate worshipping context behind and move into a different mode – that of individual pastoral ministry, with a predominantly therapeutic, rather than doxological, model. An alternative response is to reach for (or create) an act of worship in which the pastoral reality is a key starting point – a pastoral liturgy. Pastoral liturgy is a way of bridging the potential gap between the pastoral instinct and the worshipping imperative and of keeping a communal focus for pastoral care rather than an individualized one. Sometimes that act of worship will mean a public service, but it can also encompass much more small-scale acts of worship which happen in domestic contexts and private pastoral meetings. For instance, the offering of prayer and anointing to someone who is sick can take place in a formal healing service, but could equally take place as an informal act of prayer and worship in someone's home or at a hospital bedside.

In this more focused act of worship, a map is again being provided, but this time it is on a much bigger scale, showing a route through this particular junction in much more detail. Perhaps a better analogy here is a sophisticated Sat Nav, which zooms in for more detail at a complicated junction to help the driver to find the right lane. To use Paul Sheppy's phrase, the rite connects with the pastoral reality by 'rehearsing' the stages of the journey.[1]

The placing of pastoral care in a worship framework, rather than merely in a pastoral ministry framework, is one of the ways of keeping the divine story in view.

> Whereas conventional practices of public worship tend to focus almost exclusively on the story of God at the expense of human stories, the contemporary impetus in pastoral care has been to attend so carefully to human experience that the divine narrative is often muted or ignored.[2]

If we imagine the telling of the God story and the telling of the human story as the two channels of a stereo sound output, then we might picture things as in Figure 1.

- In regular Sunday worship, the volume of the God story will be loudest. The context is essentially corporate and focused on the gathering of all God's people. The God story will be expressed loudly and clearly, told through Scripture and song and liturgical text as well as in preaching and other ways. The

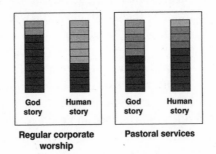

Figure 1

---

1 Paul Sheppy, *Death, Liturgy and Ritual. Volume 1: A Pastoral and Liturgical Theology*, Aldershot: Ashgate, 2003, p. 83. He applies the same map analogy to funerals on p. 104.

2 Herbert Anderson and Edward Foley, *Mighty Stories, Dangerous Rituals: Weaving Together the Human and the Divine*, San Francisco: Jossey-Bass, 2001, p. 46.

human story will be present as well, though more implicitly. It may emerge in prayers of intercession and in the application of the sermon to those present, but it will necessarily be relatively quieter, or at least less specific and more generic, as it will need to be applicable to a range of possible contexts. Individual stories will not necessarily be articulated.

- In a pastoral service, the volume of the human story will be much louder. The God story will be present and heard in scripture reading and in other ways, but the human story (this particular individual, or couple, or need for healing, etc.) will be at least as loud, possibly louder, and clearly articulated.

Understanding ritual

One of the chief ways that the 'map' (or Sat Nav) is provided is by means of the tools of ritual. Ritual is a term which is viewed with suspicion by many Christians. They associate it with 'ritualism' (an unbalanced concern for the minutiae of vesture, gesture, symbol and movement) and with worship which is dry, dull, and focused on the outer actions rather than the inner belief or faith. For some, then, ritual suggests insincerity and spiritual deadness. This is partly due to its origins as a concept at the Reformation, when people began to see true religion as what I do, and empty ritual as what you do.[3] It is important that we recognize these associations, but also resist allowing them to shape our use of the word here.

THEORY – Ritual and rites

Ritual is also a term used in a neutral sense by anthropologists, as Mary Douglas explains: 'They are in the habit of using ritual to mean action and beliefs in the symbolic order without reference to the commitment or non-commitment of the actors.'[4] Note that there is reference to beliefs here, but those beliefs are not just those of the people

---

3 Edwin Muir, *Ritual in Early Modern Europe*, Cambridge: Cambridge University Press, 2nd ed. 2005, p. 9.

4 Mary Douglas, *Natural Symbols: Explorations in Cosmology*, London: Routledge, 1996, p. 2.

most closely involved in the ritual – the beliefs are in 'the symbolic order'. Like the actions, they are connected to the worldview which is being articulated, whether they are shared by the actors or not. However, although ritual does not *guarantee* sincerity in the person speaking or acting, neither does it rule it out. Here we need to recognize the power of ritual not only to express what is true within us, but also to shape it; ritual can change what people feel or experience, or what they commit themselves to, as well as bearing testimony to these things.

The perception of insincerity which hangs around ritual finds its roots here in something which is significant; ritual does not depend on pre-existing feelings for its power. There are conditions for ritual to be effective, but these conditions do not necessarily include the right feelings of those involved. Feelings may be part of the bigger picture, but they are not determinative for the ritual. For instance, it would be natural for parents to approach the church for the blessing of their child because they are thankful to God and wish to express that – but the service does not depend on them *feeling* that thankfulness in an intense way in the service itself. The expression of thankfulness and the giving of God's blessing are both things which are formalized – not in the sense that they are meaningless or insincere, but in the sense that they are given structure and physical shape through conventional words, symbols and actions. This should mean that emotions are neither excluded nor suppressed, but are 'held'. As Jan Berry puts it:

> Ritual provides a framework in which powerful emotions can be confronted and expressed. It allows participants to enter a space beyond words, where symbols, bodily movement and symbolic action are the vehicles of meaning. It provides a physical and time-limited space, made safe by a structure which provides shape and boundaries to experiences and feelings which can otherwise feel dangerously chaotic and overwhelming.[5]

---

5 Jan Berry, *Ritual Making Women: Shaping Rites for Changing Lives*, London: Equinox, 2009, p. 2.

This giving of physical shape in the outer world is another important aspect of ritual. Such an event in the outer physical world can be seen, recorded and remembered by others, and ceases to be something which is purely personal to those most closely involved and their feelings. So, for instance, two people know they are married because of the evidence of the real-world rite, and not just their own sense that, 'I feel in love.' Not that the feelings are unimportant – on the contrary, they can become more real when put into that external world, and this is one of the ways that ritual helps us to deal with feelings, whether they are happy or sad.

For the purposes of this book, ritual is being used to mean a combination of words and physical actions or gestures. Often those words and actions are repeated, or are connected with other words and actions which carry meaning through regular use.

A rite is a specific occasion which includes the use of these rituals – in our case, a Christian act of worship. For the reasons outlined above, a rite does not assume a sincerity of heart on the part of all those involved, and for this reason is often preferable for our purposes to the term 'worship', which does suggest a particular internal orientation of the participants. In a Christian pastoral rite, there must be some belief and faith, but it is not necessarily on the part of those for whom the rite is prepared and to whom it is offered – instead it may be that the Church holds that belief, and offers to pray with its faith for those who turn to it for help.

For Christians, of course, there is more than just ritual – there is God, and faith and the belief in the power and desire of God to change us and care for us. But that does not mean that we do not need to understand ritual at all, or can simply expect God to make it work 'as if by magic'.

Public worship is sometimes treated as if it were of an entirely different nature than other forms of human ritualization. While a distinctive form of ritualizing, it is not altogether different. A faith-filled public ritualization cannot achieve its purposes apart from the means that humans employ in other ritualized aspects of their lives.[6]

We therefore need to understand ritual as one of the tools which God has given us to facilitate transformation.

A ritual map

Ritual, then, is one of the ways that people draw a map to help them to make sense of the changes which they are encountering in their lives. Running alongside the physical stages of birth, growth and approaching death are a series of social changes – changes of status, or role or self-understanding – which are not inherently tied to those stages but which are ascribed to them by human beings. The meanings are not fixed but may vary from culture to culture depending on time and place. Sarah Farrimond describes how the map of ritual connects with the reality of actual events of life:

> [Humans] impose an order on life, which derives from physi-cal realities, but imputes meaning to them. Social states or-ganize physical exigencies into a story with a clear direction, not only in terms of ultimate destination, but as regards the meaning and significance of the journey . . .
>
> The movement from one social state to another is, in most cultural contexts, an occasion for ritual, for prescribed se-quences of purposeful actions and words.[7]

In this last sentence we find some useful guidance about how to understand ritual – and all the words are significant.

First, ritual combines actions and words (and, we might add, often uses significant objects in those actions). Ritual is physical as well as verbal. Second, the combination of actions and words is *purposeful* – there is a deliberate intention to achieve something.

---

6 Anderson and Foley, *Mighty Stories*, pp. 42f.

7 Sarah Farrimond, 'Weddings and Funerals', in Christopher Irvine (ed.), *The Use of Symbols in Worship* (Alcuin Liturgy Guides 4), London: SPCK, 2007, p. 93.

The actions and words do not merely describe something, they intend to mark or change something. Finally, ritual is *prescribed*. It may be that it is literally set down and fixed by some external authority (such as the legal words required in a wedding service) but more often ritual is prescribed in the softer sense of being shaped by external expectations from tradition and history or by assumptions from the surrounding culture.

Rites of passage

The specific services, large or small in scale, relating to life events are often known as 'rites of passage'. This terminology is drawn chiefly from the work of Arnold van Gennep (1873–1957). van Gennep was a French anthropologist, ethnographer and folklorist (though born in Germany). His seminal book, *Les Rites de Passage*, was first published in 1908 and in English translation in 1960. van Gennep's research was worldwide in scope, but connected also with practice in contemporary Europe. His theories were widely influential, and have had a significant impact on the more recent field of ritual studies, and its application to Christian worship.[8] van Gennep developed a careful categorization of what he called rites of passage, the rites which mark a person's transition from one state or stage of life to another.

> For every one of these events [*birth, puberty, marriage, etc.*] there are ceremonies whose essential purpose is to enable the individual to pass from one defined position to another which is equally well defined.[9]

Pastoral rites, in the sense in which I am using the term, are usually rites of passage, acts of worship which help us to negotiate,

---

8 Key names include Victor Turner, Mary Douglas, Catherine Bell, and Ronald Grimes. For a good introduction to the field of ritual studies, see Paul Bradshaw and Paul Melloh (eds), *Foundations in Ritual Studies: A Reader for Students of Christian Worship*, London: SPCK, 2007.

9 Arnold van Gennep, translated by Monika B. Vizedom and Gabrielle L. Caffee, *The Rites of Passage*, London: Routledge, 1977, p. 3.

or make sense of, changes in our lives. They tackle life situations which cannot be held sufficiently by Sunday worship, because they mark significant changes or experiences for particular individuals which are not necessarily being experienced in the same way or at the same time by other members of the church. They are specific to *this* life, at the stage it is at *now*.

Are all rites of passage equal?

For some pastoral situations the Church has a ready answer, services in a book, and clear expectations. Weddings, funerals, healing services, these are all 'standard' and there is plenty of material to draw on for the minister, and plenty of expectation on the part of the individual or group concerned. For other pastoral needs, the Church is less sure how to respond, and sometimes is not sure even how to name the reality being experienced. It is much harder to find services which acknowledge divorce or the ending of a relationship, or which connect with the experience of childlessness or miscarriage or abortion. However, over time, the Church does change its ability to relate to these experiences and to provide resources for them.

One way to picture this is to consider a table with three columns and then to consider how items may move around from one column to another. In Table 1, opposite, I have used arrows to indicate where things are (or might soon be) on the move from one column to another, and *italic* to indicate previous or future positions.

Column 1 is the easy one. These are the events which the Church feels confident about celebrating or recognizing and they usually end up in official service books. Expectations are clear and patterns are well established. The God story that we are putting alongside the human story is understood. The other columns are more difficult to work out.

The second column will include events in life which are not usually recognized in special services in church, but which might well be mentioned in the prayers at a Sunday service. In some churches or circumstances these events might be accompanied by

1	2	3
Life events routinely marked with special services	Life events which are acknowledged, but not routinely marked with special services	Life events which are rarely or never mentioned or recognized in church
Death	Getting engaged	Bankruptcy
Marriage	*Divorce* ◄——————— Divorce	
Marriage after divorce ◄— *Marriage after divorce*		Abortion
Birth of a child	Retirement	Miscarriage
	Moving home	Release from prison
	Graduation, or taking exams	Suffering abuse
Same-sex relationships? ◄— – – – *Same-sex relationships?* ◄———		Same-sex relationships
Adopting a child	'Significant' birthdays	Discovering your baby will have special needs
Renewal of marriage vows ◄—— Wedding anniversaries		
Adolescence? (Confirmation[10])	Redundancy	Onset (or end) of menopause
Ordination	Entering a nursing home	Suicide

Table 1: *Life Events and Church Services*

more formal prayer and worship, and you might be able to find something like them in a book of unofficial resources or creative liturgies, but they are unlikely to be in official service books.[10]

In the third column we will find events in life which are rarely or never mentioned in church. These are the things which we know happen, but are unlikely to get included in prayers of intercession, and would almost certainly not feature in official service

---

10 Confirmation is technically a rite of commitment and strengthening for someone who has been baptized. There is nothing that inherently ties it to adolescence, but in the Roman Catholic and Anglican traditions (among others) the practice of confirmation being routinely given to children at or around adolescence has, in some contexts, led to it being perceived as a rite of adolescence. The Methodist rite of Reception into Membership, which may or may not accompany confirmation, does not have the same associations, because it has remained more clearly a rite for affirming adult membership of the church.

books. These include the sort of things which are 'not supposed to happen' to Christians, or about which Christians disagree so profoundly that it is impossible yet to come to a common mind about what a service would say.

Which events get put in which column depends hugely on which sort of church you go to and where you are in the world when you do this exercise. It also depends on whether you are thinking about your own particular congregation's practice or the official stance of a denomination or national church. Some things which go into column 3 if you are thinking of a fairly traditional or conservative church in a British context might be in column 1 if you are considering a 'radical' church in a North American context. Some things in column 2 for the Church of England might be in Column 1 for the Methodist Church in Britain, or the Anglican Church in Australia, and so on. In Table 1 I have assumed a British context, considering 'middle of the road' churches, but your experience may be different.

Life's unacknowledged events

Why do things end up in columns 2 or 3, rather than column 1?

- It could simply be that the event in the particular human story is too specific and individual, and is not shared generally enough to make it into column 1, which tends to include rites to recognize events which are general to a large proportion of people. Of course, it could be that a story is more generic than we realize or are willing to acknowledge.
- It could be because the human story does not have a natural (or easily spotted) God story in Scripture to put alongside it. This can happen simply because of the difference between biblical and contemporary culture. For instance, graduation, moving home, being made redundant are events which do not have straightforward biblical equivalents, even though more subtle connections can be made with a little effort.
- It could be because the Church is not sure or is divided about the God story which goes alongside this human story,

and therefore is not ready to 'put its cards on the table' in a public rite, which might be expected to reflect official doctrine. The Church simply doesn't know what to say and one feature of this is that it is unsure which are the Scripture passages that can help us make sense of this part of a human journey.

- It could be because the Church *is* sure, but feels negative about the human story being reflected – essentially, it cannot find a God story which fits it, other than a negative one. Either at local church level or more widely, it may have taken a decision on theological grounds that something is not acceptable to God, and therefore may not appropriately be celebrated in church. Interestingly, sometimes churches (or their leaders) are happy to respond privately to a situation in someone's life, but not in a public service.

- It could be because the leaders of the Church, locally or more widely, simply do not recognize certain life stages in their own experience, and therefore have never given attention to them as a need. Here it is the human story which cannot be recognized. For instance, if leadership in a church is dominated by men, it is not surprising that liturgies which recognize the menopause are thin on the ground.[11] Or if the culture of a church is focused on particular models of success and health, then the reality of mental illness is unlikely to find a space in worship, except as something which needs 'sorting out' in a particular form of healing.[12]

---

11 There are such rites in 'unofficial' books, of course: see, for instance, Diann L. Neu, *Women's Rites: Feminist Liturgies for Life's Journey*, Cleveland, OH: Pilgrim Press, 2003, pp. 160–70, 180–9; Rosemary Radford Ruether, *Women-Church: Theology and Practice of Feminist Liturgical Communities*, San Francisco: Harper and Row, 1985, pp. 204–6. Jim Clarke's *Creating Rituals*, Malwah, NJ: Paulist Press, 2011, also considers menopause (pp. 40f.) and, more unusually, rites for midlife for men (pp. 41f.).

12 Janet Walton, *Feminist Liturgy: A Matter of Justice*, Collegeville, MN: Liturgical Press, 2000, gives examples of forms of worship which take seriously the experiences of depression and mental illness, being a survivor of sexual abuse, and undergoing a mastectomy (pp. 55–71) – all very common human experiences, but ones about which the Church is often silent.

- It may be because the people involved themselves do not want a public rite or public mention of what is going on in their lives. They may feel shame or guilt, or it may simply be that the transition which is taking place is one that they do not wish to mark publicly.

Human journey and spiritual journey

There is a further possible reason why some events in people's lives do not end up in column 1 of Table 1, and that is because some events can easily be seen as part of one's spiritual journey, whereas others cannot. Those which belong most easily in column 1 are often those which have been traditionally recognized as sacraments (or sacramental). They are seen as part of a person's Christian or spiritual journey through life. Events such as moving house, retiring, graduation, and so on, are seen as important on our human journey, but not on our spiritual journey. They are not expected to be 'means of grace', and hence can be excluded from attention in the Church and from public prayer.

By extending the bounds of pastoral services to embrace things which fall outside of the traditional sacramental model, I want to reinforce the idea that pastoral liturgy works by helping people to grow in their humanity, as well as their spiritual growth, by using ritual with a Christian worldview. This provides a big map, with the largest number of possible routes. Retirement may not be a sacrament in the traditional sense, but being helped to prayerfully negotiate that new phase can be a way of recognizing and receiving God's grace and help.[13]

Transitions without rites

The result of this very mixed picture about which events get associated with Christian liturgy is that people's journey through

---

13 There is a reflection on the construction of retirement rites in Ronald L. Grimes, *Deeply into the Bone: Re-inventing Rites of Passage*, Berkeley, CA: University of California Press, 2002, pp. 323–32.

life can include many transitions, but not all of them will have rites. Does this matter? In the big scheme of things, not necessarily, but there may be implications.

> Passages can be negotiated without the benefit of rites, but in their absence, there is a greater risk of speeding through the dangerous inter-sections of the human life course . . . Unattended, a major life passage can become a yawning abyss, draining off psychic energy, engendering social confusion, and twisting the course of the life that follows it. Unattended passages become spiritual sinkholes around which hungry ghosts, those greedy personifications of unfinished business, hover.[14]

That may be a bit of an overstatement as a general principle, but as a description of what may happen in particular circumstances it contains more than a grain of truth. In practice, what happens is that where the Church (or another religious institution) does not, or feels it cannot, provide a rite, informal and non-religious ritual-like behaviour develops instead. This ritual-like behaviour does not structure the journey in the way that a full rite of passage does, but it can carry some of the weight of a fuller rite, for instance, in giving a sense that the transition has happened, and has been negotiated 'properly'.

TO THINK ABOUT – Passages without a rite, but not without ritual

Think of the changes in life which are not marked with a Christian rite, the sorts of things that we put in columns 2 and 3 of Table 1, above. In these situations there are often elements of ritual, even if there are no Christian rites. Graduation is an obvious example, but in some of the other examples it is also the case. For instance, moving home is often marked by the sending of cards and holding of housewarming parties. When children move from one school to another, there may be special assemblies, teachers may give the children symbolic gifts (for instance, cards with good wishes and

---

14 Grimes, *Deeply*, pp. 5f.

wise tips) and practical things take on symbolic significance, such as buying a new school uniform (I still have a photograph of my daughter wearing hers after we returned from the shop). Among the children themselves there may be the signing of shirts and blouses on the last day of term, not to mention the end of year prom. At retirement, there may be a gathering of some sort, someone will be called on to 'say a few words' and there may be the giving of a gift.

Beyond the immediate impact on those involved, there is a further formational implication when some transitions are marked with Christian rites and others are not. Events which are marked with Christian liturgy, especially if they are marked with services in official books, will be seen as those which the Church views as normative, or at least acceptable. The corollary of this is that if 'your' event is not reflected in this official or accepted provision, it suggests that your life story contains elements of failure, weakness, or marginality.

A moving target

I have already indicated the difficulty of allocating events to the different columns of this table, but the situation is further complicated if we allow for the fact that in these matters the Churches are in a constant state of flux (like the wider society, but often a decade or two behind). We find that some life events or pastoral situations move from one column to another. Sometimes things which are seen as unacceptable in one generation – and therefore impossible for the Church to recognize, let alone bless – can become run of the mill in the next. Or perhaps something which is relatively commonplace, but taboo, becomes more widely recognized and acknowledged in society. Suicide, abortion and miscarriage would be examples of such events, about which society generally is becoming more willing to talk openly, and the Church (often through chaplaincy specialists) is more able to provide liturgical and pastoral resources to help.

In the table above I have indicated with arrows some of the events in life which in recent years, at least in some churches, have moved or are moving, from one column to another. Your experience may be different, and you may feel I have been too radical or too conservative, but what I have tried to indicate here is not what I think *should* be happening, but what I observe *is* happening, whether all Christians agree with it or not. Whether you think that the Church should be catching up with the world, or resisting the world, will depend on your own theological assumptions. Let us acknowledge that there is some movement, even if we do not all feel comfortable with it.

For instance, divorce has moved from being one of the taboo subjects unmentionable in church circles, to something which is increasingly acknowledged. Why? Partly because it has moved from something which was socially rare and unacceptable to something which is very common and no longer carries stigma. Not least in this is the impact of having Christian leaders who are themselves divorced or married to people who are divorced. In other words, the simple statistical 'normalizing' of the experience of divorce, both in society in general and within the Church, has had a liturgical impact.

The first change is to do with whether divorced persons can marry again in church. In the Church of England the change to allow for such marriages has happened over recent decades; in the Methodist Church in Great Britain the change happened earlier; and in many other churches it would still be frowned upon. The reason that it became a regular and pressing issue is because of changes in society which made divorce easier, and therefore more common. Suddenly, requests from divorced persons to marry in church were not an occasional interruption into a standard pattern, but became part of the standard pattern, and it became harder for the Church to maintain a 'stand' for the permanence of marriage, and yet still to be perceived as responding pastorally and lovingly to those who had been divorced. Church congregations increasingly included divorced persons, and so did church leadership. And so the marriage in church of divorcees moves from column 2 into column 1, at least in some churches. But what of the marriage service itself? Should it recognize a former relationship in the act of forming a new one? When the Church of England set about revising its marriage service for *Common Worship*, one of the issues was whether to incorporate a compulsory confession (for the bride and groom) in a marriage where one or both parties was divorced – a course of action which was not pursued in the end (though a general confession for everyone present is part of the order of marriage when it includes Holy Communion).[15]

This then raises the next liturgical implication: if divorce is being acknowledged in marriage rites, is it also appropriate to recognize the divorce itself, to offer pastoral care through a liturgical rite which might be part of a need to 'let go' before entering a new relationship? Here the Church has found it harder to respond to a pastoral need, partly because of the uncertainty about what the God story is and what the parallels are with other pastoral rites. Some Christians are looking for rites by which to recognize the 'death' of a relationship and perhaps to grieve, and so might draw on funeral models. Others might wish to acknowledge responsibility or to seek forgiveness for the part they have played in that breakdown, and would look more naturally to models drawn from services of confession and reconciliation. Yet others might be seeking healing for the damage sustained in the relationship or during its breakdown, and so would turn to models drawn from services of wholeness and healing.[16]

Some rites have been devised on a private and ad hoc basis,[17] but increasingly these rites are entering the mainstream, recognized (if not 'authorized') by church authorities. For instance, the recent Methodist publication, *Vows and Partings*, while not

---

15 See the Church of England report, *Marriage in Church after Divorce: A Discussion Document from a Working Party Commissioned by the House of Bishops* (GS 1361), London: Church House Publishing, 2000, pp. 16–18. For a more positive view about the value of a confession for bride and groom, see Kenneth Stevenson, *To Join Together: The Rite of Marriage*, New York: Pueblo, 1987, pp. 202f.

16 See Elaine Ramshaw, *Ritual and Pastoral Care*, Philadelphia: Fortress Press, 1987, pp. 51–4, and John H. Westerhoff III and William H. Willimon, *Liturgy and Learning Through the Life Cycle*, Akron, OH: OSL Publications, revised ed. 1994, pp. 109–18.

17 For instance, see Hannah Ward and Jennifer Wild, *Human Rites: Worship Resources for an Age of Change*, London: Mowbray, 1995, pp. 170–94.

exactly including a liturgy for divorce, does contain a section of prayers surrounding 'Separation'.[18] And so divorce itself moves from column 3 into column 2, and potentially into column 1.[19]

Is a similar change happening with regard to the blessing or affirming of same-sex relationships? For some Christians this is still very much a 'column 3' matter, not to be talked about or encouraged in any way. For others, the reality of knowing gay people, and perhaps openly gay Christians, means that congregations are more likely to be ready for relationships to be acknowledged, albeit in mainly low-key, informal or implicit ways. For some churches, a move to column 1 has already happened, as the Anglican Communion knows only too well.[20]

IN PRACTICE – Changes in the Church

Sometimes life events move from one column to another because of changes in the Church rather than changes in society. One example of this would be individual prayer of confession and reconciliation (sometimes known as sacramental confession). For the Roman Catholic Church this practice would be a clear column 1 rite. Official forms are provided and all Catholics are expected to make use of the provision. Indeed, it has become so commonplace that it has ceased to be associated with particular life events (although first confession would still feel

---

18 Methodist Church, *Vows and Partings: Services for the Reaffirmation of Marriage Vows and Suggestions of How to Pray When Relationships Change or End*, Peterborough: Methodist Publishing House, 2001, pp. 35–45.

19 For example, The Anglican Church of Canada already has a service 'At the Ending of a Marriage' in its *Occasional Celebrations* material, Toronto: Anglican Book Centre, 1992, pp. 66–72, but it is not insignificant that these resources were published in a ring binder rather than a book (and are now available from The Anglican Church of Canada website), and that the service in question is largely derived from an unofficial source – Anne Tanner, *Treasures of Darkness*, Toronto: Anglican Book Centre, 1990. See Muir, *Ritual*, p. 48 for a reminder that at other times in history so-called customary rites have also ritualized the ending of a relationship.

20 Though worldwide Anglican angst and North American practice tends to dominate the headlines, more quietly the Lutheran Church of Sweden has responded to its government's decision to make marriage gender neutral by offering a marriage service suitable for a same-sex couple.

like a significant milestone) and become instead something which is part of regular discipleship.

For other churches, this sort of individual confession in the presence of an ordained minister has been, since the Reformation, either anathema, or reserved for situations of extreme need. Generally speaking, the more evangelical a church or an individual the more likely they are to put such a rite in column 3, and the more 'catholic' they are, the more likely to put it in column 2 or column 1. And yet if we look in *Methodist Worship Book or Common Worship*, we now find rites provided for this by Churches which had previously resisted any such rite.[21] The rites are by no means compulsory, and their presence in official books is not the same as their regular use in practice, but the shift is nonetheless significant. The reasons for the change are complex but are largely connected with the ecumenical movement of the last hundred years. Christians who had been used to firing rhetorical shots at one another across theological battlefields began instead to talk and listen to one another. Commonalities were discovered, defensive positions retreated from, and a new willingness to learn from one another, as well as to rediscover aspects of our own heritage, grew.

A less dramatic example would be the provision in *Methodist Worship Book* for a service for blessing a home (pp. 504–6). The experience of moving home has not become any more common, nor was it ever taboo in wider society, but a Church which had no history of such rites has responded to a perceived need and received from traditions in which a home blessing would be a more common occurrence.[22]

---

21 *MWB*, pp. 422–5; *CWCI*, pp. 266–89.

22 The Roman Catholic Church has texts for the blessing of a home in the *Book of Blessings*, Collegeville: Liturgical Press, 1989. The Church of England has no official rites for home blessings, but the practice is common and there are plenty of unofficial resources. See, for instance, David Silk (compiler), *Prayers for Use at Alternative Services*, Oxford: Mowbray, 1980, pp. 138–40; John Leach and Liz Simpson, '*Bless this House*' (Grove Worship Series 204), Cambridge: Grove Books, 2010; Dilly Baker, *A Place at the Table: Liturgies and Resources for Christ-centred Hospitality*, Norwich: Canterbury Press, 2008, pp. 9–13.

It is also important to acknowledge that although I have drawn the arrows all moving from right to left, it is possible to imagine things moving the other way. An example might be the service of Churching of Women.[23] Though services for the blessing of a child continue to be popular,[24] the older service of Churching has largely died out. There are a variety of possible reasons for this (which will be explored later in Chapter 4), but it is an example of where a service which was once in an official prayer book has dropped out of use, albeit replaced by something else which takes a different approach (in this case, focused on the child rather than the mother). Not only has the service disappeared, but the underlying theology (or the popular superstition which grew up round it), which can suggest a need for a mother to be 'cleansed' in some way, has become unacceptable. It has truly moved to column 3. However, it is worth noting that in this shift, as in so many of the shifts the other way, the Church is following wider society, rather than leading the way.

One of the aims of this book is to help us to identify some key principles from the events in column 1, which we can then apply to events and life stages which are more likely to fit in columns 2 and 3, and for which ready-made resources are much harder to find. For more on this, see Chapter 8.

What makes a rite 'Christian'?

If you had to answer the question, 'What makes a wedding a *Christian* wedding?' what would your answer be? It is much easier to answer the question, 'What makes a Christian *marriage?*'

---

23 See Chapter 4 for more on services surrounding childbirth.

24 Church of England statistics show that there were 4,190 services of Thanksgiving for the Gift of a Child for infants under 1 in the year 2009, with a further 1,790 for children aged 1–12 (source: *Church Statistics 2009/10*, London: Archbishops' Council, Research and Statistics, Central Secretariat, 2011, p. 23). The Methodist Church in Britain reported 490 services of Thanksgiving for the Birth of a Child in 2007 (source: *Statistics for Mission 2005–7*, presented to Conference in 2008, www.methodist.org.uk/downloads/conf08_55_Statistics_for_Mission_report210808.doc – accessed 24/5/11).

because then we can point to particular qualities of the ongoing relationship – a commitment to a lifelong partnership, an acknowledgement of God's involvement in the relationship, perhaps shared Christian values which underpin decisions which the couple make, churchgoing and prayer as part of the life of the couple, and so on.[25]

How then shall we answer the more focused question about a Christian wedding (meaning the ceremony which marks the start of the formal marriage relationship)? When I have asked this question, groups tend to list things like these as important:

- The use of a church building or other sacred space for the ceremony.
- An ordained minister or other Christian leader to lead the service.
- There are readings from the Christian Scriptures.
- Prayers, vows, declarations, and so on, which articulate a Christian vision of what marriage is for.
- A sermon which connects this relationship to the gospel and God's love.
- Prayers which acknowledge a need for God's help and involvement in the marriage.
- Christian songs or hymns.
- A blessing of the couple.
- For some, the inclusion of Holy Communion.

It is hard to argue strongly that any of these on their own is essential for a wedding to be Christian, and one can imagine a wedding which could still be described as Christian in which one or several of these items might be absent. However, the list has a cumulative force, and it would be pretty safe to say that if none of these things were present, then it would be hard to describe the wedding as Christian in any meaningful way.

---

25 This is meant to be an indicative, rather than exhaustive list, and I am conscious that where only one party to a marriage is a practising Christian, questions about whether the *marriage* is Christian become more complex.

Where there is often disagreement among Christians is whether there should be one further bullet point:

- A couple in which one or both have a Christian faith.

Those from churches where the only weddings tend to be of members of the church assume that the faith of the couple is essential for a Christian wedding. For them, the answers to the two questions (what makes a Christian marriage and what makes a Christian wedding?) must match more closely. The wedding will assume that the relationship will connect closely with Christian discipleship.

Others come from churches where most of the weddings are between persons who are either not previously connected to the church at all, or only very tenuously. For them, the idea that what we are offering is *not* a Christian wedding seems odd. Added into this mix is a further complication: there are Christians who believe strongly that every marriage is important to God, wherever and however it is celebrated. For these Christians, a civil ceremony without any explicitly Christian content can be a 'Christian' wedding if the intention of the union (lifelong, committed, exclusive, etc.) reflects Christian, or godly, values.

Christian rites for non-Christian people?

So, is the faith of the couple, or at least of one of them, essential in a Christian wedding? Though we are asking this question of weddings, the principle is a key one behind all pastoral services. Can we offer Christian healing to those who don't have faith? Can we offer a Christian funeral service to a family who do not profess to be practising Christians and whose deceased loved one was, at best, an agnostic? Questions such as these raise big questions of integrity for many Christian ministers and for some members of congregations too.

The answer I want to suggest is, 'No, you do not have to be a Christian to gain benefit from these services, and yes, we can offer Christian rites to those who do not necessarily profess a Christian faith.' There is a sense in which any wedding, whatever its format, can be a Christian wedding in that it gives shape to the values of the kingdom of God, even if those involved in it would not express it like that. More specifically, it can be Christian because the view of marriage being given expression draws on specifically Christian insights and emphases.

So, what do Christian rites provide for those who would not identify themselves as practising Christians? At the most basic level, the offering of these services to one and all is simply an expression of Christ's love: it is the Church serving the world, using the skills and experience it has and doing something it is generally good at.

But is there more than this? There are several possible things which a Christian rite offers:

- Encouragement to 'come on board' and perhaps join the church. This is certainly one way of seeing the mission potential in pastoral services.
- An opportunity to consider the spiritual aspect of life.
- A possible new way to understand the journey of life, including its ultimate purpose and destiny.
- God's grace. This would be the first answer from a sacramental perspective. A pastoral service articulates this, and can be itself a means of receiving grace and blessing from God. If the sacramental model is applied in a more restricted way then God's grace is given to people through the sacrament, mediated by the Church and its ministers. This still sounds generous, but in practice it can lead to the Church taking a 'gatekeeper' approach to the question of who might benefit from the sacrament. For instance, the Roman Catholic Church sees marriage as a sacrament, but the sacramental aspect does not benefit couples in which one of them is not baptized.

Pastoral services as invitations and gifts

The model I am working with is that pastoral services offered by the Christian Church are invitations to see one's life through a

Christian lens in the context of prayer and worship. If you share the Christian faith, that will be the natural way to see life, and the services will make perfect sense. But even if you don't have an active Christian faith, the Church can offer, for instance, a Christian wedding, or a Christian funeral, as long as you are happy to work with the worldview and assumptions that come with that. These acts of worship are essentially invitations to put your story, the story of your life, alongside what I am calling the God story, and to see the connections. Seeing those connections may cause you to want to build on them, to make the connections stronger, to explore deepening your faith and awareness of God . . . or it may not. The Church's role is missional in inviting you to explore the God story and its connections with your story, but it does not depend on you signing up to the God story before you start. The services are offered as gifts to those who will receive them.

A Christian understanding of the journey

One way to understand our journey through life is to see it in relation to its beginning and end. Every life event (and especially every *marking* of those life events) is, in one way or another, looking back to our birth and ahead to our death and recognizing our movement from one towards the other. It may not be a happy thought, but a birthday party is essentially a way of noting that movement, and it is significant that whereas our childhood birthdays are focused on how far we have moved from birth ('Hasn't she grown!'; 'I remember when he was born'; and so on), our later birthdays can carry an unspoken edge of, 'Not much further to go . . .' ('Enjoy life while you can'; 'You only live once'; and so on). Each event thus celebrated (whether a birthday or an anniversary of some other sort) is both a birth and a death: it carries a sense of a new phase beginning (even if that phase is in strong continuity with the last one) and a phase ending. Christian pastoral rites will not only mark the particular event, but will also help us to see how this event fits the bigger life journey; they will help us to see the whole map as well as to negotiate this particular junction.

Part of the distinctive aspect of a Christian map through life is the recognition that though this life may be bounded by birth and death, the Christian hope is that death is itself a phase on a bigger journey. This gives a different feel to the way the map is articulated. For instance, a humanist funeral may have a strong sense of thanksgiving for a life, just as a Christian funeral will have. The difference will be that the Christian funeral also has a sense of pointing ahead to the future for the person who has died, as well as looking back to the life they have lived.

Pastoral rites as eschatological pointers

For this reason Christian pastoral rites need to have an essentially eschatological edge to them. This is why the reading of the story of the wedding at Cana (John 2.1–11) at a marriage service is not only a reminder of the way that Jesus brought joy into one particular human marriage, nor even a prompt to pray that he will do the same in the relationship being celebrated in this service. Rather, it is a reminder that the turning of water to wine points ahead to a heavenly banquet and to God's ultimate destiny for the whole cosmos. Similarly, in a funeral, it is not just the future of the deceased which is in view, but a reminder of mortality for all present, and the need to be ready for the day when we too will see our creator face to face. In a healing service, though the immediate easing of suffering is always in view, there is again that recognition that even those who are physically healed now will meet their death one day and the ultimate healing can only come when God has made a new heavens and earth and all creation is restored and healed and humankind finds its destiny in that renewed creation.

3

A Pastoral Liturgy Toolkit

I find the metaphor of a pastoral liturgy toolkit helpful when thinking about the ways that pastoral rites can care for people. A pastoral liturgy toolkit will consist of two sorts of things:

1. Actual physical resources which can be used in pastoral services. While I am thinking of the toolkit primarily metaphorically, there will be some literal 'tools' that can be used, including service books which include pastoral rites.
2. A set of principles, skills and practices which will be part of most pastoral services but which need to be applied sensitively and contextually.

Christian ministers need to have both at their fingertips. Resources without principles will lead to a paralysis of action in contexts for which the books contain no resources. The principles without the established resources can lead to a creativity gone mad, which is unconnected to the wider Christian tradition across time and space, and which can leave those who are involved unsure as to whether what has been done has been 'proper'. As we shall see, this is a key factor in making pastoral services 'work'.

Physical resources

There are several obvious starting points when seeking to equip yourself for pastoral liturgical ministry.

- The official published resources of your denomination or tradition will be the natural starting point for some. Even in Churches that do not publish their own official services, there will be some contexts in which using particular words will be important – for instance, in a wedding it is important to get the legal declarations right, even if the rest of the service is more flexible.

- Other pastoral resources published either online or on paper will be another place to turn. There is a growing market for 'creative liturgy' and these are often related to pastoral situations. Often those situations are quite unique, and the solutions offered may be quite specific, but these can form a good starting point for creativity, especially for contexts which are not covered in more mainstream publications. Make sure that something which is described as a liturgy for a life event is really a rite which will help with transition and change, and not simply a 'themed' service. With online resources, always use with care: some things are on the internet because no one could be persuaded to publish them, and there may be reason for that.

- In some contexts, Churches or traditions, pastoral liturgy is not fixed in print, but is nonetheless governed and given shape by particular expectations. For instance a funeral in some Pentecostal traditions may appear to be free-flowing and certainly will not be written down in a book, but there may be clear expectations about who will help with filling in the grave afterwards, which songs will be sung at the graveside, and so on.

- As well as words, there are some physical objects which may form part of the toolkit. That might include a home communion kit, oil for anointing, incense, candles (for instance, for lighting as part of prayer, or as a symbolic action at a wedding), an MP3 player for music to set a mood, and so on.

Although these physical books, texts and objects will be important resources in pastoral liturgy, the more important tools in the toolkit are the metaphorical ones – the deep structures, the principles and the skills that are needed in pastoral rites. Some of these are specific to pastoral services, others are the same tools that are used in regular Sunday worship, though they may be used in slightly different or more focused ways.

In the rest of this chapter we will explore some of these principles and practices. They need to be so deeply understood by both lay and ordained ministers, that they become the toolkit we carry round with us wherever we are, and which we can draw from in flexible and creative ways to serve new needs as well as to improve our practice of existing pastoral rites.

Scripture – telling the God story

Throughout this book I refer to the 'God story', and in general this will be a reference to the reading of the Bible in pastoral rites (though sometimes it has a broader reference). I recognize that calling Scripture 'the God story' is simplistic, to say the least, but for our purposes here it will stand as a shorthand way of saying 'the story of God's action in the world, especially as revealed in Jesus Christ, and available to be applied to our individual lives.'

CASE STUDY – Speaking for God at a funeral

Karen, the minister of a local church, was taking the funeral of Jason, a young man in his early twenties, who was killed in a tragic accident. His funeral was packed, and many of those present were also young. One of those attending the service was Chris, whose mum was a regular member of the church where the funeral was held. After the service, Chris said to his mum, 'Why did Karen go on about God and the Bible? I thought the service was about Jason.' His mum's answer? 'Because that's what Karen is there for.'

There are many ways in which a Christian minister's role overlaps with the roles of others in the process of caring which surrounds pastoral services. Ministers may be called on to work with registrars, funeral directors, counsellors, medical specialists and many others. What makes the minister's role unique is that she or he is specifically there to talk about God.

Though the formal Bible reading is the most obvious place where Scripture, and therefore the God story, will feature, there are other ways that it is part of a pastoral service too. Scripture, either quoted explicitly or paraphrased more subtly, may feature in the spoken liturgical texts or in the songs or hymns which are sung. The God story more generally may also be 'told' in other ways, such as through the physical symbols and space of a church building.

The particular story of someone's life, as told at a wedding or a funeral, for instance, may also include testimony to the work and love of God, but here I am reserving the phrase 'God story' to refer to the bigger picture of God's action more generally in all people and across time, into which we place our own experience, our human story.

The human story

If telling the God story, especially through Scripture, is one of the key roles of the Christian minister and a Christian pastoral rite, the other key part of a pastoral service is the telling of the other story, the human story which has brought us together for this act of worship. That story might be the birth of a child, the formal-izing of a relationship, or the ending of a life. Whatever the story is, it provides the particular context in which we are hearing the God story and finding connections between the two.

In some services there will be a very explicit place for the hu-man story to be told: the so-called eulogy (or tribute) at a funeral is the most obvious example. It may also happen when someone shares their reasons for seeking prayer for healing, or when par-ents bring their child for baptism or God's blessing and share something of their story, or perhaps the reasons for the choice of the child's name. There are other ways too in which the human story can be shared. The hymns or songs that are chosen – and particularly the 'secular' pop songs which are increasingly asked for – may well be a part of the telling of the story: a favourite track of someone who has died; the pop song which was playing when the couple now marrying first met; and so on. It is becoming more common for the story to be told in pictures too – a slideshow of photos playing on screen of the happy couple (or the lately deceased) as the congregation assemble for the service, for instance.

CASE STUDY – Is secular music wrong at a funeral?

The Roman Catholic Archbishop of Melbourne, Australia, hit the headlines recently when he issued guidelines forbidding the use of secular music at Catholic funerals.[1] Was he right to do so? Many Christians will have sympathy with a desire to keep the focus of a service on God, and to avoid inappropriate choices for an act of Christian worship (Meat Loaf's, 'Like a bat out of hell', for instance, might be one to avoid at a funeral, no matter how important it was to the person who has died). In this case the issue is further complicated by the fact that a Catholic funeral is normally a Requiem Mass. This means that it is clearly connected to a sacramental model, and to the Church's regular worship. It is primarily a Mass with a particular intention – the rest of the soul of the departed – rather than a celebration of that person's life. Hence the Archbishop encourages families to keep the telling of the human story and the sharing of memories to social occasions before or after the funeral Mass itself.

However, the danger of such bans is that they risk disconnecting the telling of the human story from the God story. Perhaps in a Christendom context, or for a Christian family, this matters less, because God is perceived as the thread connecting all parts of life. However, if the Church is to offer Christian pastoral rites generously to those who are not regularly part of its life, it will be important that the human story is part of those rites. For many who are not used to church (and, increasingly, those who are), aspects of popular culture, including pop songs, are a key way of understanding themselves and telling their story, and so we must expect them to be part of those services.

---

1   www.bbc.co.uk/news/world-asia-pacific-11256843, 10 September 2010.

Sometimes the human story is not told 'fresh', but is formalized as part of the service, something for the minister to read out, as if we do not trust that it will be told properly if real people speak about their actual experience. Usually this involves making assumptions or generalizations about the human story. Formal introductions to services such as funerals or marriages sometimes do this, as do some forms of prayer. If a prayer tells God how we all feel, then you know that the human story is being told for you, and it may not be reflecting reality. Churches tend to do this when they want to tidy up the human story, but such tidying up is counterproductive in the long run, because 'ritual loses its power when it fails to address all of the human story, including its shadow side'.[2]

Making the connection

The telling of the human story is not just the preserve of the Christian minister, of course, nor is it confined to explicitly Christian services – a humanist funeral will also tell the story of the deceased's life, and a civil wedding at a hotel or a civil partnership ceremony will be just as concerned with celebrating the love between two people. However, the key principle in a Christian pastoral service is that these two stories need to be brought into close contact, allowed to sit alongside one another so that each may inform the other. The minister's job is to help all those present to see how our human story can be part of God's story and how God's story can impact on our human lives.

This bringing together of the stories is one of the keys to the success or otherwise of a pastoral rite, and it will happen in several ways through the service. The sermon will hopefully be a central place to connect the Scripture reading with the story of the individual or family which the service centres on. Prayers of intercession, thanksgiving or petition will be another place

---

2 Herbert Anderson and Edward Foley, *Mighty Stories, Dangerous Rituals: Weaving Together the Human and the Divine*, San Francisco: Jossey-Bass, 2001, p. 54.

where the connections can be explored. Usually at some point there will be an action which explicitly brings the two together: it might be the commending of someone who has died into God's care, it might be the blessing of the couple after the exchange of wedding vows, it could be the laying on of hands or anointing of someone who has sought healing.

IN PRACTICE – Using the principles in pastoral visiting

As well as the more formalized healing services, we can see how some of the key principles outlined above are applied in the most simple pastoral context where prayer and worship are part of pastoral care. Imagine a simple visit to the bedside of someone ill at home or in hospital, hospice or care home. The minister first listens as the person shares the latest news, and tells how they are feeling, what is on their mind, and what they would like from God (the human story). The minister then reads a psalm or other passage of Scripture, perhaps prompted by the story just told, or simply a passage which might be generally applicable to times of trouble (the God story). Finally, the two stories are connected as the minister prays, turning the stories into prayer, and concluding by drawing on the resources of the Christian tradition as they say the Lord's Prayer together.

Using words

Words are a central part of most acts of Christian worship. I am aware that silence – the absence of words – is also a key part of Christian worship, but I suggest that even the use of corporate silence is a form of communication, either between humans or between us and God. By words, I also want to include forms of communication such as British Sign Language, in which words may not be 'spoken' but ideas are clearly given articulation and communication is the result. Prayers, readings and the telling of the human and divine stories will all, generally speaking, include the use of words, even if they are not exclusively restricted to words.

Powerful words

Those words need to speak to the heart as well as the head, for these are emotive times in life and this must not be denied or ignored. As Paul Sheppy puts it in regard to funerals, the language 'must address the heart with imaginative fire'.[3] This is not the same as saying the language must be 'poetic', for poetry often expresses a more individual perspective, but some of the same power and force of language will be needed. A pastoral rite must find a way of expressing feeling as well as faith, with emotional connection but not idiosyncratic or self-indulgent content. It must work for 'us' as well as for 'me'.

In a reaction against what is sometimes perceived as cold or formal liturgical text there is a move towards prayers which are much more 'raw' in expressing emotion. As a balance this can be helpful, but there is a danger that such prayer will assume too much, both about the intensity of the emotion and about the extent to which those feelings are shared by all who are present. This is focused particularly sharply when the minister or the service book not only tries to articulate emotions on behalf of everyone present, but puts the words into their mouths too.

> It is true that ritual can shape our attitudes after the pattern of Christ. It does this, however, not by imputing feelings to us which we do not feel, but by engaging us in actions we might not spontaneously perform.[4]

If it is not to alienate some of those present, emotion expressed in liturgy must have integrity with the *corporate* context, and therefore with the range of both persons and emotions present. Here is an example of a prayer designed for use at the funeral of someone who has been murdered:

---

3 Paul Sheppy, *Death Liturgy and Ritual. Volume 1: A Pastoral and Liturgical Theology*, Aldershot: Ashgate, 2003, p. 19.

4 Elaine Ramshaw, *Ritual and Pastoral Care*, Philadelphia: Fortress Press, 1987, p. 28.

O God, we are angry,
we have been robbed of N,
and *she* has been robbed of life.
We have wept
till there were no tears left to shed;
and still we weep . . .[5]

The prayer addresses God with admirable frankness, and a refresh-
ing honesty about the feelings which have been evoked by this tragedy. However, its content might be more suited to an extempore
prayer on a pastoral visit, where those present have themselves expressed these feelings, than to a funeral service, when it may not
ring true or may not tell the whole story for all those present. At
the funeral, those very strong feelings are often best shared and
articulated in the sermon, where they can be placed in context.

Performative words

Perhaps the most significant aspect of the use of words in pastoral
rites is what is sometimes referred to as 'performative language',
'performative utterance', or simply 'performatives'. The term 'performative language' has little to do with dramatic performance
(though that can sometimes be part of it) and everything to do
with using words in ways that 'perform' in the sense of producing a result or causing something to happen. The key ideas were
given classic exposition by J. L. Austin in *How to Do Things with
Words*.[6] The title is self-explanatory. He explores the ways that
words do more than simply describe, but also 'perform' – that
is, they are tools of transformation. Because pastoral services are
not merely services that describe, but also tools of transformation

5 Paul Sheppy, *In Sure and Certain Hope: Liturgies, Prayers and Readings for
Funerals and Memorials*, Norwich: Canterbury Press, 2003, p. 44.

6 J. L. Austin, *How to Do Things with Words*, Oxford: Clarendon Press,
1962. The book contains his 1955 William James Lectures, delivered at Harvard
University. The lectures were edited for publication by J. O. Urmson. He presents
similar material in a more concise way in 'Performative Utterances', in J. L. Austin,
J. O. Urmson and G. J. Warnock (eds), *Philosophical Papers*, Oxford: Clarendon
Press, 1961, pp. 220–39.

through which God changes us, understanding how to use words in a performative way will be key to constructing pastoral services which not only *mean* something, but *do* something.

THEORY – Performative language

Austin gives several examples showing the way that performative language works in ordinary life and contrasting it with other uses of language. Descriptive language, for instance, includes statements such as, 'The grass is green.' The statement itself can be contested, but it does not itself do anything. By contrast, a sentence such as, 'I name this ship the *Queen Mary*,' does not make a statement but intends to perform what it says. It is in the act of speaking the words (perhaps with accompanying action, such as smashing a bottle on the side of the ship) that the ship is named: before it was not the *Queen Mary*; now it is.

Austin gives other examples of performatives: 'I bet'; 'I declare war'; 'I bequeath my watch to my brother'.[7] Though he begins with the relatively straightforward contrast between statements and performatives, he goes on to develop a much more complex set of categories, including different sorts of performatives. He helpfully points out situations in which the edges are blurred. For instance, 'I am sorry' can be a statement, along the lines of 'I regret that this has happened' (a phrase much loved by politicians), but in the right context it could be an act of contrition or apology. Austin categorizes it as 'half-descriptive'. 'I apologize', however, is more clearly performative because it is an act of apology in itself.[8]

There are usually other conditions which make the performative 'work', it must be:

- said in the right context (for instance, marriage vows do something in the context of an actual wedding which they do not do when a primary school class act out a wedding as part of their learning)

---

7 Austin, *How to*, pp. 5–7.
8 Austin, *How to*, pp. 150ff.

> - spoken by the right person (that is a person with the appropriate authority or role in this situation)
> - said with the right intention (for instance, not ironically, or as quotation, or as a joke) and often following a conventional form
> - accompanied by the right conditions (for instance, saying the word 'Snap' in the card game has no effect unless the two cards actually are the same).

It is easy to think of examples of the performative use of words in Christian worship.

- 'I baptize you in the name of the Father, the Son, and the Holy Spirit.'
- 'I now proclaim that you are husband and wife.'

Here words are being used in a way that parallels a traditional understanding of how sacraments work. If a sacrament is a sign that delivers what it signifies (to put it simply) then here are words which do the same: they do not simply point towards what they articulate, they do it. 'I baptize you,' is not the same as, 'I remind you that you are baptized,' or as, 'I hereby show that you belong to Christ'. However, the use of performatives is not 'word magic'. The words alone do not cause things to happen, but only in their rightful place in a bigger context, as Austin's conditions make clear.[9] Christians might want to add that those conditions include a context of prayerful faith and the action of God in and through the words, symbols and actions.

In pastoral rites, words can be active in other ways too. These services often include vows, promises, questions, namings, commitments and pledges – words used to enact or prepare for significant life changes.

---

9 For more on this, see A. C. Thiselton, *Language, Liturgy and Meaning* (Grove Liturgical Study 2), Nottingham: Grove Books, 1975, pp. 18–19.

'Proper' words

There is a further sense in which words matter in pastoral services, and this is to do with the language register, the style of language and the mood it evokes. Pastoral services (as with all corporate acts of worship) will often preserve more archaic or formal modes of language. This is not unique to Christian worship – any ritual context will tend, all other things being equal, to be conservative in matters of language and ritual. So, for instance, even though the law courts are constantly being modernized in language and practice, the desire to make them accessible is countered by an equally important sense that they must feel 'proper', weighty and significant. An important part of that may be that they are *not* the same in every respect as other everyday places and experiences. This does not mean that all pastoral prayer and worship needs to be archaic and formal to be 'proper', but it does mean recognizing that the way words are used in these contexts may need to be different from the use of words in other contexts.

This has implications not only for the content and form of the words used in pastoral rites, but also for the way the leader of the rite delivers them. The minister is not the only person who needs to be aware of this, but the minister's role is crucial for setting the sense that the rite is doing its job – ministers are not simply there as themselves, they are in role. As Sarah Farrimond puts it, 'The minister in a pastoral rite is there to fulfil a role for the benefit of people at a critical point in their lives, not to display deliberately or carelessly their own personality.'[10]

Symbols

The use of objects in symbolic (some may say, 'sacramental') ways is common in Christian worship, but is particularly important

---

10 Sarah Farrimond, 'Weddings and Funerals', in Christopher Irvine (ed.), *The Use of Symbols in Worship* (Alcuin Liturgy Guides 4), London: SPCK, 2007, p. 97.

in pastoral services. Candles, rings, Bibles, oil; these are all objects used in symbolic ways in pastoral rites, as well as in other Christian worship.

Actions

Alongside the use of objects is the use of action. Sometimes the two go together (that is, it is not just the object, but what you do with it that matters). Here are some examples:

- The *exchange* of wedding rings.
- Bride and groom arriving separately at a wedding and then leaving together.
- Anointing with oil or laying on hands for prayer in a healing service or commissioning for particular service.
- Coming forward to touch or kiss a coffin, or placing flowers on it.
- Taking a child in your arms and placing a hand on its head as you pray a prayer of blessing.

Liminal moments

Think about pastoral rites that you are familiar with. Often the key moments are marked by word, symbol and action coming together – in other words, by a moment of ritual.

THEORY – Juxtaposition: making meaning

The American Lutheran liturgical scholar Gordon Lathrop has helped us to see how Christian worship is shaped and gains some of its impact from the way its structure places things next to one another in such a way as to make new meanings.[11] Among other things, he applies this concept of juxtaposition to the shape of Sunday services, and to the patterns of Christian daily prayer, weekly worship

---

11 Gordon Lathrop, *Holy Things: A Liturgical Theology*, Minneapolis: Fortress Press, 1998.

and annual calendar. We have already seen an example of this idea in the way that pastoral rites juxtapose the human story and the God story in such a way as to let each interpret and enrich the other, to make connections between the two and thence to apply the gospel to the particular situation being marked.

Here I want to take his principle of juxtaposition and apply it at a more detailed level. It is vital to recognize that it is not just the combination of word, symbol and action that is effective in pastoral rites and in Christian worship generally, but *how* they are combined. I suggest three different ways that they are commonly combined.

1   Explanation

In explanation, an object (and action) is given one simple meaning which is then spelt out, just in case anyone misses it. A classic example is the way that candles on an Advent ring are given meanings: 'We light this candle to remember that John the Baptist prepared the way for Jesus,' and so on. Lighting candles is probably the most common context in which this mode is exhibited, but it can apply to other actions too.

2   Reinforcement

Here the words and action are placed next to one another, but without the meaning being explicitly spelt out. This allows more room for imagination and work of the Spirit to make meaning. Simply saying 'Jesus is the light of the world' as we light a candle is an example of reinforcement: we are not saying 'this candle is Jesus', or that this is the only thing it can mean; rather, we provide a context of interpretation but leave the way open for other meaning to be made.

3   Subversion

The most powerful way to combine words and actions is when we juxtapose them in ways that are not obvious, and in which each element is allowed to subvert and challenge the other. Back to our candle: if we light the candle and say, 'The world is full of sorrow,

> pain and hatred,' then we are doing something very different with juxtaposition. Here the candle does not represent the sorrow, pain and hatred, but it might represent the solution to them or at least a response to them. The candle flame can be hope, or Jesus, or prayer, or whatever the Spirit puts into our heart. Think how often the most powerful moments in Christian worship are when elements are juxtaposed in subversive ways. For instance, singing 'Thine be the glory' as the coffin is carried out at a funeral; or saying 'The body of Christ' as you give someone a piece of bread. These are the times and places where God is given space to make new meanings for us, and to do new things in us.

In a pastoral rite, these key stages might be called the liminal moments (though 'moment' does not necessarily imply something instantaneous). These are the points of transition, when things happen and the service *does* what it is intended to do.

The idea of liminality is drawn chiefly from the work of Arnold van Gennep (1873–1957) whom we came across earlier in our discussion of rites of passage. For van Gennep, rites of passage mark a person's transition from one status to another or from one stage of life to another. He described a threefold process of transition and three different types of rites (see Figure 2):

- The separation phase, in which a person lets go of, or is separated from, their current state or stage (Pre-liminal rites).
- The incorporation phase, in which a person joins, or is incorporated into, a new phase which marks their new position or role in life and society (Post-liminal rites).

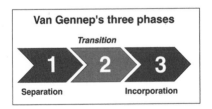

Figure 2

- Between these two comes a transition phase (Liminal rites, from the Latin word *limen* for threshold).

van Gennep talked about rites of these different types, and worked on a careful pattern of categorization. In real life the categorizations do not always feel so neat or clear, and undoubtedly there are other ways of understanding the process of moving through life and the changes that occur. I prefer to think of three phases in a process, in which the liminal moment can be thought of as the point at which you cross the threshold or pass through a doorway. Once you have passed through, you are in a new room: your reality has changed. Hence in pastoral rites, the liminal moment often marks the point at which the service shifts from looking backwards at what is being left behind, to looking forwards at what the new phase holds.

In some services different parts of the process will feel more significant. For instance, in a funeral, the separation phase will usually feel dominant, as the mood will inevitably be focused on looking back, even though a Christian funeral seeks to encourage a hopeful approach to looking forward, for the deceased as well as for the bereaved. By contrast, a wedding will tend to focus on the future, and be more heavily weighted towards the incorporation phase.

THEORY – Questioning van Gennep's model

van Gennep's work has been developed further by others; notably by Victor Turner, who focused on the liminal phase and the way that a shared experience of being 'in between' can build a particular sense of community between those involved.[12] However, van Gennep's theory and the development of it by others has not gone unchallenged. Some have questioned his use of initiation rites as the default pattern, suggesting that he projects that

---

12 See, for instance, Victor Turner, *The Ritual Process: Structure and Anti-structure*, London: Routledge, 1969. His theory has been criticized; see Caroline Walker Bynum, *Fragmentation and Redemption: Essays on Gender and the Human Body in Medieval Religion*, New York: Zone Books, 1991, pp. 27–51.

model onto other forms of rite. Others have suggested that his model assumes a male pattern of initiation rites and does not take account of female perspectives or rites.[13] Jan Berry draws on her own experience as well as the experience of others to suggest that Victor Turner's writings assume a primarily male experience of life as a series of relatively sudden and decisive changes, rather than a more gradual process of change, which she suggests is more typical of women's experience of life.[14] These perspectives are important reminders that the action which the rite 'performs' may not be about changing, solving or completing something, but might be about recognizing, accepting, marking or acknowledging something – 'putting down a marker' in the outer world. In other words, pastoral rites include elements of continuity as well as change.

Though questions can be asked of van Gennep's model, for our purposes, we will simply recognize the basic usefulness of the idea of the three stages, and note how they can be applied to pastoral situations and pastoral services. So, for instance, when someone dies, it is possible to see how a time of illness approaching death is part of the separation phase for those who are close to the person. The death itself is the limen, the threshold. Beyond that comes the phase of grief, loss, and coming to terms with new realities and patterns of life.

In real life the phases are not neatly defined – for instance, grieving may begin before someone has actually died. Equally, it is possible to see how the process can be disrupted. For instance, when someone dies suddenly the separation process may not have happened and this helps us to understand the different role that the funeral then has. The period between death and the funeral takes on a heightened role in helping with the separation phase, and the funeral itself may feel like a recapitulation of the moment of death, helping the close family and friends to be ready to make the next step on their journey.

---

13 Some of the criticisms are well summarized by Grimes, *Deeply*, pp. 103–7.

14 Jan Berry, *Ritual Making Women: Shaping Rites for Changing Lives*, London: Equinox, 2009, pp. 90–4.

In particular we note that the idea of liminality, of transition, can be applied both to periods in our lives, and to specific moments within rites (see Figure 3).[15] For instance, if we step back and consider the whole process of meeting and marrying another person, between the 'moment' of engagement and the 'moment' of a wedding, lies the liminal *state* of being 'engaged' – neither single nor married, but on the way between one and the other.

If we zoom in more closely and look at the rites at stages 1 and 3, we can apply the same model to the actual wedding service. In this case, 'engaged' becomes the *state* from which the couple are being separated, and 'married' becomes the third phase, the state into which they are being incorporated. In between comes a liminal *moment*, the point in the wedding at which vows have been exchanged and the couple are declared wife and husband.

van Gennep's theory was, of course, descriptive, not prescriptive. He was not setting out to show how rites of passage should be, but simply noting patterns that he observed in particular circumstances. However, by being aware of the patterns he observed we can find clues to help us with pastoral rites:

> van Gennep's three stages are not only accurate renditions of what goes on in primitive societies, but they also point to new ways in which rites of passage can be understood and celebrated by Christians.[16]

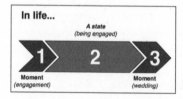 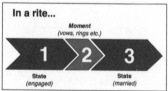

Figure 3

---

15 van Gennep himself recognized the nature of this 'nesting' of the threefold process. See, *The Rites of Passage*, London: Routledge, 1977, p. 11.

16 Kenneth Stevenson, *To Join Together: The Rite of Marriage*, New York: Pueblo, 1987, p. 190.

Often the key to a pastoral service feeling that it has 'done the job' is that there has been a liminal moment which has been handled well and clearly marked, so that it has felt like a significant point in the service, and not been lost. In a Christian marriage service (for instance), the signing of the legal registers is important, but it ought not to feel more important (because of the fuss that surrounds it, or the symbols and ritual that accompany it) than the declaration of the marriage, or the exchange of vows or the blessing of the couple. Liminal moments need to stand out as key parts of the rite. They are by no means the whole story of what pastoral rites are about, but they are often central to their success.

CASE STUDY – A Christian Bar Mitzvah equivalent

Martyn Percy, in *Engaging with Contemporary Culture*,[17] describes a rite which is intended to be a Christian equivalent to the Jewish Bar Mitzvah or Bat Mitzvah, marking at age 13 the process of a young Christian taking on more adult responsibilities within the church and entering adolescence. This is a point at which many churches would use the rite of confirmation. However, this rite took place at Toronto Airport Christian Fellowship in Canada, which practises adult baptism and does not have a rite of confirmation. Instead, they have invented (drawing on Jewish precedent) a rite which helps Christian teenagers to mark a significant stage in their lives in the context of Christian worship. The ceremony includes blessing by pastors and parents and, most significantly, walking across a precarious bridge! This is a liminal moment writ large, making sure that the moment of transition cannot be missed, as each young person makes a literal journey of separation from childhood through to incorporation into adulthood.

One of the principles in van Gennep's thinking was that the process is one-way. Once you have been separated, gone through a transition, and been incorporated into something new, you cannot go back. You can change further, but only by moving forward,

---

17 Martyn Percy, *Engaging with Contemporary Culture: Christianity, Theology, and the Concrete Church*, Aldershot: Ashgate, 2005, p. 175.

crossing new thresholds. So, for instance, though a marriage may be concluded with the death of one of the partners or by divorce, you do not thereby go back to your previous single state, as if reversing the wedding process. Instead you have to go forward, and enter a new state of 'having been married'. This may be marked by other liminal moments (a funeral, or the issuing of a decree absolute).[18]

From 'moment' to 'process'

In recent liturgical revision there has been a greater appreciation of how liturgy needs to parallel the pastoral process of change and transition. This means taking account of the shape of a service itself, making sure that the service allows for a proper preparation and marking of the separation phase, not moving too quickly to a liminal moment or the incorporation phase. It also means making sure that the last part of the service recognizes the new state, and does not go backwards or try to resist the forward journey. In addition, it has influenced thinking about the place of pastoral rites in the bigger pastoral processes of people's lives. The phrase 'from moment to process' sums up this idea that the focus needs to shift from the idea of a moment in a rite to the idea of a continuum of care expressed through a range of different pastoral services, whether formalized or more informally shaped. van Gennep himself talks about life as a sequence of events and accompanying rites, in a constant rhythm:

> For groups, as well as for individuals, life itself means to separate and to be reunited, to change form and condition, to die and to be reborn. It is to act and to cease, to wait and rest, and then to begin acting again, but in a different way. And there are always new thresholds to cross . . .[19]

---

18 This principle of one-way movement is important when working on pastoral rites which intend to 'undo' something, such as a ritual to mark a divorce. Herbert Anderson and Edward Foley describe such an event and call it an *anti-ritual*. However, the marking of a divorce in this way is not so much an anti-ritual but a ritual marking of an anti-wedding. See Anderson and Foley, *Mighty Stories*, pp. 135f.

19 van Gennep, *Rites*, p. 189.

He goes on to recognize that this is not just about events of crisis or joy, but about the natural rhythms of nature and the year which also help us to mark our journeys through life.

This has helpfully reminded us that pastoral rites must not be disconnected from pastoral care more generally. For instance, in churches which provide central resources for funerals, there has been increasing provision for rites which help people to prepare for death, and which surround and follow the funeral itself. For instance, the Church of England's *Common Worship* services include provision for ministry at the time of death, and material for use before the funeral and for those who are unable to be present at the service.[20] *Methodist Worship Book* similarly provides Prayers with the Dying, Prayers in the Home or Hospital after a Death, and an Office of Commendation for use either on hearing of a death or at the time of the funeral for those unable to attend.[21] For the period after the funeral, a welcome example of what is often needed is Paul Sheppy's 'Affirmation of the Living', for use when someone feels that their time of intense grief is over, and they wish to mark a turn towards the future (including, perhaps, the possibility of forming a new relationship for someone whose spouse or partner has died).[22]

This extending of provision from core rites to a series of pastoral liturgical resources is sometimes referred to as providing 'staged rites'. Again, this is not about how the rites are 'staged' in the sense of put on or performed, but is about the way that the rites themselves recognize the bigger process of which they are a part.

A sense of journey through the service

The idea of worship as a journey is a key principle in any act of worship. Much worship that happens on a Sunday is theme-based, and the danger with theme-based worship is that it becomes static, rather than dynamic – we learn lots about God,

---

20 *CWPS*, pp. 216–35, 236–9, and 240–1 respectively.
21 *MWB*, pp. 426–32, 434–6, and 437–41 respectively.
22 Sheppy, *In Sure and Certain Hope*, pp. 84–9.

and express it too, but we are not necessarily *changed* by the act of worship.[23] This is unfortunate when it is the case in Sunday worship, but when it is true of a pastoral rite, it is disastrous. A service needs to have a clear shape which is dynamic and which lends itself to transformation rather than information. The journey model is intended to help with this. Know where you need to start, and where you hope to finish (i.e. have an aim, rather than a theme) and then think about how you will get there – the route, the stopping places, and the potential diversions.

A fourfold shape

One way of shaping the journey is to think of four key sections to a service:

1. Gathering (Why are we here?)
2. Word (What does God have to say?)
3. Response (What should we do about it?)
4. Dismissal (How then shall we live?)[24]

It is possible to describe the same process from God's perspective too:

- God gathers us.
- God speaks to us.
- God changes us.
- God sends us.

This basic shape, however it is articulated, has found much ecumenical favour in recent years as a common structure for

23 See Mark Earey, *Leading Worship* (Grove Worship Series 152), Cambridge: Grove Books, 1999, for more about the difference between 'jigsaw' and 'journey' approaches to planning and leading worship.

24 For some ideas about how this pattern for worship connects with God's pattern for working in and with us, with the shape of the Christian year and the shape of Christian ministry, see David Stancliffe, *God's Pattern: Shaping our Worship, Ministry and Life*, London: SPCK, 2003. Stancliffe finds the fourfold pattern originally in the account of the Road to Emmaus in Luke 24.

understanding the shape of the Eucharist, though the exact naming of the four sections varies considerably. The shape developed from an emphasis on the twin foci of the liturgy of word and table (or sacrament) at the heart of the Eucharist, supplemented by a gathering rite and a dismissal rite.[25] From there it has become more widely adopted, with a recognition that the sacramental section could, in other non-sacramental acts of worship, be named as the section for response or transformation.

In *Methodist Worship Book*, for instance, non-eucharistic Sunday services are introduced in this way:

> They [*the services which follow*] share a common fourfold structure of Preparation, Ministry of the Word, Response and Dismissal . . .[26]

It is possible to see this basic shape in many of the Church of England's *Common Worship* services (either explicitly, or implicitly) through the main section headings,[27] and the principle is spelt out in the Preface to the main volume:

> In each case the journey through the liturgy has a clear structure with signposts for those less familiar with the way. It moves from the gathering of the community through the Liturgy of the Word to an opportunity of transformation, sacramental or

---

25 For more on the eucharistic structure see Thomas F. Best and Dagmar Heller (eds), *Eucharistic Worship in Ecumenical Contexts: The Lima Liturgy – and Beyond*, Geneva: World Council of Churches, 1998, pp. 35 and 140–1.

26 *MWB*, p. 26.

27 For instance, in Holy Communion Order One, the headings are: Gathering; Liturgy of the Word; Liturgy of the Sacrament; Dismissal. In the marriage service the headings are not so clear, but the basic structure is the same. There are other ways to imagine or articulate this structure, such as the dynamic shape focused on gathering and sending suggested in the Baptist Union's worship resource, Christopher J. Ellis and Myra Blyth (eds), *Gathering for Worship*, Norwich: Canterbury Press, 2005, pp. 4–13. Ellis's later book, *Approaching God: A Guide for Worship Leaders and Worshippers*, Norwich: Canterbury Press, 2009, shows how the models can be seen together, pp. 47–61.

non-sacramental, after which those present are sent out to put their faith into practice.[28]

This simple shape makes a great framework for planning worship, whether it is a large-scale service on a Sunday morning, a funeral or wedding service, or a more informal healing service or a simple pastoral encounter involving prayer.

CASE STUDY – The fourfold structure in informal contexts

People were leaving church after the morning service, and Joel, one of the ministers, was busy shaking hands when he saw someone out of the corner of his eye, clearly waiting to speak to him. It was Claire. Claire was facing surgery later that week, and when he spoke to her she asked if they could pray together. Joel suggested that they move to the prayer corner of church, where they could be more focused.

The first thing that Joel did when they were sitting in the prayer corner was to ask Claire to share how she was feeling and what it was that was particularly troubling her. Were there any particular fears? Was there anything she especially wanted to ask God for? (**Gathering** – why are we here?).

Joel then turned to his Bible and read out Psalm 23, verse 4, 'Even though I walk through the darkest valley, I fear no evil; for you are with me; your rod and your staff – they comfort me' – a verse which assures us of God's presence even in the most frightening of circumstances (**Word** – what does God have to say to this situation?).

Joel then asked Claire if he could pray for her. He asked Valerie to join them and suggested that Claire might want to light one of the candles in the prayer corner as a sign of her prayer and her trust that God's light is stronger than the shadow of fear that was troubling her (**Response** – what then shall we do?).

Finally, after they had prayed and laid hands on Claire, Joel used the standard dismissal which had been used at the end of the service that morning: 'Go in peace, to love and serve the Lord,' and Claire responded, 'In the name of Christ. Amen' (**Dismissal** – how then shall we live?).

---

28 *Common Worship: Services and Prayers for the Church of England*, London: Church House Publishing, 2000, p. x.

The idea of journey is not restricted to the act of worship itself. It also applies to the wider pastoral context into which a pastoral service fits. For instance, if a funeral is to do its liminal job, the work of helping the bereaved to engage with the separation phase will need to have begun already, so that the service connects with reality. Those who take funerals often do this through their visiting of the bereaved before the service. Simple actions such as listening (often more than once) to the story of how the person died, and naming the death rather than using euphemisms, is one of the ways that the minister can prepare a family. If a funeral does not feel as if it has done its job, then it may be because some who are present are not ready to make the transition that a funeral marks. Their pastoral reality gets out of step with the liturgical journey, and the result is a perceived lack of integrity to the rite.

Pastoral care and corporate worship, then, will often flow together and interact, and each affects the other. Ensuring that both are serving the same journey will make the pastoral care that results all the more effective. It is easy to get that wrong, and to find that a well-intentioned and theoretically helpful pastoral intervention can fail to reach its full potential, not because it wasn't the right thing to do, but because it didn't come at the best place in the pastoral or liturgical journey for that person.

CASE STUDY – A wedding without dad

When Jen and Matt came to see Marilyn, their local minister, about getting married, it was obvious that Jen was troubled about something. In conversation it transpired that Jen's father had died in the previous year. Though she was intending to ask her brother to walk her down the aisle, she was very upset that her father would not be there to 'give her away' at the wedding, and so she asked if Marilyn would say prayers with her at her father's grave after the wedding. Marilyn readily agreed, seeing it as an important aspect of the pastoral care needed at the wedding.

However, when Marilyn reflected after the meeting she thought again and instead suggested that she went to the grave with Jen and her brother on the day *before* the wedding, and said some prayers to 'pass on' Jen's hand from her father to her brother (to use Jen's way of describing it). Marilyn had realized that when Matt and Jen, as husband and wife, walked down the aisle to the open door, it was important that they went out into the world together and not (symbolically) straight back to her father.

A clear sense of expectations – getting it 'right'

With many (but not all) pastoral services – certainly the ones that are well-established – there are expectations about mood, style, content and structure. We will see how important this is when we come to consider particular services in more detail. For now we simply note that the trend in many churches (and in society) is towards individualizing services in the belief that what is personal and creative is therefore sincere, and has integrity. This can only be a good thing – no one would want a return to the time when funerals at crematoria were led by a duty minister who had never met the family before, or to funerals in which the deceased was not named, but simply referred to as 'our dear brother/sister' (delete as applicable). On the other hand, the very nature of pastoral rituals as corporate repeated events, owned by the wider community, gives a strong sense that certain things have to happen as part of them for the rite to be 'proper'.

> The repetition of ritual also helps create a sense of continuity in our lives by linking the past to the present and the present to the future. In the midst of life's discontinuities, rituals become a dependable source of security and comfort.[29]

This becomes more difficult when a service is being prepared for which there is little established precedent, few published resources, and no official provision – the sorts of events which appear in columns 2 and 3 of Table 1 in the previous chapter. Here it is more tempting to have a blank sheet of paper and a world of possible directions in which to go. However, it is good to remember that

---

29 Anderson and Foley, *Mighty Stories*, p. 49.

part of the challenge of creating these 'new' sorts of service is how to maintain that sense that they 'work' and do something. This will often require connections with forms of service that people are already familiar with, or with principles and tools which people have come across in other pastoral services. These can reassure them that this service too is doing the job properly. We will reflect further in Chapter 8 on creating rituals and services for new pastoral situations or for particular individual needs.

The dangers of expectation violation

In the meantime, for more established rites there usually are expectations. If you are the minister leading such a service, you need to be aware what those expectations are and to recognize that the service does not belong to you, or even to the individual or family which the service is focused on.

Those expectations may sometimes be false or unhelpful, and they may sometimes need to be challenged – but they cannot be ignored or trampled over. As Elaine Ramshaw puts it: 'Anyone who doesn't have deep respect for that hunger for continuity should not be messing around with other people's ritual practice.'[30] Her comment comes in a discussion about regular Sunday worship, but it applies equally to pastoral rites.

IN PRACTICE – Familiar words

One aspect of this need for continuity might be as simple as the use of particular words or phrases. For instance, the phrase, 'Earth to earth, ashes to ashes, dust to dust,' has been associated with the committal at a funeral in England since the first English Prayer Book of 1549. There is nothing which says that these words could not be replaced with others, and sometimes alternatives might be used. In some traditions this phrase will never have been central in the first place. But in traditions and sections of the population where that phrase *will* have been heard at funerals for generations, its absence can leave a gap.

---

30 Ramshaw, *Ritual*, p. 25.

The same principles can apply in Christian traditions which do not rely on printed texts and fixed forms of words. There will still be particular expectations about the sorts of things that will be said, the order in which things happen, the practicalities of how the service takes place, which are violated at your peril.

Evolution not revolution

This is not to say that changes can never happen – they happen all the time, and perhaps that change will accelerate in a fragmenting culture in which expectations are not shared so widely. But generally in pastoral rites too much is at stake for change to happen quickly or too regularly. Ronald Grimes memorably sums up the tension between expectation and creativity, between tradition and transition: 'Rites are not givens; they are hand-me-downs, quilts we continually patch.'[31] In general changes come gradually, by evolution and bit by bit. They can happen more quickly, but this will occur only when a large part of the wider population are exposed to a change in a context that suggests this is now 'okay'. Nowadays this sort of relatively quick change comes through things people see on television or other mass media. If they show a wedding on *EastEnders* or *Coronation Street*, for example, people tend to think that what they see is what 'everyone is doing', and so a new idea can quickly catch on (in the same way that names of children tend to follow the trends set by the rich and famous).

One example was the impact of the funeral of Diana, Princess of Wales in 1997.[32] In my own pastoral practice I sensed that after that service, ordinary funeral practice shifted slightly. Two things particularly seemed to impact on this. The first was the

---

31 Ronald L. Grimes, *Deeply into the Bone: Re-inventing Rites of Passage*, Berkeley, CA: University of California Press, 2002, p. 12.

32 As Paul Sheppy points out in *Death*, Vol. 1, p. 101, the service at Westminster Abbey had more in common with a memorial service, and the funeral service itself was the Burial service from the *Book of Common Prayer*, which took place privately later that day. He also suggests that the idea of a Christian funeral which is 'not too religious please' gained credibility that day.

'eulogy' given by Earl Spencer, and the second was Elton John singing 'Candle in the Wind'. After that, I found that it became more common for families planning a funeral to consider the possibility of someone from among the close family and friends saying something about the deceased, as well as, or instead of the minister. It also became more common for people to request recordings of popular music in the service, which reflected something of their loved one. It is not that these things never happened before, or that they became universal afterwards, simply that people had seen a model of what might happen and felt emboldened to apply it to their own context. More recently, it will be interesting to see the impact of the royal wedding in April 2011 on the practice of weddings. Will couples be more willing to consider a traditional language service (William and Catherine chose to use the Church of England's Series One marriage service, which is a revision of the service in the *Book of Common Prayer*)? And will everyone want trees lining the aisle at their weddings, like the ones which lined Westminster Abbey?

However, though change can happen, leaders of pastoral services (and the individuals and families they work with) do well to remember that anything that might leave people afterwards not sure if it has 'done the job', or that it was 'proper', will be a hindrance rather than a help. This is an important reminder that creativity is at its most powerful in these rites when it is a creative variation on something that people can still recognize, not when it begins from scratch. Catherine Bell is one of several writers to consider the Soviet Union's attempts to invent new rituals for life events to replace what they saw as the superstitious ones of the Church.[33] This required creativity on a massive scale, but what resulted was connected with what it was intended to replace, as well as different from it. Something which is 'new' is still interpreted and understood in terms of what it is over-against, what it is different from.

---

33 Catherine Bell, *Ritual: Perspectives and Dimensions*, Oxford: Oxford University Press, 2009, pp. 223–9.

This should all give us pause for thought when we are tempted to invent a ritual, or be creative with existing services, or when we pull down from the shelves one of the increasing number of creative resources for pastoral services.

Who is the service for?

Both pastorally and evangelistically it is important to remind ourselves that pastoral services are not just for those who are most closely involved. Others who are present may be going through their own pastoral situations, happy or sad, which are very different from that being celebrated in the service itself. How will the service speak to them? How will the service, while doing its job for the immediate pastoral concern, also articulate a gospel which is good news for those at other stages of life, feeling very different emotions and asking other questions? This question of 'who the service is for' is one that we will come back to in later chapters.

Summary

Perhaps the key principle to have at the back of our minds throughout is that a pastoral rite must, above all, *do* something and not just *mean* something, if it is to be effective. A funeral (to use just one example) is not a service where the theme is death and resurrection – a funeral has to enable us to commend someone we love to God's care. We must not just think about the meaning of what is happening in our lives, we must not simply bring that thinking to God, we must actually feel and know that we have crossed a threshold, that the journey has moved on, that God has helped us and is present to act in our lives.

I have outlined in this chapter some of the key principles of pastoral liturgy, which I have called tools for a pastoral liturgy toolkit. They are not only useful for pastoral and liturgical practice, they are also useful tools for evaluating the services and resources which already exist. In the chapters that follow we will see how these tools are applied in particular pastoral rites. This will not be a systematic look at every tool for every rite, but rather an opportunity to focus on different areas in each particular rite, seeing where the challenges and issues are focused today and using the tools for evaluation and reflection on practice. For more thorough guidance about theory and practice for these individual rites, see the Further Reading suggestions for particular services at the end of the book.

4

Birth Rites

A birthday party as a pastoral rite

Most of us will be familiar with what happens at a birthday party. In the UK, a typical birthday party (for a child or an adult) might include some or all of the following:

- Balloons, decorations, banners.
- The giving of cards and gifts to the person whose birthday it is.
- A cake, decorated with candles.
- The bringing in of the cake with the candles alight (often other lights will be turned out to heighten the experience), with exclamations of 'Ah!', as if no one were expecting this to happen.
- The singing of 'Happy Birthday' to a traditional tune, expected to be known by all, followed by applause.
- The blowing out of the candles by the birthday person (preferably with one breath – everyone will be watching closely to make sure this happens), along with a 'wish' being made.
- The cutting and sharing of the cake with the guests, either now or for them to take away.

It is not hard to see in this description many of the elements which I have called principles or tools to use in pastoral rites – for instance, there is a liminal moment marked by the use of objects with symbolic meaning (the cake and candles), the use of actions (bringing in the cake, blowing out candles, clapping), accompanied by specific words (usually the singing of 'Happy birthday to you'). There is also the clear sense of needing to meet existing expectations. Well-meaning as you might be, if you suggest cutting the singing of the song, 'because it's so old-hat', and 'while we're at it, let's not have the cake or the candles', your suggestions would not be well-received. That is not to say that you cannot change some things – for instance, if you hate cake, you might get away with a box of doughnuts, but the chances are that someone would suggest putting candles in them to make them 'birthday doughnuts'. Or maybe you could sing a different version of Happy Birthday. In extreme circumstances, you might need to improvise (birthday crisp packet?), but in general, even if people play around a bit with the tradition and the expectations, what everyone recognizes is what the improvised item is *not* being, or what the change is *from*.

Let us now imagine, just for the sake of argument, that we wanted to turn a birthday party into a Christian pastoral rite. What is missing from the birthday party? It already has its liminal moment. What would we need to add or change to make it a pastoral rite?

The God story

The first thing that is missing is the God story. What Scripture passages would you suggest for a birthday party service – a deliberate attempt to take a birthday party and make it a Christian rite? The answers that come up if you ask this question often fall into two basic categories. If people are thinking primarily of a child's party they tend to suggest a range of passages themed around children:

- Passages about honouring your parents (such as Ex. 20.12; Eph. 6.1; and Col. 3.20).
- Hannah longing for the gift of a child (1 Sam. 1).
- The boy Samuel being called by God in the middle of the night (1 Sam. 3) (incidentally, they don't normally suggest the passage between these two, where the child Samuel is left at the temple with Eli! – 1 Sam. 2.11).

- Young David defeating the giant Goliath (1 Sam. 17).
- Jesus setting children as an example of humility for his disciples (Mark 9.35–37).
- Jesus welcoming and blessing the children (Mark 10.13–16).
- Jesus himself as a child, either the birth narratives or the accounts of him being presented at the temple (Luke 2.22–38) or being left behind at the temple when he was 12 (Luke 2.41–52) (another passage with potential for suggesting unhelpful patterns).
- Paul's exhortation to Timothy not to let anyone look down on him because of his youth (1 Tim. 4.12), or other passages from 1 and 2 Timothy, as tender advice from an older person to a younger one about how to live the Christian life.

If people are thinking more generally of a party which could be for a child or an adult, they tend to suggest passages about the bigger picture of life and God's involvement in it, such as:

- Psalm 139.13–18 – God knowing us since before we were born.
- Ecclesiastes 3.1–8 – there is a time for everything (though perhaps not the section about there being a time to die . . .).
- Romans 8.31–39 – in all circumstances God is for us, and nothing can separate us from God's love.

What is immediately obvious is how the different passages would give very different interpretations to the event, reflecting very different ways of putting the God story alongside the human story and finding the connections.

The human story

Though the God story would be the obvious thing which might need to be added to a birthday party to make it a Christian rite, the other part which might need to be strengthened is the human story. At a birthday party, in general, most of those present know (or are assumed to know) the story of the person whose birthday it is. At some birthday parties we do tend to make more of the human story. When it is someone's 21st, or 40th, or 80th birthday party, there is more likely to be more explicit story-telling. That might come via some short speeches, or it might consist of a display of photos. But these do not tend to happen so much for a 'normal' annual birthday party. To make the rite 'do' more, one might want to increase the explicit story-telling part of the party/service, perhaps through the birthday person telling their own story, giving testimony of what God has done in their life in the last year, or simply recounting some of the highlights or challenges which have filled the space since the last birthday.

Other elements to add

Are there other things which might make a party into a rite (or, at least, add a rite into a party)? The cake is already a central element – might we say a prayer over the cake, giving it symbolic meaning? Should we say grace before eating the party food, and if so, how would we use that prayer to connect the thanks for God's goodness in supplying physical needs with thanks for the year in the life of the person being celebrated? Perhaps we might include special prayer for the child or adult whose birthday it is, asking for God's grace and strength to accompany them in the year to come.

It is immediately obvious that we would need to structure this party rite carefully. A prayer for the future would most naturally come near the end, as part of the incorporation phase (to use van Gennep's model). The human story, in testimony, or speeches or photos, needs to come early and be followed by the God story in the shape of a reading from the Bible or a paraphrased Bible story. The turning point from thanks for the past to looking to the future comes with the cake, the candles and the wish, turned instead into prayer for the future.

And would the person whose birthday it is have to be a Christian? It would certainly make most sense and be most comfortable (for the guests as well as the birthday person) if this were the case, but it is possible to imagine a scenario where someone with no particular faith wished to celebrate another year of their life 'in the sight of God' and might turn to the church for help to do so. It is possible . . . but don't hold your breath.

CASE STUDY – Celebrating birthdays in church

Though the scenario envisaged above, of turning a birthday party into a Christian rite of passage, has not been a regular part of the Church's offering of pastoral services, many churches do celebrate birthdays in the context of Sunday worship. I have been part of several churches which, at their monthly all age service, invite anyone (of any age) whose birthday falls in that month, to come to the front. Once at the front, some or all of them might be invited to tell us how old they are going to be. Usually we would then sing Happy Birthday to them, often using a Christianized version of the Happy Birthday song – something along the lines of, 'Happy birthday to you, to Jesus be true, may God's richest blessings be showered on you.'[1] This was usually followed by a round of applause. Some of the key elements were present (human story, ritual acts, prayer). What was missing?

From birthdays to birth days

Though the Church does not have a history of providing birthday party rites, it does have a history of rites which surround the birth of a child. However, that history is complex and not straightforward, as we shall see.

Baptism as a birth rite

It is an undeniable fact that, 'through a series of historical accidents baptism has come to fulfil the function of a birth rite in

---

[1] This is one version which was sung at a church I belonged to. I have no idea if it had been created by someone at that church or whether they got it from somewhere else. I apologize if I have infringed anyone's copyright by reproducing it here.

many Christian denominations'.[2] During the era of Christendom in the West, the baptism of infants was seen not only as entry into the Church, but as entry into society; indeed, the two were seen as synonymous. Not only so, but high levels of infant mortality and a fear of infants dying unbaptized led to baptism taking place very soon after birth. In the medieval period, it became common practice for midwives to baptize newborn infants in the home, but even if the child was brought to church for baptism, it would take place very close to the time of birth. Because of the dominance of infant baptism there were few candidates for adult baptism (hence the original *Book of Common Prayer*, whether the 1549 or 1552 version, makes no provision for adults to be baptized at all). No wonder, then, that baptism became that 'accidental' birth rite. However, as soon as we consider adult baptism, it becomes harder to see baptism in this way, as Aidan Kavanagh reminds us:

> For baptism is indeed about birth, but it is not about birth in the natural order . . . There is nothing intrinsically infantile about Christian baptism, nor is there anything intrinsically adolescent about confirmation.[3]

The key word in this quotation is 'intrinsically'. The dominance of infants as candidates for baptism in the past has skewed our thinking about baptism overall. When you can assume that all or most infants will be baptized, it is possible to lose the sense that baptism is something which marks out those who are Christians. When 'everyone' is a Christian, baptism ceases to be marker of that, and instead it is tempting to think of it as essentially a sign or instrument of God's grace which welcomes a new baby into the world. Baptism certainly is about grace, but it is also crucially about response to God's grace – there is no way to read the

---

2 Paul F. Bradshaw and Lawrence A. Hoffman (eds), *Life Cycles in Jewish and Christian Worship*, Notre Dame, IN: University of Notre Dame Press, 1996, p. 13.

3 Aidan Kavanagh, 'Life-cycle events, civil ritual and the Christian', in David Power and Luis Maldonado (eds), *Liturgy and Human Passage* (*Concilium* 112), New York: Seabury Press, 1979, p. 16.

New Testament and escape this emphasis. It is not that baptism is the sacrament of grace, to which we then respond; rather, being baptized *is* the response to God's grace, which is held out to us through the preaching of the gospel, the message of the Scriptures and the witness of creation.

Baptism is therefore not simply a birth rite; it is a rite of new birth, which for some candidates takes place close to their physical birth, but is not *intrinsically* related to it. In a pastoral rite, the God story that is told certainly needs to fit the human story; so in an infant baptism there must be some point of contact with the fact that the candidate is a baby. But that is not the same as saying that the God story can be completely determined by the human story. 'Although baptism is a family event, it is not simply a continuation of a family story.'[4] The core God story in baptism both liturgically and theologically is along these lines: 'Creation is spoiled; God wishes to put it right, and in Christ he has done so and will do so; come and join in by letting God put your own life right and by working with God for the putting right of the whole creation.' The core human story to which that God story connects is, 'Someone is going to join in.' That human story will have different details depending on whether the candidate is two months old or 30 years old, but the core story is the same. What cannot happen, if baptism is to still be baptism, is for the core human story to become, 'Someone has recently been born,' or for the God story to become, 'God loves children and wants to show us his love from the very beginning of our lives.' This is an important God story, but it is not the God story of baptism.

Effectively, this was the God story which was inserted into baptism when the account of Jesus welcoming and blessing the children became the Bible reading.[5] In a Christendom context

---

4 Herbert Anderson and Edward Foley, *Mighty Stories, Dangerous Rituals: Weaving Together the Human and the Divine*, San Francisco: Jossey-Bass, 2001, p. 65.

5 Mark 10.13–16 was the Bible reading at baptism in the 1549 Prayer Book. This replaced the Sarum rite, which had used the parallel passage from Matthew 19.13–15. The Eastern Church used Romans 6.3–12 and Matthew 28.16–20, passages about baptism rather than about children. See Charles Neil and J. M. Willoughby, *The Tutorial Prayer Book*, London: Harrison Trust, 1912, p. 384.

one can see why it happened, but it distorted the Church's understanding of baptism thereafter. The Methodist and Church of England rites of recent years have tried to turn back that particular tide by making the default baptism service in their books simply a rite of baptism, whether for adults or infants, rather than assuming children as the default candidates and then providing a separate service for adults.

In some ways, of course, baptism is a pastoral rite like any other that we are considering. It is occasioned by the particular needs of an individual at a particular point in their life – whether that is a young baby or child whose parents wish them to be baptized, or the candidate is an adult who has come to a life-changing encounter with Christ which they wish to mark. Its practice will also, no doubt, benefit from the application of some of the principles of the pastoral liturgy toolkit, and particularly the careful use of symbols and action to ensure that baptism feels like the liminal moment it should be. Many readers, I know, will wish that this chapter was devoted to the challenges of caring pastorally through infant baptism services, and I omit it reluctantly, and not because I do not think it matters.[6]

At root, however, baptism is a rite of passage *into* the Church, and not just a rite of passage celebrated in a church. This means that it cannot be treated in the same way I am treating other pastoral rites, as *invitations* to consider the God story and put it alongside our human story. Baptism marks the next stage, a *commitment* to respond to the invitation and to keep on connecting the human story with God's story, even if that commitment is ill-articulated or is at the very early stages. Baptism is increasingly recognized as the sacrament of spiritual rebirth and of welcome into the Church for people of all ages, and only secondarily (if at all) as a welcome into society and into a child's human family.

---

6 I refer frustrated readers to the many books which do focus on good practice in infant baptism, including Mark Earey, Trevor Lloyd and Ian Tarrant (eds), *Connecting with Baptism: A Practical Guide to Christian Initiation Today*, London: Church House Publishing, 2007.

Finally, we note that even when infant baptism is chosen, whether by churchgoing families or not, it is often delayed considerably beyond the child's actual birth and may take on other roles, such as marking a deepening commitment in the relationship between the parents and thus becoming either a substitute for marriage or a step on a journey to it.[7] Baptism is no longer seen as obviously and naturally related to birth, even though it is still often thought of as something for children. It is time to look at other possibilities for a contemporary birth rite.

Other possibilities

The churching of women

The other obvious possibility from church history is not promising. In Western Europe the most widely known and practised service associated with childbirth (at least since the eleventh century) was 'The Thanksgiving of Women after Child-birth, commonly called The Churching of Women'. This is its full title in the English *Book of Common Prayer* of 1552 (retained in the later 1662 version) and shows that at that time the use of the service was already a well-established tradition. The title in the earlier *Book of Common Prayer* of 1549 is somewhat different: 'The Order of the Purification of Women'. This gives an indication of the understanding of the service inherited from the medieval period, being a translation of the Latin title of the medieval Catholic service in the Sarum Manual. The change in title in 1552 shows a significant shift taking place, removing the association of the service with purification and making it explicitly an act of thanksgiving.[8]

---

7 See Alan Billings, *Secular Lives, Sacred Hearts: The Role of the Church in a Time of No Religion*, London: SPCK, 2004, pp. 52–4.

8 See Natalie Knödel, 'Reconsidering an obsolete rite: The Churching of Women and feminist liturgical theology', *Feminist Theology*, 14, Jan. 1997, pp. 106–25. A similar change in title and emphasis takes place in the Roman Catholic *Rituale Romanum* of 1614; See Walter von Arx, 'The Churching of Women after Childbirth: History and significance', in Power and Maldonado,

Though the Churching of Women is a service surrounding childbirth, it is primarily a service about the mother and not the child, which is one of the things which makes it so different both from infant baptism and from other more recent services surrounding childbirth.[9] The birth rite itself (that is the rite focused on the child) would have been baptism, which happened soon after birth and before the churching service. Nonetheless, churching was a significant part of the way that the birth of a child was marked for many centuries.

The woman, 'decently apparelled', would come to church 'at the usual time after her Delivery' (traditionally this had been 40 days). She would come fully into the church ('in some convenient place, nigh unto the quire door' – 1549) and not just the church porch as during the pre-Reformation period.[10] Here the woman would kneel while the minister would remind her of how important it was to give thanks to God for her safe delivery through the perils of childbirth. Then he would read out either Psalm 116 ('The Lord hath heard the voice of my prayer . . . The snares of death encompassed me round about . . . I will pay my vows now in the presence of all his people: in the courts of the Lord's house . . .) or Psalm 127 ('Lo, children and the fruit of the womb are an heritage and gift that cometh of the Lord . . . Happy is the man that hath his quiver full of them . . .').

Liturgy pp. 65–9. For other background about churching see Joanne M. Pierce, '"Green Women" and blood pollution: Some medieval rituals for the churching of women after childbirth', *Studia Liturgica* 29, 1999, pp. 191–215.

9 The Orthodox Church also has a service of Churching, which follows 'Prayers on the First Day after a Woman has Given Birth to a Child' and the 'Naming of a Child' (on the eighth day after birth). Unlike the Western form, the Churching is a service for both mother and child, and the child is assumed to be still unbaptized. Any idea of purification of the mother attaches more to the Prayers on the First Day than to the Churching. See Alexander Schmemann, *Of Water and the Spirit: A Liturgical Study of Baptism*, London: SPCK, 1976, pp. 131–47; and Ron Grove, 'Baby dedication in traditional Christianity: Eastern Orthodox "churching" of forty-day-olds', *Journal of Ecumenical Studies*, 27, No. 1, Winter 1990, pp. 101–7.

10 There is a brief description of what a churching might have been like in medieval England in Roy Strong, *A Little History of the English Country Church*, London: Vintage, 2008, pp. 46–7.

This was followed by the Lord's Prayer, some versicles and responses and a final prayer for the woman, that she might live faithfully in this life and come to everlasting glory. Finally, the rubric requires the woman to 'offer accustomed offerings' and 'if there be a Communion, it is convenient that she receive the Holy Communion'. Note that there is nothing in the service which requires the presence of the child at all, or the presence of the father. The mother could come on her own or with others to support her, and the service could take place even if the child had died (which perhaps explains the choice of psalms – one focusing on deliverance from peril and the other emphasizing the blessing of children). It is the mother's deliverance, rather than the child's arrival, which is being celebrated.

CASE STUDY – Churching in modern Britain

When I was vicar of a church in West Yorkshire, someone discovered a number of copies of our parish magazine from the early 1890s. In these magazines the front page gave the times of regular services, which included baptisms and churchings. Simply turn up at church at 2.15pm or 3.45pm on the first Sunday in the month, or at 7pm any Wednesday evening (that is, before the regular Wednesday evening service) and you could be 'churched'.

Many of the older women in the congregation could remember churchings from their own lives, though for most of them it was the stories from their own mothers, and not their own experiences. By the time most of them were mothers (in the 1950s and 1960s) churching was already dying out, and the women were the ones who were causing it to die. I remember Elsie telling me how she refused to be churched after the birth of her child. Churching was seen as necessary before a woman who had given birth could re-enter society – to receive an unchurched mother into your home was to invite bad luck. Elsie was having none of it – against the advice of her own mother, she refused churching, and was one of a whole new generation who refused to see themselves as unclean and giving birth as something that excluded you from society.

By the early part of the twenty-first century, when my ministry was beginning in the parish, no one asked for churching, and most people had never even heard of it. But the modern service of Thanksgiving for the Gift of a Child in *Common Worship* was increasingly popular, while infant baptisms continued their slow decline.

The extinction of churching

There are several overlapping reasons why churching has declined to the point of extinction in Britain today.[11] Most significant among these reasons is that women became increasingly empowered and confident to challenge existing patterns and traditions and to decide for themselves how they wish to engage both with the experience of childbirth and with the Church. They are certainly not prepared to be considered unclean because of giving birth. This is evident in Elsie's story, even as early as the 1950s.

TO THINK ABOUT – How did the idea of uncleanness attach to giving birth?

The churching service in the *Book of Common Prayer* has, since 1552, not contained any reference, either in the title of the service or in its content, to childbirth making a woman unclean. The only hint of a need for purification comes in the retention of the rubric at the very end of the service which requires the woman to 'offer accustomed Offerings'. Yet 400 years later, there was still a common belief that the main purpose of the service was to purify the mother, or to make her fit to re-enter society. Clearly the purification 'story' had become very closely associated with the service, even when the text of the service had moved on. (This is a salutary point for all those who revise liturgical texts and think that by

---

11 It should be noted that churching has not died out in other parts of the world. A friend recently sent me a photograph of a packed Anglican church in Tanzania, full of families attending a churching service.

doing so they will quickly change people's understanding.) So where does that part of the 'story' come from?

The biblical starting point is Leviticus 12, which sets out the uncleanness which was believed to follow childbirth and establishes the need for a religious rite of purification, the making of animal offerings, and the period of time during which the mother was to be considered unclean. The making of an offering is something which is echoed in the churching service, where it refers to an offering of money. It is this Bible passage which lies behind the purification of Mary, the mother of Jesus, in Luke 2.22–24 (though in Luke it is described as 'their' purification, rather than Mary's alone). One can see how easy (though mistaken) it is to make the jump: 'If even the Blessed Virgin Mary was unclean after giving birth to the Son of God, how much more must ordinary women be unclean after delivering their children.'

But there are other reasons for the extinction of churching too. Giving birth is still potentially dangerous, and for millions of women in the world it is truly life-threatening. But in the West it is now generally seen as something which is *normally* safe. Unlike previous generations, when a large proportion of women could expect to die in childbirth, nowadays a birth which results in the death of the mother is seen as an unusual and tragic occurrence. When the human story of giving birth is seen as more 'normalized', the God story of near-miraculous preservation, which not only invites but demands thanksgiving, does not make so much sense, and new God stories need to be heard.

Churching also marked the point at which the mother left the home environment and rejoined wider society. The growth of hospital births, as opposed to home births, changed that dynamic. The woman could hardly be confined to hospital for 40 days, and the fact that the birth itself took place outside the home made any restriction to the home context thereafter feel odd. Giving birth is no longer something which takes place 'behind closed doors', doors which traditionally excluded men and added to the sense of childbirth being a mysterious and marginalizing experience.

Women's more prominent role in society generally means that the story and understanding of what childbirth involves is 'out there' in the public domain. The presence of fathers at the birth of their children (again, a relatively recent change) means that the story is not confined to the women. None of this makes bearing a child an easier experience (though pain relief and other medical support has helped), but it does reduce its marginalization.

In the church context, the growing numbers of single mothers affected practice. (Actually, it was not so much a growth in numbers as a growing refusal of such women to be 'hidden'.) Churches might refuse churching to single mothers, and therefore risk looking very unwelcoming and judgemental, but women in that situation became more likely to take control and refuse to ask for churching.

Finally, the extinction of churching is partly because of its lack of emphasis on the child. In a society which increasingly romanticizes children, seeing them as central, where families generally have fewer children than in previous generations, and therefore may tend to see each as even more precious, it feels more natural to look for a service in which the child is central – being named, or blessed, or having thanks offered for them.

Birth rites in use today

Although churching has all but died out, and infant baptism is in decline, surveys show that a significant proportion of people want to mark the birth of a child with some kind of religious ritual.[12] Many Churches now offer a service to recognize the birth of a child which is very different from churching. As Trevor Lloyd puts it:

---

12 In the Soul of Britain survey, 53 per cent of respondents expressed a desire for a religious ceremony to mark a child's birth, see Paul Avis (ed.), *Public Faith? The State of Religious Belief and Practice in Britain*, London: SPCK, 2003, p. 98.

It does not start with the mediaeval question, 'How can we encourage and allow this woman back into our holy building?' but with the more homely and contemporary question, 'Tell us how you feel about the arrival of this child, and we will see if we can express that in prayer and thanksgiving.'[13]

Now that many people choose a church on grounds such as worship style or provision of children's activities rather than denomination, congregations often include a range of views about baptism and churches therefore need to have a mixed economy in terms of what is offered as a rite to celebrate birth. In the same church, some children may be brought for baptism while other parents want a blessing or a dedication service for their new baby.

TO THINK ABOUT – Infant dedication

Baptist churches and others which practise only believers' baptism will often offer a service of 'dedication'. Here it is important to ascertain who is being dedicated and to what. Is it the dedication of the child to God? Or is it the dedication of the parents to bringing their child up in a Christian home so that the child can make his or her own decision for Christ in due time?

In addition, beyond the church, though 'christening' still probably conjures up images and ideas which are primarily related to baptism (the use of water and white robes, for instance) what is actually sought is often more to do with blessing a child and welcoming it into its human family.[14]

The titles of the new services are revealing:

---

13 Trevor Lloyd, *Thanksgiving for the Gift of a Child: A Commentary on the Common Worship Service* (Grove Worship Series 165), Cambridge: Grove Books, 2001, p. 5.

14 Helen Sammon has done some interesting research about what parents are hoping for from a christening service. A summary of her findings was published in *Church Times*, 9 September 2011, pp. 19–20.

- Methodist Church: *An Act of Thanksgiving for the Birth or Adoption of a Child.*[15]
- Church of England: *Thanksgiving for the Gift of a Child* (the name was designed to allow for its use where a child has been adopted, and in cases where the child is older, rather than recently born).[16]
- United Reformed Church: *Thanksgiving for the Birth of a Child: The dedication of parents and the blessing of children.*[17]

In each case the focus is on the child and in each case the focus is on thanksgiving. The URC service name makes explicit what is also present in the Methodist and Church of England services, which is the blessing of the child and an opportunity for parents to make commitments about the child's upbringing. The Methodist and Anglican services also include an element of naming – not the giving of a name, but a question asking what the name is, and the formalized using of that name in thanksgiving and blessing.

Part of the challenge for churches offering these services in a British context is the huge shadow of christenings (infant baptisms) which hangs over them. Because for many centuries, Christian baptism was the default rite surrounding the birth of a child, anything else which is offered has to distinguish itself and justify itself against that folk memory backdrop. Even for those who have no regular church connection, any notion of what the church might have to offer is probably connected with christening. For churches which offer Thanksgiving services but also baptize infants there also has to be some careful footwork

---

15 *MWB*, pp. 399–403. For commentary on the service, see Neil Dixon, *Wonder, Love and Praise: A Companion to the Methodist Worship Book*, Peterborough: Epworth, 2003, pp. 152f.

16 The service can be found in *Common Worship: Pastoral Services*, pp. 200–12. It is also printed in the *Common Worship* main volume and in *Common Worship: Christian Initiation*. For commentary on the service, see Lloyd, *Thanksgiving*, and Earey, Lloyd and Tarrant, *Connecting with Baptism*, pp. 54–8 and 126–31.

17 *WURC*, Part 1, pp. 77–81.

to make sure that the offering of these other services does not suggest a retreat from infant baptism. So, the Methodist service includes this explanation at the start of the service:

> In the Methodist tradition, the children of Christian parents are normally brought for Baptism, but there are occasions when An Act of Thanksgiving . . . may be helpful, either suggested by the minister or requested by the parents . . .[18]

This is followed in the service itself with a prayer which specifically mentions baptism, just to make it clear that this service is *not* baptism, and to remind everyone that baptism is still where we are aiming:

> May *she/he* come to know you
> and to share with all your people
> the life of the baptized, the bread of heaven,
> and the joys of your kingdom;
> through Jesus Christ our Lord. Amen.[19]

The *Common Worship* Thanksgiving service has a similar prayer,[20] and a clarification that this service is *not* baptism, and that you should ask the minister if you are interested in finding out about baptism.[21]

These services are also part of a wider ritual landscape beyond the church. The British Humanist Society offers, through its website, advice about secular naming ceremonies, and publishes a guide to them.[22] The Family Covenant Association is a

---

18 *MWB*, p. 399.

19 *MWB*, p. 401.

20 *CWPS*, p. 204.

21 *CWPS*, p. 201. This is in the Pastoral Introduction, which is designed to be read by those waiting for the service to start. In many actual services the congregation might never see this, especially if a locally produced booklet is used which does not include it.

22 The guide is Jane Wynne Willson and Robert Ashby, *New Arrivals: A Guide to Non-religious Naming Ceremonies*, London: British Humanist Association, 1991.

non-religious, but not anti-religious, organization which exists to foster the use of rituals surrounding the birth of a child. Many local authorities also offer a naming ceremony, performed by a trained celebrant, as an alternative to religious rites.

These ceremonies draw on many of the key tools in our pastoral liturgy toolkit (some doing so better than others), but the key elements that are missing or potentially missing are the God story and the eschatological perspective. The reference to baptism in the Anglican and Methodist Thanksgiving rites, mentioned above, has the effect of noting the future spiritual journey of the child as well as general hopes that the child will be happy and healthy and loved by family and friends. It points to God's grace and the fullness of life which, in Christian understanding, depends on that grace. And ultimately the Christian rites recognize that final threshold, the doorway of death, which every human being must one day cross, and does not shy away from that. This is what the Christian Church has to offer in a society in which it is just one among competing voices. Perhaps we should be bolder in offering it?

Some issues for church practice today

Reclaiming a positive focus on the mother

Today, the idea of uncleanness and purification which has been associated with the churching service is rightly rejected. However, some have questioned more recent services, which tend to focus on the child and to recognize the important role of the father, as well as the mother.[23] Feminist theologians, in particular, see potential losses in these moves, as well as the more obvious gains, and remind us of the need to recognize in ritual ways the particular journey of the mother, separate from the journey of the child

---

23 *CWPS* includes in the supplementary prayers a prayer specifically for the father (Prayer 5, p. 209) as well as for grandparents, siblings and health workers, but no prayer specifically for the mother, except after a difficult birth (Prayer 8, p. 210).

or the father.[24] Despite the negative associations of uncleanness, the expectation that a woman would not re-enter normal society for 40 days after giving birth was, in its own way, a form of protection for her. In this way she was spared the pressure to take on her normal responsibilities too soon, and given the space and time to recover physically and emotionally from labour and delivery.

In his book, *Staging Posts*, Roger Grainger describes a service for celebrating the birth of a child.[25] It is interesting because of the way that it retains a special role for the mother, while not losing the focus on the child. He does this by separating out the thanksgiving for a safe delivery and the mother's journey, from thanksgiving for the child and welcoming the child into its whole human family, including the wider community of friends.

What is also notable is the way that he uses movement to emphasize the liminal shift from the mother's primary responsibility for the child to a sense of corporate responsibility, shared by the father and the wider family. After an opening hymn and introduction there is a reading chosen by the mother (which can be from any source), and a Bible reading. Then the service comes to the central section.

- The mother (alone) comes to the front of the church.
- The minister takes the mother's hand and asks: 'Do you thank God for all he has done in giving you this child?' and she responds. Then the minister asks, 'Is there anyone else you would like to thank?' and the mother may name others.
- A hymn is then sung, during which the mother goes to the back of church and collects the child (presumably from a relative or friend).

24 See Knödel, 'Reconsidering an obsolete rite'; and Thelma Aldcroft, 'Childbirth, liturgy and ritual: A neglected dimension of pastoral theology', in Elaine Graham and Margaret Halsey (eds), *Life Cycles: Women and Pastoral Care*, London: SPCK, 1993 for careful reappraisals.

25 Roger Grainger, *Staging Posts: Rites of Passage for Contemporary Christians*, Braunton, Devon: Merlin Books, 1987.

- At the same time, the father and other representatives of the family get up and come to the front of church and stand to one side.
- When the hymn is over, the mother walks down the aisle to the front, carrying the child, and presents the child to the minister.
- The minister lifts the child in her/his arms, moves to the family group and presents the child to the father.
- The father passes the child to another family member and joins the mother. They join hands and ask the minister to bless the baby.
- The minister moves to the group, blesses the baby and the family and walks among them, greeting them and shaking hands.

There are several things worth noting in this outline. First, the way that the tools of pastoral liturgy have been employed:

- There is space for the human story, in this case not just about the child, but particularly for the mother, who is asked about those who have supported her. Grainger suggests that the mother chooses the first reading from any book, magazine or other source of comfort to her during pregnancy. This might not be realistic in many cases (many mothers might not get their comfort from written sources), but it is another way of exploring the human story ready to connect it with the God story. It would be interesting to explore ways to also express the father's story in the service, recognizing that the story will be different from the mother's, but avoiding reinforcing a division between the two stories and two parents.
- Action and movement is used a lot – moving from one part of the church to another, using the different spaces to show a movement through the service and enact a sharing of responsibility for the child.
- Words are used in active ways. Note the use of questions to the mother.

All of these contribute to a strong sense of liminality in this service. There is a blessing of the child, but this is just one part of a much bigger journey which is taking place, and the different parts of the service recognize that this journey involves the parents as well as the child.

Telling the God story

The ideas we gathered at the start of this chapter for readings for a birthday party 'rite' are the sort of readings that one might also use for a service to recognize the birth of a child. The Methodist and URC services which we considered earlier focus on two suggestions for readings:

- Deuteronomy 6.4–7: the command to love God and to pass on the words of God to your children.
- Mark 9.36–37: 'Whoever welcomes one such child in my name welcomes me . . .' (Methodist); or Mark 10.13–16: Jesus blessing the children (URC).

The *Common Worship* service gives an appendix with a list of 17 possible readings (with a note adding that any suitable reading could be used).[26]

A careful look at the readings shows how the particular God story that we choose to put alongside the human story can dramatically shift the interpretation of both the human story and what the service itself is doing.

- Passages about thankfulness or the wonder of creation give one focus for the service.
- Passages about the birth of Jesus would give a different 'spin' (that we are like Jesus, or maybe that Jesus is like every other child?).
- Passages about honouring parents or passing on the faith (such as the reading from Deuteronomy 6 included in the

---

26 *CWPS*, p. 207.

Methodist and URC services) suggest an emphasis on parental dedication to particular ways of bringing up a child.

- The passages which record Jesus blessing children (Mark 10.13–16) act as a warrant for the service which is taking place and also point to children as not merely recipients of God's love, or objects of adult gratitude, but as those who have things to teach adults about what it means to see and enter God's kingdom ('. . . whoever does not receive the kingdom of God as a little child will never enter it', Mark 10.15).

And what if, in a particular case, the arrival of the child has brought particular worries or concerns, perhaps because the child has a disability or because the child's life is still at risk? In that case, the God story from Scripture might need to be more about God's faithfulness in times of challenge and uncertainty, rather than the more obvious passages about children.

Who is the service for?

We saw at the end of Chapter 3 that one of the questions to ask of any pastoral service is 'Who is the service for?', recognizing that the answer will often extend beyond those most closely connected to the individual or family at the centre of the service. In a service to mark the birth of a child, the parents and the child will be the key persons in the service, and the sense of thanksgiving, the need to bless the child, will be uppermost in the mind of any minister leading such a service.

But others at the service may have very different needs. How can the service care for them – or at least, not cause them unnecessary pain? Sitting in the congregation could be:

- A couple who are the child's Supporting Friends,[27] and who are currently in the middle of a third round of IVF treatment.

---

27 The *Common Worship* service of Thanksgiving for the Gift of a Child allows for the parents to appoint Supporting Friends, who have a particular role in the service, and beyond it. Their commitments are to help and support the

- Someone who has been recently turned down by an adoption agency as a potential adoptive parent.
- A woman who has had a miscarriage in the last year.
- A couple who have recently discovered that their unborn child has Down's Syndrome.

And this is not to mention those who may be bereaved, have lost their job, or who have had bad news from the doctor in the previous week. How does the service care for them? Clearly the service cannot be geared to all of these different and conflicting needs. But what it can do is make sure that, in the midst of the joy and thanksgiving about this birth, there is room for recognizing that life also contains hard times and that the gospel has something to say in those circumstances too. This recognition might come through a sermon, or be present in the prayers, but it needs to be present somewhere.

It also means that those who write prayers and liturgies for services surrounding childbirth need to do so carefully, avoiding any sense of taking the joyful for granted or implying that anything other than the most happy outcome is a sign of God's displeasure or even punishment. Children may be a blessing from the Lord (Ps. 127.3), but this must not be portrayed in a way that suggests a lack of children is a sign of God withholding blessing, for instance.

Summary

In this chapter we have seen how one life transition can be given different understandings (including, in the case of churching, very negative and damaging interpretations) by putting different Scripture passages alongside it. We have also begun to see how action and movement can support the sense of journey in a service and help a liminal moment to do its work.

---

parents in the bringing up of the child, but they do not make promises or have a necessary role in the spiritual upbringing of the child.

In the next chapter, on marriage, we will see two sorts of disconnection which can occur in pastoral rites. The first is when inherited symbolic actions in a service clash with contemporary intentions and understandings of what is going on. The second is the gap that can open up between the God story the service tells and the human story of the key participants.

5

Marriage

Relationships and celebrations

Any discussion of marriage rites in Christian churches, and of the potential for services which recognize and celebrate other forms of committed relationship, immediately hit the complexity caused by different Christian views about the rightness or wrongness of certain forms of relationship – same-sex relationships are the obvious example which is prominent as I write, but even questions about sex before marriage, and about the appropriateness of offering Christian weddings for those who have been divorced are other topics of disagreement between Christians. It is tempting, therefore, to think that until we have sorted out what sorts of relationships we can corporately, as a Church, affirm, we cannot begin to discuss the form which the celebrations of those relationships might appropriately take. However, while there is truth in this view (and, indeed, in many Churches, this is exactly the process which seems to be taking place), it is also true that the process works the other way round: if weddings give *expression* to a theology of relationships, they also *shape* theologies of relationships. For those whose only contact with the Christian Church is through weddings and funerals (and the occasional christening), then what they hear and see at a wedding in church will shape their understanding of what a Church believes about relationships – even if what they see and hear seems wildly disconnected from their own experience or views.

For this chapter, then, I recognize that there are within the Church different views about marriage and about other forms of committed relationships. The analysis here will focus on Christian marriage services, first, because those are the 'official' rites currently offered by most Churches, and second, because what is being expressed in these services will also be having an impact on other forms of service and may be shaping the Churches' ability (or not) to see beyond rites for heterosexual marriage.

Putting the life journey in order

Let us think about the various things that might surround the celebration of a marriage or other relationship:

- starting 'going out'
- becoming 'an item' (being willing to be known as partners, not just people who are dating)
- making the relationship public and permanent – a church or civil wedding, or a civil partnership ceremony
- moving in together
- having sex
- buying a first home together
- having a baby
- marking anniversaries.

I have listed these things in roughly the order in which 'traditional' Christian morality expects them to happen.[1] In van Gennep's three-stage process, sex, living together and having children would traditionally all have been seen as part of the incorporation phase, which marriage represented.

The order given above is reflected in the marriage service of most Christian Churches. The service itself articulates that marriage

---

1 This order is also reflected in the order in which the services of Marriage and Thanksgiving for the Gift of a Child come in CWPS (see the contents list at the beginning of the volume) – marriage comes first, then the service which might follow the birth of a child. The same is true of Marriage and Thanksgiving for the Birth of a Child in MWB (see the Contents, pp. iii–iv).

is the point at which a (relatively) new relationship is made permanent, that sexual relations begin and within which children are born. Here is the articulation of that view of marriage from the Church of England's *Common Worship* service:

> The gift of marriage brings husband and wife together
> in the delight and tenderness of sexual union
> and joyful commitment to the end of their lives.
> It is given as the foundation of family life
> in which children are [born and] nurtured
> and in which each member of the family,
> in good times and in bad,
> may find strength, companionship and comfort,
> and grow to maturity in love.[2]

The suggestion is clear that this, the wedding, is marking the beginning of sex and the possibility of children.

A different order for the life journey?

So what is the Church to do when the human story of most of the couples who want a church wedding does not fit the God story that we are telling? How should we respond when the order of things is mixed up, so that sex, living together and having children are now often part of the liminal phase of engagement, or may even be the prompt to get engaged?[3] Often today it is the imminent birth of a child (or the decision to start 'trying for a family') that prompts a couple to move from open-ended cohabitation to engagement and making plans to get married. This may seem a long way from 'traditional Christian values' for some in the Church, but history shows that in many ways it is a pattern which would have been familiar to a lot of people in a lot of places for a lot of the time.

---

2 *CWPS*, p. 105.

3 For good summaries of some of the history and analysis of contemporary issues, see Adrian Thatcher, *God, Sex and Gender: An Introduction*, Oxford: Wiley-Blackwell, 2011.

An outline of some history

In the earliest decades of the Church, it seems that Christians married according to whatever local customs existed, perhaps with specifically Christian prayers afterwards.[4]

By the early second century, Ignatius of Antioch was urging that Christians should at least have the goodwill of their local leader before getting married, and possibly that the Christian leader should preside at the ceremony, or have some other part to play in it.[5] Even if the leader were involved in the ceremony itself, it is unclear whether this would take place in the home context, or as part of a gathering of the church – and anyway, it is unclear whether Ignatius is following common patterns or trying to change them.

By the ninth century we see clear evidence of a full Christian marriage service (that is, a nuptial Mass including a nuptial blessing, either of the couple or of the bride alone).[6] This service in church was followed by domestic rites, which varied from place to place. Whether the full provision was widely experienced by those at the bottom of the social pile is unclear. This was the pattern for those who were respectable and wealthy – for the rest, customary rites at home may have been all that was possible or, indeed, desired.[7]

---

4 The outline given here relates primarily to the Western pattern as it influenced marriage in Britain. For liturgical detail (and information about rites in the Eastern Churches), see Kenneth Stevenson, *Nuptial Blessing: A Study of Christian Marriage Rites* (Alcuin Club Collections 64), London: SPCK, 1982. For a briefer historical overview and some views about the direction revision should take, see Kenneth Stevenson, 'Setting the Scene: Background and Developments', in Kenneth Stevenson (ed.), *Anglican Marriage Rites: A Symposium* (Alcuin/ GROW Joint Liturgical Studies 71), Norwich: Hymns Ancient and Modern, 2011. German Martinez, *Worship: Wedding to Marriage*, Washington, DC: Pastoral Press, 1993, also contains a useful account of the liturgical history, and some agonizing over issues of sacramentality relating to marriage from a Roman Catholic perspective (especially pp. 51–98).

5 Stevenson, *Nuptial*, pp. 13f.

6 For detailed information about the nuptial blessing, see Kenneth Stevenson, *Worship: Wonderful and Sacred Mystery*, Washington, DC: Pastoral Press, 1992, pp. 85–118.

7 See Edwin Muir, *Ritual in Early Modern Europe*, Cambridge: Cambridge University Press, 2nd ed. 2005, pp. 38–41. Muir notes the absence of the Church in the marriage rites of even the wealthy in fifteenth-century Florence.

By the later medieval period some of the customary rites had now been brought before the nuptial Mass. The giving of consent took place at the church door, which was the normal place of ratification of all civil contracts. This rite at the church door also included the exchange of a ring and the 'giving away' of the bride. The nuptial Mass in church was followed by more prayers, this time in the home of the newly married couple, where the marriage bed would be blessed. Whatever its official hopes, however, the striking fact is still the relative absence of the Church from the process of getting married for most people, as Thomas Cooper starkly reminds us:

> Always and everywhere the same pattern emerges: the church held up public betrothal as the ideal but never incorporated it into the liturgy. Where a priest attended the signing of a marriage contract (usually after the betrothal), it was as a literate and credible witness and not as one called upon to bless the couple or offer prayer. Liturgical celebrations of betrothal were unknown and church weddings rare.[8]

The Church itself stressed that the key element necessary for a valid marriage was the mutual consent of the couple, rather than any particular ritual, religious or otherwise.

The idea of a specifically Christian rite of marriage was solidified at the Council of Trent (1563), at which marriage was formally defined as a sacrament. The supporting evidence for Christ's institution of marriage as a sacrament was drawn from the Latin translation of Ephesians 5.32: '"For this reason a man will leave his father and his mother and be joined to his wife . . ." This is a great *mysterion* . . .' (*sacramentum* in Latin). This had implications which were both practical and liturgical. In practical terms it meant that marriage became seen as indissoluble in the West. Liturgically, it changed the role of the priest: previously he had been present to bless a marriage; now he was

---

8 Thomas Cooper, '"Wilt thou have this woman?" – Asking God's Blessing', in Stevenson, *Anglican Marriage Rites*, p. 33.

necessary to 'create' a sacramental marriage (though a marriage which was not conducted by a priest could still be counted as valid if there was mutual consent, even though it was not sacramental). In Catholic Europe this marked a shift from marriage in the domestic context to marriage in church.

The Reformers rejected the idea of marriage as a sacrament, and returned to the idea of marriage as contracted by the couple, with the minister as chief witness, and leader of prayer. However, the result was an increasingly legalistic approach to marriage as covenant between the couple, rather than as a gift from God. They brought the giving of consent inside the church building, making one seamless service which included the consent, the exchange of vows and the reading of Scripture. Holy Communion continued to be encouraged, but in practice rarely took place as part of the marriage service.

In 1753 in England the Hardwicke Marriage Act pushed aside customary marriage and required that marriages were registered and that they took place in public in the parish church (the only exceptions being the marriages of Jews and Quakers). This raised the profile of church weddings considerably, and cemented the alliance between Church and state where marriage was concerned.

The 1836 Marriage Act made provision for civil registration and also made possible Free Church and Roman Catholic wedding services, in which the marriage was registered within the service itself. In recent years, civil registration has mushroomed, being extended to include venues of all sorts, which has made a church wedding not the default mode, but a particular choice for an increasingly small number of couples.[9]

So, why does all this matter? Primarily because it reminds us that so much of what is assumed to be 'normal' or 'traditional' Christian practice around marriage is mainly a middle class Victorian invention. As Adrian Thatcher reminds us, we find it hard 'even to imagine that strange and informal world of conjugality

---

9 Church marriages (of all denominations) have declined from just over 50 per cent of all marriages in England in the early 1980s, to just over 30 per cent since the turn of the century. Source: *Church Statistics 2009/10*, London: Archbishops' Council, Research and Statistics, Central Secretariat, 2011, p. 32.

that lies behind the veil of modernity'.[10] Even in Britain (without even taking into consideration the rest of the world), brides have not always worn white, arrived at church as virgins on their father's arm, been joined to an equally inexperienced groom, and then set up home for the first time. Church weddings have not been the norm, from which recent society has fallen, and the idea of civil ceremonies, supplemented by subsequent religious rites, is not some radical sub-Christian idea but the earliest Christian pattern. This reality, rather than the late Victorian myth, is the background against which Churches need to think about their provision of marriage services.[11]

TO THINK ABOUT – Civil ceremonies for all?

Some have suggested that everyone, Christians included, should have some form of state-registered wedding, with Christians coming to church for their religious bit afterwards (and a similar practice for those of other faiths). In this pattern the Christian service is not a wedding as such; it is, rather, a seeking for and articulation of God's blessing on a marriage which has already been inaugurated.[12] There are strong parallels here with the pattern which dominated for the first thousand years or so of the Christian Church, though in those early centuries, the marriage which the Church blessed had not been 'made' by registering it with the civil authorities but by fulfilling whatever customary rites or practices were expected (which might have been as simple as setting up a household together).

---

10 Adrian Thatcher, *Marriage after Modernity: Christian Marriage in Postmodern Times*, Sheffield: Sheffield Academic Press, 1999, p. 108.

11 See Thatcher, *God*, Chapter 5, pp. 76–93 for a good overview and Frank C. Senn, *The People's Work: A Social History of the Liturgy*, Minneapolis: Fortress Press, 2006, pp. 214–23 for some helpful analysis.

12 See, for example, Cooper, '"Wilt thou have this woman?"', p. 46. Cooper suggests that what is registered with the civil authorities is the mutual consent of the couple, from which point they are counted as married. What the Church offers subsequently (or at the same time) is a service of solemnization, which effectively would be a service of prayer for God's blessing.

The Church of England and the Methodist Church already have services which can be used following a civil ceremony.[13] They are already often used for couples who choose to get married abroad, and then wish to have a service on their return to which they can invite more of their family and friends. They are also sometimes used (especially in the Church of England) when a priest is not able to offer a couple a church wedding (usually because of the priest's conscientious views about the marriage of divorced persons in church). What is being suggested by some is that these services, or ones like them, should become much more commonly used by Christians, not just in particular circumstances.

Fitting a God story to a human story

In any pastoral service the God story and the human story will often not fit neatly with one another – that is part of the purpose of putting them together, so that we can see how change may occur. For instance, when the Church offers prayer for healing to someone who is ill, their story of suffering is put alongside God's story of hope and God's desire for salvation (in its fullest sense) and the idea is that the latter encourages a trust in God and allows for transformation.

Does there, though, come a point where the two stories, the one told in the service and the one being lived out, are so far apart that it looks like dishonesty rather than formation?

The power of ritual to communicate meaning is vitiated when ritual is known to lie or to contradict clear experience. Of course, there are differences in interpretation, and some people may call

---

13 'An Order for Prayer and Dedication after a Civil Marriage' (*CWPS*, pp. 173–83) and 'The Blessing of a Marriage Previously Solemnized' (*MWB*, pp. 385–97). The Anglican service specifically excludes from its title and its content a blessing of the marriage. This is because of the origins of the service as a pastoral option when a church wedding could not be offered to a couple because one or both of them was divorced.

a lie what others would call an expression of hope, but downright dishonesty should be avoided whenever possible.[14]

If the bride and groom have been living together for years and have three children, is that something which we need to play down so as not to clash with the rite, or is it something that the service can and should acknowledge, both verbally and in the way it is presented? Should the Christian marriage service continue to tell the old story, setting before the couple and the congregation (and therefore, before society) a different map from the one they have been following – a challenge to change and a call (albeit implicitly) to repent? Or should we change the map? Can we recognize God speaking to the Church through the lives of those in society seeking to make sense of their own relationships? And if that is the case, how can the Church avoid becoming nothing more than a mirror of society?

IN PRACTICE – Two approaches to a clash of stories

One response to the clash of the human story and the God story is to try to adjust the human story, at least in a nominal way. So, couples who have already had sex are encouraged to consider refraining from doing so until after the wedding, so that, at least in some way, the God story told in the marriage service can match the reality.

A completely different response would be to recognize the reality and affirm the positives, changing the God story which is expressed. An alternative story could be that the couple, as far as God is concerned, are already married in all but name, and therefore the church wedding is not starting a new relationship but is adding God's blessing to an existing relationship, along with a new and deeper level of commitment. This would need a re-writing of the introduction to the marriage service and of other parts of it too – a step that few Churches have been willing to take.

---

14 Elaine Ramshaw, *Ritual and Pastoral Care*, Philadelphia: Fortress Press, 1987, p. 26.

Changing the map

Of course, historically the Church *has* changed the map and the story to reflect a changed society and new readings of Scripture. Take the introduction to the Solemnization of Matrimony in the *Book of Common Prayer*, which gives the following 'causes for which Matrimony was ordained':

> First, it was ordained for the procreation of children, to be brought up in the fear and nurture of the Lord, and to the praise of his holy Name.
>
> Secondly, it was ordained for a remedy against sin, and to avoid fornication; that such persons as have not the gift of continency might marry, and keep themselves undefiled members of Christ's body.
>
> Thirdly, it was ordained for the mutual society, help, and comfort, that the one ought to have of the other, both in prosperity and adversity.[15]

In this list it is the begetting of children which is given as the primary reason for marriage, and though the Church of England had a go at revising its Prayer Book in the 1920s, the version which was proposed simply tidied up the language a bit, and did not change the basic content or the order in which it was laid out.

TO THINK ABOUT – Acknowledging the shadow side of relationships

The Prayer Book seems pretty grudging about sex, and modern marriage services tend to put things much more positively. But not everything about this is necessarily helpful. Pastoral services need to acknowledge the whole human story, including the untidy parts and the shadow side. Robin Green (commenting in 1987 on the then 'new' Church of England services in the *ASB*) challenges the Church to acknowledge some of that reality and ambiguity about relationships:

---

15 *BCP*, Solemnization of Matrimony, from the opening words.

> What the new liturgy has sacrificed is an honest recognition of the ambiguity of human sexuality. Although the 1662 Anglican liturgy was at fault in many ways, it did show a more realistic grasp of the destructive, as well as creative, power of sexuality: '. . . to satisfy men's carnal lusts and appetites, like brute beasts that have no understanding.' The new Anglican liturgies have an aura of middle-class respectability about them. But you do not have to wander far in any city to recognize that the 1662 liturgy also had part of the truth. Can liturgy care for people if it does not recognize honestly the ambiguous nature of human sexuality?[16]
>
> His challenge is powerful. How could a wedding service articulate that today without sounding either ridiculous or judgemental?

The Prayer Book map for the journey is quite different from the one given in *Common Worship*, in which the order of the reasons for marriage is completely reversed, and becomes:

- mutual love and support
- sex and intimacy
- children.[17]

The Methodist marriage service takes a similar line:

It is the will of God that, in marriage,
husband and wife should experience
a lifelong union of heart, body and mind;
comfort and companionship;

---

16 Robin Green, *Only Connect: Worship and Liturgy from the Perspective of Pastoral Care*, London: Darton, Longman and Todd, 1987, pp. 101f. The quotation from the *BCP* is from the introduction to The Form of Solemnization of Matrimony.

17 This summary is drawn from the Preface to the Marriage Service, *CWPS*, p. 105. The order (though not the detailed wording) is the same in the alternative Preface on p. 136. The reversal of the order is not a new idea: Martin Bucer recommended it in his comments on the 1549 Prayer book and the Puritans advocated it too (Bufford Coe, *John Wesley and Marriage*, London: Associated University Presses, 1996, pp. 52–5).

enrichment and encouragement;
tenderness and trust.
It is the will of God that marriage
should be honoured as a way of life,
in which we may know the security of love and care,
and grow towards maturity.
Through such marriage,
children may be nurtured,
family life strengthened,
and human society enriched.[18]

This is still a very traditional model in many ways (there is a clear statement in the next paragraph, for instance, that 'marriage involves the giving of a man and a woman wholeheartedly to each other', so no room here for same-sex relationships sneaking in). However, the explicit reference to sex has been taken out, much to the relief of ministers and congregations alike. And the overall sense is less explicitly of a relationship just starting and much more of it stabilizing and becoming secure ('lifelong union' and 'security of love and care') and of the persons within it maturing (that phrase, 'grow towards maturity', is very telling). Children get a mention, but they are to be nurtured within a marriage, not necessarily born within it.

The Roman Catholic Church is, as one might expect given its stance on contraception, the most explicit about the importance of the potential for children to be born. Its rite includes a question of intent about children:

Will you accept children lovingly from God, and bring them up according to the law of Christ and his Church?[19]

However, interestingly, it is also the form of service most explicitly sensitive about the potential embarrassment of this question,

---

18 *MWB*, p. 369.
19 Roman Catholic Church, *The Rites of the Catholic Church, Volume 1*, New York: Pueblo, 1976, p. 540.

and the instructions give specific permission to omit it, 'if, for example, the couple is advanced in years'. There may be other reasons to omit it, of course.

TO THINK ABOUT – A new introduction?

If you were writing a marriage service 'from scratch', what material would you put in the preface, the introductory material which sets out the God story at the start of the service? Try something which begins, 'Marriage is given by God so that . . .'

Though Christian Churches have moved a long way to change the order in which children, sex and companionship are presented in a marriage service, the three are still there . . . at the moment.

TO THINK ABOUT – Beyond the traditional God story?

There are many reasons why Churches and individual Christians have different views about the appropriateness of same-sex relationships, and those reasons are spelt out at great length in other places. Here, we simply note that from a liturgical point of view one of the sticking points, even if one did want to produce a service of same-sex marriage, is a problem about the God story which is articulated in weddings.

While the Church relies on a procreation basis for the God story it tells in weddings, it will not be straightforward to extend the service to gay couples. For services which would work for gay and lesbian people the God story would need to shift to one, for instance, about covenanted friendship as the core of what marriage is about. The care of children within a committed relationship might still be part of the story for particular couples, but it would be harder to see *procreation* as one of the standard norms of marriage. For some Christians (gay and straight), this is a sign that *marriage* is not an appropriate model for same-sex committed relationships; for others, it is a sign that marriage services need to change.

Modern marriage service structure

The English marriage rite, for complicated reasons of history, inherited two forms of giving consent:

- An interrogatory form, in which the couple were asked questions and gave an answer ('Will you take this woman/man . . .?' / 'I will.').
- A declaratory form, in which the couple make affirmative statements ('I take you to be my wife/husband, to have and to hold . . . till death us do part.').

These ended up in the same service, effectively duplicating the consent part of the rite.[20] Many recent revisions of the marriage service have re-structured the service to separate the questions from the statements by the readings and sermon. The Episcopal Church in the USA led the way in its 1979 *Book of Common Prayer*, and by calling the questions 'The Betrothal' suggested (incorrectly) that this was their origin.[21]

Though the history may be bogus, the separation of what feels like a statement of intent (the opening questions and answers[22]) from the solemn vows and the exchange of rings does give a journey through the service which echoes the bigger life journey of separation and incorporation and matches the fourfold structure outlined in Chapter 3:

- **Gathering** (Why are we here? The human story, including the questions of intent/consent).
- **The God story** (We hear what God has to say about relationships through Scripture reading and sermon, and connect that to this couple).

---

20 Cooper, '"Wilt thou have this woman?"', pp. 27–32.

21 The fact that the question and answer use the 'Will you?' / 'I will' form has led some to conclude, incorrectly, that they are questions in the future tense. For the argument that they were historically seen as in the present tense, see Cooper, '"Wilt thou have this woman?"', pp. 27–31.

22 These are labelled 'the declarations' in both *CWPS* and *MWB*. Kenneth Stevenson describes the new sequence as something which 'heightens the importance of intentionality', Stevenson, *Anglican Marriage Rites*, p. 8.

- **Responding** (We proceed with the vows and rings on that basis, and pray for God's blessing on the couple).
- **Dismissal** (We are all sent out with God's blessing, to live the reality we have celebrated).

This has become a common overall structure, being followed by the Church of England, Methodist, United Reformed Church, Baptist (First Pattern) and Joint Liturgical Group (JLG) services.[23] However, the detail of the placing of different elements, and the wording of them, varies considerably.

IN PRACTICE – Blessing of the couple

In some Anglican churches the tradition has been to take the couple to the holy table (the 'high altar') for the prayers and possibly for the blessing. This pattern clearly does not work with all church layouts, and even where it does, it is worth thinking differently. The message is that the couple are being taken away from the congregation and 'nearer to God'. This may give a sense of heightened importance to the moment, but it also signifies that the congregation have little role in this part of the service. A very different message is given if the newly married couple are led to the centre of the congregation, who are asked to turn and face them, and there, surrounded by family and friends, they are blessed, and prayers are said for them.

It is easy to see how the traditional pattern of putting the signing of the registers at the end, just before the blessing, can wreck this journey, by introducing a hiatus at just the point at which the service should be gathering momentum to send couple and congregation out into the world. For this reason, it works better for the journey through the service if the registers are signed

---

23 In the *Common Worship* services, the parallel with the fourfold shape is seen most clearly in the structure outline for the Marriage Service within Holy Communion, *CWPS*, p. 115. The JLG service is published in, Joint Liturgical Group, *An Order of Marriage for Christians from Different Churches*, Norwich: Canterbury Press, 1999.

closer to the proclamation of the marriage. In practical terms (especially if the signing is done in the church itself) it also gives a chance to invite photographs and generally to tap into the mood of celebration and relief that follows the vows and rings.

IN PRACTICE – Giving the new shape a try

In my experience, many clergy are nervous about the structure in the recently revised services, and tend to revert to an earlier pattern in which the couple give their consent, and move straight into the vows and exchange of rings, so that they are married within ten minutes of the start of the service. I have heard clergy say that they do this for the sake of the couple (who, apparently, are so nervous that they want it all over as quickly as possible).

However, I find that the new pattern gives the couple time to take in what is happening. Early on in the service they hear themselves speak out loud in public (a big worry for many) as they give the answers to the questions about consent. Then they get a chance to sit down, hold hands, smile at each other, take lots of deep breaths, while the readings and sermon take place, before returning to the front for the vows and rings. This puts the main action more centrally in the service, giving a sense of time to build up to it. I have never found a couple too paralysed by nerves to do it this way, and many in the congregations have said that it made the wedding feel more like an event, rather than something which is over so fast that if you blink you miss it, followed by a slow anti-climax, filling the rest of the hour.

What makes a wedding Christian?

We asked this question earlier, in Chapter 2, when we were establishing some general principles about how Christian pastoral rites can work for those who are not practising Christian believers. In summary we suggested that a Christian wedding might be given its Christian 'nature' by some or all of the following:

- The officiant (a Christian minister).
- The venue (a Christian church building).

- The expectations (of marriage itself and of God's involvement, or at least interest, in that marriage).
- The content of the service (vows, hymns and songs, and so on) assuming and pointing towards the bigger Christian story.

We stopped short of saying that the faith of the couple was also required, on the grounds that a Christian *marriage* might need that faith, but a Christian *wedding* is more about offering a prayerful interpretive context through which to begin to see the marriage.

The core elements which articulate the God story in a wedding are the words of the service and what they say about God, relationships and this couple. We have already seen how parts of the service (the introduction or preface, for example) express this in terms which are explicitly about God, but even the expectations of the relationship itself, expressed in vows which are made 'for better, for worse', can be significantly counter-cultural and suggest a need for God's transforming help. However, vital as the words are, the other factors are important too.

Worship space

A wedding can have Christian content without taking place in a church (though, at the time of writing, civil ceremonies in the United Kingdom must *not* have any religious content to them), but a church building can also contribute to the God story. Its layout, decoration, furnishings can all speak of the Christian story, as can the simple fact of its association with worship. The holy table, whether it is used for communion or not in the service, reminds all present that at the heart of the Christian God story is self-giving love, expressed in Jesus with an invitation to all to share. This may be reinforced by aspects of church decoration – stained glass windows, crosses, banners, and so on. If we recognize, as we did in the last chapter, that those who come to the service will not all be in the same emotional place as the couple, it is important that the gospel is seen to encompass things which go beyond the schmalzy sentimentality which can surround weddings so easily in contemporary culture. The church building is the place for saying goodbye to those we love as well as for welcoming those recently born. The words of the vows about 'for better for worse, in sickness and in health, till death us do part' take on a very different feeling in a building where death is remembered as well as health and joy.

No hotel can do this, even if the words of the service itself speak of a gospel that is big enough to embrace all this. A Christian wedding ceremony in a secular venue would be perfectly possible, of course,[24] but like a Christian funeral at a crematorium, it has to work extra hard to evoke the Christian worldview on which the service rests.

A secular wedding venue could become 'sacred' to a particular family, of course. And if the same venue were to be used for baby naming ceremonies and perhaps for a reception after a funeral then one could see how the place could begin to acquire associations for that family with significant times of both joy and sadness. A church building, however, is more likely to feel sacred to a whole community as well as to particular families, and it is sacred at a whole different level – not merely 'special' in the sense of familiar and carrying memories, but sacred because it carries echoes of a bigger narrative which transcends the events of any one family or group. The problem with a hotel or other venue for a wedding, is that it too can carry echoes of a bigger narrative, but not necessarily one that helps. Alan Billings discovered this when a woman who enquired about a church wedding described to him how she understood the difference between a church wedding and one at a hotel:

> A church wedding is a proper wedding. I never quite believe a wedding in a hotel is a proper one. Hotels are for, well, a night out and enjoying yourself.[25]

Not that this is an argument for weddings in traditional church buildings – any space where Christian worship takes

---

24 Though not under current UK law.
25 Alan Billings, *Secular Lives; Sacred Hearts*, London: SPCK, 2004, p. 77.

place will begin to take on those bigger echoes – but it means that a church building can have a part to play in the service, and ministers are wise if they use the space to speak in the service itself, making connections with the particular symbolism of the building or the decorations of the church at the time of year the service is taking place.

The presiding minister

The same principles apply to questions about who presides at the service. For some Churches it will be important that it is an ordained minister, in other traditions, as long as legalities are fulfilled, lay leaders can officiate. Again, this does not matter in any absolute sense. And yet . . . as with the building, the person leading the service carries connotations of other stories which are not the focus of this service but which connect with those who are present. Christian ministers, like church buildings, carry with them the echoes of the other parts of life which they serve – the sickness, the dying, the new births, the big questions, the quiet listening, the nursing homes, the council initiatives, the school assemblies . . . No civil registrar, no matter how professional and caring, can carry quite so many associations, even though the connection between registering births, marriages and deaths does encompass something of the 'all life is here' kind.

Key moments, symbols and actions

Weddings are rites in which action and movement plays a significant part:

- How the bride and groom enter the church.
- How they make the separation from one state (being engaged) to another (being married) and what they understand that new state to mean for them, and how it is different from the state in which they began the service.

- What vows and promises they make, and how they make them (for instance, where in the church they stand, which direction they face).
- How the bride and groom leave the church.

In all these areas, the way the actions are given shape will speak just as loudly as the words that are spoken.

Some typical elements

It is worth analysing some of the key symbolic moments and actions in a wedding service. Typically in Britain a wedding might include any or all of the following:

- Arrival of the bride and of the groom (though the focus is usually on the bride, the groom's arrival is just as significant, even if only for the fact that it is not usually treated as such – it is the fact that they do not usually arrive together which is the key here). This might include the bride, wearing a veil, carrying flowers, being escorted down the aisle on the arm of her father or some other male relative. It may include numbers of bridesmaids, and often now includes the rings being processed in on a cushion carried by a page boy.
- Giving of consent, via questions about willingness to enter marriage.
- Turning to the best man, and asking him to produce the rings.
- Possible 'giving away' of either bride, or of both parties.
- Exchange of vows with joining of hands.
- Exchange of rings or ring.
- Declaration of the marriage (sometimes these days accompanied by applause).
- Permission to kiss (also sometimes accompanied by applause).
- Binding of hands with a stole.[26]
- Blessing of the couple, often with laying on of hands.

---

26 In the Methodist service this is spelled out as a possibility in the instructions in the service text (*MWB*, p. 376) whereas *Common Worship* mentions the joining of hands, but not the stole, though it is a common practice in many Anglican weddings (*CWPS*, p. 110).

- Prayers – often with the couple moving to the high altar, in churches which have that tradition and layout.
- Signing of the register – increasingly done in church in view of everyone, followed by a ritual of photograph-taking, which is often as carefully controlled and choreographed as anything in the liturgy.
- The departure of bride and groom (this time definitely together), followed by the wedding party, often in a carefully prescribed order (though these days the complexities of family relations make this harder to comply with).

These are by no means the only symbols and actions that are possible, and each cultural or ethnic group will have its own variations and additions, but they give a sense of the sheer number of key moments and expected elements that might be present in a typical church wedding.[27] They are, of course, supplemented by a whole range of other customs and practices which butt up against the church wedding: the arrival of the bride in some form of special transport (white Rolls Royce, horse and trap, stretch limousine, motorcycle and sidecar, etc.); the reception afterwards, including speeches and cutting of the cake; and the departure of bride and groom for their honeymoon, in a car suitably decorated for the purpose.

IN PRACTICE – Being 'given away'

The idea of the bride being 'given away' by her father and her hand given to her husband – literally passed, like a piece of property from one man to another – derives from the era when this is exactly how society understood what was happening in a wedding and what would be reflected in the relations between husband and wife in the marriage. Of course there were marriages where women were treated with respect as equal parties by their husbands, but these were exceptions – the law was on the side of those who saw a woman as dependent on her husband's goodwill for all that she owned and did.

---

27 For further lists, see Kenneth Stevenson, *To Join Together: The Rite of Marriage*, New York: Pueblo, 1987, pp. 194–9 and Charles Read, *Revising Weddings* (Grove Worship Series 128), Nottingham: Grove Books, 1994, pp. 17–20.

Yet, as most ministers will tell you, even when you point this out, a majority of modern brides still rather like the idea of being given away. Even if it is not done by her father (because he is not present) she will often look to a male relative to do the job. Most will baulk at promising verbally to obey, but are happy to be symbolically handed over as if it is the men that matter.

Before we rush too hastily to jettison the traditional giving away ceremony, it is worth recognizing two important roles that it has in the service. First, it ritualizes the important separation phase of the rite of passage, albeit only for the bride in the traditional form. To put it bluntly: 'Cleaving . . . does not ensure leaving.'[28] A couple may have been living together for years, but not bitten the psychological or emotional bullet involved in truly loosening their respective parental bonds. Second, it is an important sign that the wedding belongs to more than just the couple – two families and groups of friends are being joined as well as the bride and groom.

For these reasons, we should rejoice that revised services provide for other, much more even-handed, ways of handling the separation of bride and groom from primary attachment to their parental families, ready for the incorporation into a new family unit which trumps those birth relationships. For instance, the Baptist resource book *Gathering for Worship* suggests that, 'The custom of the bride being given away by her father may be omitted, repeated for the groom, or extended by including other members of the couple's families and the whole congregation.'[29]

Methodist Worship Book has symmetrical words which may be addressed to a relative or friend who presents bride and/or groom to be married: 'Who presents C to be married to A?', though it is noticeable that whereas in every other part of the service the man is addressed or speaks first, here the rubric relates to the woman first and then to the man.

---

28 Herbert Anderson and Edward Foley, *Mighty Stories, Dangerous Rituals: Weaving Together the Human and the Divine*, San Francisco: Jossey-Bass, 2001, p. 83.

29 Baptist Union of Great Britain, Christopher Ellis and Myra Blyth (eds), *Gathering for Worship: Patterns and Prayers for the Community of Disciples*, Norwich: Canterbury Press, 2005, p. 186.

In *Common Worship* the words are not printed in the main service, but are hidden away in a note at the end of the service,[30] where it is stressed that they are optional, and the form of words given is watered down to, 'Who brings [*not "gives"*] this woman to be married to this man?'[31] And yet, many couples want to do the 'traditional thing', even if it is in the watered down version.

If the couple want to include a more symmetrical giving away, one of the key things to remember is the importance of action and movement. When a bride is given away, it is not just the words (important as they are) but the physical action which matters: the bride's father, physically passing his daughter's hand to the minister, and the minister handing her on to the groom, as the couple turn to face each other, and the bride's father takes a step backwards. (Incidentally, that stepping back is possibly the most significant of the actions – it is symbolic of what all parents need to do if the new relationship is to flourish.) If parents or others (it could be children, friends, the best man and chief bridesmaid) are to present both bride and groom to one another, it will be important to think through the movement and action as well as the words said.

And remember the option for the congregation to express their support, which is present in many modern rites.[32] Again, action is important, even if it is as simple as asking the members of the congregation to stand before pledging their support.

Tools of liminality

Some analysis of the elements listed above reveals two important things. First, note that some of the key tools of liminality, which we identified earlier and saw at work in the birth rites, are present here too:

---

30 *CWPS*, Note 6 on p. 133.

31 As an alternative, *Common Worship* allows for both sets of parents to entrust their respective children to one another in marriage, but if this is done it takes place earlier in the service, not at the traditional point of the giving away. Again, this is not in the main text but is mentioned in Note 6 on p. 133.

32 *MWB*, p. 373, section 10; *CWPS*, p. 106; *Gathering for Worship*, p. 192; *WURC*, p. 171; *An Order of Marriage* (JLG), p. 19, section 19.

- use of words in active ways – asking questions, making solemn vows, making declarations of new reality
- use of physical objects (rings)
- use of action (joining hands, exchange of rings, turning to face each other, kneeling to be blessed, tying of stoles round hands, etc.).

Culture – connections or challenges?

The second thing to note from the list of key moments in a wedding is that the elements, even the 'traditional elements', derive from a range of sources. Most come from a different era, or from ancient pre-Christian roots. Others are very old, but derive from primarily commercial practices (for instance the giving of consent and exchange of rings was primarily derived from normal business transactions and the forming of a binding contract). Others are relatively recent, but seen as traditional because a tradition is only a memory that is older than the generations still alive.

For instance, the wearing of white by the bride may go back to the Roman custom 'for the bride to dress in vestal white',[33] but seems to have become a universal tradition in Britain only after Queen Victoria wore white for her wedding in 1840. Up until that point and, for those of more modest means, long after it, brides simply wore their best dress, of whatever colour. The 'first kiss' is increasingly expected by both the couple and the congregation (usually the groom is told, 'You may now kiss the bride.'), though it is not explicitly mentioned in the rites of any British Church except the United Reformed Church.[34] In its current form it probably derives more from Hollywood than from Christian tradition. However, it too may go back to Roman practice, and by the medieval period kissing was sometimes part of the giving of consent and exchange of dowry at betrothal, comparable with

---

33 Martinez, *Worship*, p. 54.

34 *WURC*, p. 175, includes a rubric immediately after the declaration of the marriage which says, 'The couple may kiss. The congregation may applaud.'

a handshake to seal a deal[35] – which all goes to show that there is no 'pure' root to any tradition.

Sometimes these practices have been controversial, such as the giving of a ring. This was frowned on as superstitious and unscriptural by the Puritans and omitted by John Wesley from his revision of the marriage service for Methodists as part of his endorsement of a plain and simple style in dress and the avoidance of jewellery.[36]

In each case they remind us of the same dilemmas that face us today: how to connect with our current context, without losing the distinctive elements which should point to a Christian understanding of marriage itself. 'You may now kiss the bride' is looked down on by many Christian ministers, as pandering to a celebrity and entertainment culture, and yet those same ministers do not bat an eyelid at the exchange of rings, or the wearing of a bridal veil, whose origins are possibly as dubious – certainly not deeply or intrinsically Christian.

In our own day there are pressures to change wedding practice. The lighting of a candle, as a sign of unity and the formation of a new relationship, is becoming common, for instance.[37] Where one or both of the couple have been married before, or been in a relationship which has produced children, it is not uncommon for the bride to be 'given away' by her own children.[38] Are these examples of 'giving in' to culture, or of connecting with culture? In wedding services the classic tensions and dilemmas of Christian mission and its engagement with the surrounding culture are given powerful illustration: Christ over culture;

---

35 Muir, *Ritual*, p. 39, points out the connection with the kiss of peace in the Eucharist, which would be shared with bride and groom at a Nuptial Mass, and also notes that in Italy a kiss was common between the male guardians of both bride and groom when the initial negotiations about the marriage and the dowry were finalized.

36 Coe, *John Wesley*, pp. 96f.

37 See Read, *Revising Weddings*, p. 19, for an interesting critique of this practice.

38 *A New Zealand Prayer Book* makes explicit provision for any children of the bride or groom to promise their 'help' in the marriage (Marriage Liturgy Second Form, p. 786).

Christ in culture; Christ against culture?[39] A church which wishes to avoid looking ridiculous and to give expression to Christian truth through the pastoral services it offers will need to look long and hard at wedding services.

Yet for all the desire to change things, there is much that stays resolutely unchanged, even when all around in society has changed completely. This is also part of the nature of pastoral rites and an expression of the fact that the rites belong widely to the community and cannot be changed simply on the whim of a particular couple or minister. They have to be 'proper', even if 'proper' changes over generations.

CASE STUDY – The arrival of the bride and groom

In parish ministry, I always met with a couple who wished to get married to talk them through the service and help them to see the options and to make the service their own. I especially helped them to see those elements which were traditional, but not compulsory. One of those was the arrival of the bride.[40] Most couples were already living together, and they were not embarrassed about this. (When I was first ordained twenty years ago, couples often were embarrassed – I find them almost universally unembarrassed nowadays, unless they are practising Christians, in which case they often sense that this is frowned upon by the Church.)

That being the case, I used to encourage them to think about how the beginning of their service could reflect the reality of their relationship. What was the point, I would ask, in the groom arriving early, having not seen the bride that day, and then the bride arriving later, veiled, with her dad, and walking down the aisle to be joined with the groom and remove her veil as if they had hardly met

---

39 A classic expression of these alternative approaches is found in Richard H. Niebuhr, *Christ and Culture*, London: Faber, 1952.

40 *MWB* has an opening rubric which states: 'The people stand as the bridal *or marriage* party enters the church,' (my emphasis). The *Common Worship* service says nothing about the entry of anyone in the main text, but Note 4 says, 'The bride may enter the church escorted by her father or a representative of the family, or the bride and groom may enter church together.' *CWPS*, p. 132.

> before? If this wedding was to mark not so much the beginning of a marriage but the next stage in deepening an existing long-term relationship, had they thought about possibly arriving together, to represent that they were already 'together' in real life? There was usually a long silence and a lot of looking at each other, before one would say (usually the bride), 'Well, we see what you mean, but we'd like to do it the traditional way please.'
>
> I had no problem about doing it the traditional way, but I wanted them to think about it. Ironically, the only people who ever chose to enter together were a couple who were practising Christians. They were living together, and felt slightly awkward about representing that publicly and symbolically, but, crucially, they were confident enough about the church context and the way ritual and liturgy worked, to change the tradition and yet remain confident that it could be 'proper'. For them, the core parts were the vows and the blessing – as long as that was right, the rest was up for grabs.

Public rituals: private meanings

The example above about the entrance of the bride and groom raises again the issues about the coherence of ritual action, liturgical text and marital reality. What happens when the actions of the couple in the rite contradict both the official intentions of the liturgy and the way the couple intend to live out their relationship? J. Michael Joncas wrestles with this dilemma in some reflections on Roman Catholic weddings in the United States. He points out that though the official Roman Catholic rite intends a radical equality of the couple by directing that they enter together, this is wrecked by the couple following a historical pattern derived from the handing over of a woman from one man to another. He suggests an analysis on the basis of three levels of meaning in the rite:[41]

41 J. Michael Joncas, 'Ritual Transformations: Principles, Patterns and Peoples', in Gabe Huck et al., Toward Ritual Transformation: Remembering Robert W. Hovda, Collegeville, MN: Liturgical Press, 2003, pp. 53ff. The three-fold framework is from Margaret Mary Kelleher, 'Liturgical Theology: A Task

- The 'official' meaning is what is intended by the liturgy (in this case, equality).
- The 'public' meaning is what the couple do (in this case, echo a patriarchal understanding by having the bride enter with her father and possibly later be 'given away' to her future husband).
- The 'private' meaning is how the participants intend or understand what they are doing (in this case, seeing it as a special time for a dad and his daughter).

Joncas worries that the three meanings are, at best, not consonant or, at worst, contradictory. I share that concern, which is why I encourage couples to consider their actions in the service. However, a cooler, more distant look at the problem suggests another dimension. If, in practice, couple after couple do live as equals, but choose to use the traditional pattern, the meaning of that pattern is subverted and does not necessarily speak of a subordinate role for the woman in the relationship. The symbolism no longer either expresses or shapes the reality which once it did, but it may be performing an equally important ritual role (in this case, perhaps ritualizing, and therefore aiding, a changing relationship between a daughter and her father). It may be that what is needed to bring greater ritual coherence is an additional symbolic (and not just verbal) feature to mark the parallel changes in relationship between a daughter and her mother, and between the groom and his parents.

Connecting with the bigger journey

As Churches have revised their rites to give more emphasis to the journey within the service, there has been relatively little to engage with the bigger journey beyond the service of marriage. There is material for celebrating wedding anniversaries and the renewal of marriage vows, even recognizing that this may come

---

and a Method', *Worship*, 62, No. 1, 1988, pp. 2–25, cited in Anderson and Foley, *Mighty Stories*, pp. 28f.

after a particularly difficult period in a marriage,[42] but as we have noted, there is little material, certainly at more official level, for when a relationship has broken down irretrievably. Perhaps it is this lack of material about the ending of a relationship which makes the forming of the new one (at least at the formal level of exchanging new vows and making a fresh start) feel so difficult or problematic for some people?

But what about the stages on the journey before the wedding? If we follow van Gennep's model, and zoom out and see engagement as a liminal state, which is concluded with the marriage rite which marks incorporation into a new state, the question is, where is the separation rite at the start of that journey? Whereas historically, betrothal was a clear formal rite (whether religious or not), engagement is now more fuzzy. Despite its importance historically, few Churches have connected with engagement or provided prayerful pastoral resources for this important stage.

It is still marked, of course. The stages on the way and the rites that mark them include:

- proposing – these days this does not necessarily mean the man proposing to the woman
- buying and exchanging engagement rings
- informing relatives and friends, often by hosting an engagement party
- cards and gifts sent to the couple.

The key thing is that these are essentially privatized and non-religious rites. They are neither publicly controlled nor religiously supported. Is that part of the problem for Christian wedding rites? We have ended up adding a Christian God story

---

42 *CWPS* includes an outline order and sample service for a 'Thanksgiving for Marriage' (pp. 184–93). This can be used as a service for several couples, or as something more personal for one couple, and it specifically mentions in the opening note that it can be used 'after a time of separation or difficulty in marriage' (p. 184). See also, *Pastoral Prayers*, pp. 32–8, for a service of Renewal of Vows, and *Gathering for Worship*, pp. 214–19, for a service of Thanksgiving which includes Renewal of Vows which can take either a 'thanksgiving' or a 'recommitment' emphasis.

with all its assumptions at the incorporation end of the process, but that process has begun somewhere else with some very different controlling stories.

Many Churches will use marriage preparation meetings or the wedding rehearsal as an opportunity for informal prayer with and for the couple, but there is little that is more formalized. The most significant opportunity is probably for couples getting married in a Church of England church, who need to have their banns of marriage read out, and *Common Worship* provides a choice of prayers which could be used on that occasion in regular worship.[43] Other Churches would also encourage couples to come to church before the wedding and might pray for them publicly when they do.

Summary

This look at marriage rites has shown the importance of action and movement within a pastoral service, but has also explored how complicated it can be to match the God story and the human story in a situation where people's life patterns are changing rapidly. In the next chapter, we look at a very different sort of pastoral service, the Church's offering of prayer for wholeness and healing. However, though very different, we will see again how important it is to get the God story right if the pastoral service is truly to care for people and not leave them even more damaged.

---

43 *CWPS*, p. 135.

6

Healing and Wholeness

Healing is big in the Church today. Pentecostal Churches and other churches influenced by the charismatic movement have reminded the Church that healing was a key part of the ministry of Jesus, frequently mentioned in the same breath as his teaching (and indeed, as his casting out evil). For instance,

> Jesus went throughout Galilee, teaching in their synagogues and proclaiming the good news of the kingdom and curing every disease and every sickness among the people. (Matt. 4.23)

Not only did Jesus' own ministry include healing alongside preaching, when he sent his followers out the same two-pronged approach is apparent again:

> Then Jesus called the twelve together and gave them power and authority over all demons and to cure diseases, and he sent them out to proclaim the kingdom of God and to heal . . . they departed and went through the villages, bringing the good news and curing diseases everywhere. (Luke 9.1–2, 6)

This re-discovery of healing in the ministry of Jesus, coupled with 'healing' being one of the gifts of the Holy Spirit specifically mentioned in the New Testament (1 Cor. 12.9), means that healing is a key focus for many churches. Not only is prayer for healing offered regularly during services (or at the end of them) as part of what is often called 'prayer ministry' (or just 'ministry'), it is also seen as part of a strategy for evangelism, being offered at large-scale evangelistic events, or as part of smaller-scale local evangelism, through initiatives such as Healing on the Streets.[1]

But healing is not just big in charismatic and Pentecostal Churches. Healing services have taken off too, in a very different form and style, in churches which are much more traditional in style and in those which are broader in theology. In the Church of England this was given a massive boost by the report by the House of Bishops, *A Time to Heal*.[2] This report both recognizes the growth in healing services and other forms of healing ministry, and also encourages churches to see it as a normal part of the pastoral ministry which they offer. It is this 'normalizing' of healing which has been so significant.

The growth of prayer for healing

Why has regular prayer for healing within worship gone from being something which was limited to a few churches and some para-church organizations, to something which is so common? There are several factors:

- The influence of the charismatic movement and the re-discovery of healing as part of the work and gifts of the Holy Spirit.
- The recovery of interest within New Testament studies in Jesus as a healer and exorcist.
- The impact of medical advances, which, in many parts of the world, make 'health' the normal state, from which

---

1 Healing on the Streets began in 2005 as an initiative of Causeway Coast Vineyard church in Coleraine, Northern Ireland, and is now being adopted by many other churches. See www.healingonthestreets.com for more information. Interestingly, the recent document, *Christian Witness in a Multi-Religious World: Recommendations for Conduct*, published jointly by the World Council of Churches, the Pontifical Council for Interreligious Dialogue and the World Evangelical Alliance (2011), also mentions healing in the section headed 'Principles': 'As an integral part of their witness to the gospel, Christians exercise ministries of healing. They are called to exercise discernment as they carry out these ministries, fully respecting human dignity and ensuring that the vulnerability of people and their need for healing are not exploited' (Paragraph 5).

2 *A Time to Heal: A Report by the House of Bishops on the Healing Ministry*, London: Church House Publishing, 2000.

illness and ill-health feels like an unnatural departure. This contrasts with the situation in the past (and, of course, in the present in many parts of the world) where ill-health and the danger of death was all too common. The Churches' affirmation of health and healing is thus, to a certain extent, a mirroring of society's expectations.

- The growing interest in the wider world in 'wholeness' and well-being, as witnessed by the groaning shelves on 'mind, body and spirit', 'wellness' and 'self-help' in any library or bookshop. This connects with what Alan Billings calls a 'therapeutic culture' with its emphasis on how we feel, and he notes that Christian prayer ministry is often not just about physical cures but about memories, emotions and our psychological well-being.[3]

- Ironically (given the impact of medical advances above), the increasing suspicion of 'scientific' modes of healing (or modes which are solely scientific) and the growing interest in holistic, homeopathic and complementary therapies, including both herbal and other medicines, and forms of therapy using touch, such as reiki and massage.

Different patterns

Whatever the causes, healing is on the agenda in most churches, though in many different ways. In some churches it is largely informal, spontaneous, and extempore, offered at most services, perhaps by a large 'prayer team' consisting of trained lay people supported by the clergy. The extempore prayer, accompanied by laying on of hands, might be quite lengthy and may be preceded by some conversation about the issue which is to be prayed about.

In other churches it is more likely to manifest in the form of more formal 'healing services', which happen less frequently and are planned carefully, in which prayer is offered mainly by ordained ministers, perhaps supported by lay people. The prayer

---

3 Alan Billings, *Secular Lives, Sacred Hearts: The Role of the Church in a Time of No Religion*, London: SPCK, 2004, pp. 23f.

itself might consist of brief fixed forms of words, drawn from published or denominational resources, and be accompanied by laying on of hands and anointing with oil.

Though I have described these as two very different scenarios, as if they were at two ends of a spectrum, it is possible to draw on the different elements in a range of combinations. For instance, one church might only offer this ministry at occasional healing services, but the prayer at the healing services could be informal and extempore and involve a large team of lay people. Another church down the road might be offering more formal ministry of prayer with laying on of hands and anointing at the end of all its services. At a third church in the town, monthly formal healing services with anointing with oil are offered alongside informal prayers for healing at the end of any Sunday morning service.

IN PRACTICE – Using the full range

Though some churches are operating with combinations of the different models offered above, in many churches and for many ministers, their offering of the ministry of healing tends towards one particular form. Perhaps they are most comfortable with informal prayer and laying on of hands in pastoral contexts or as part of prayer ministry offered in regular services, or maybe they are only happy to anoint with oil using fixed forms of prayer and to offer this as part of formal healing services or at home or in hospital.

Pastorally, however, there can be good reasons to be comfortable with a range of different modes, so that you can fit the ministry to the needs of the context or the individual. On the one hand, for someone who needs the ministry to feel 'proper', the use of fixed forms of words taken from a service book, with anointing from a 'proper' oil dispenser might be helpfully reassuring. On the other hand, for someone involved in youth ministry who is asked on the spur of the moment to pray with someone after youth club, it might be important to be able to offer something more 'low-key' and informal, which does not require books and preparation.

How has healing in worship developed?

We have already seen that healing was a part of Jesus' own ministry, and in this he followed the path trodden by others in the Hebrew Scriptures. Elijah and Elisha were both known for their miracles of healing – Elisha's raising of the dead foreshadows Jesus' similar miracles (John 7.11–15 and Mark 5.35–43).

The Church has followed Jesus' use of touch through the laying on of hands in prayer, but has added to it the use of anointing with oil. Not surprisingly, the Church has tended not to repeat Jesus' use of spit and mud (Mark 7.33 and John 9.6) in its own ministry of healing (at least not in recent years in the West).

The development of a ministry of healing in the early Church is evidenced initially from the epistle of James, in which prayer for the sick and anointing are clearly mentioned.

> Are any among you sick? They should call for the elders of the church and have them pray over them, anointing them with oil in the name of the Lord. The prayer of faith will save the sick, and the Lord will raise them up; and anyone who has committed sins will be forgiven. Therefore confess your sins to one another, and pray for one another, so that you may be healed. The prayer of the righteous is powerful and effective. (James 5.14–16)

Several things are worth noting:

- It is the responsibility of the sick person to seek prayer.
- It is the elders of the church who are to be called to pray, not someone who necessarily has a charismatic gift of healing.
- Anointing with oil is mentioned, though there is no indication of whether the oil has been prayed over in any way.
- A connection is made between sin and sickness – not in a direct causal relationship ('you are sick because you have sinned'), though it could be read like that, but simply noting that healing involves spiritual 'wholeness' as well as physical.

IN PRACTICE – Oil in healing ministry

There is no evidence that Jesus himself used oil in his healing miracles, though it is recorded that when Jesus sent out the twelve they 'anointed with oil many who were sick and cured them' (Mark 6.13). Elizabeth Stuart reminds us that the fact that Jesus himself received anointing may also be significant (Mark 14.3–9).[4] However, it was the passage from the letter of James which became the most significant for the use of oil to accompany prayer for healing.

There are many meanings given to oil in the Old Testament.[5] Oil is associated with joy and gladness (Isa. 61.3 'the oil of gladness instead of mourning'; Ps. 45.7 'God has anointed you with the oil of gladness beyond your companions');[6] with blessing, abundance and God's approval (Ps. 23.5 'you anoint my head with oil; my cup overflows'; Ps. 104.15 'wine to gladden the human heart, oil to make the face shine'; Jer. 31.12 'they shall be radiant over the goodness of the LORD, over the grain, the wine, and the oil'; Joel 2.24 'The threshing floors shall be full of grain, the vats shall overflow with wine and oil'); and with God's choice and equipping of priests and kings (for instance, Samuel's anointing of Saul in 1 Sam. 10.1, which is followed by Saul prophesying).

---

4 Elizabeth Stuart, 'The Sacrament of Unction', in Jonathan Baxter (ed.), *Wounds that Heal: Theology, Imagination and Health*, London: SPCK, 2007, p. 198. She suggests that Jesus being anointed by the woman gives a pattern which was followed in the Church in the same way that Jesus being baptized by John sets a pattern about the importance of baptism. However, as she also notes, this fits better with the later development of anointing as a rite before death than with the early development of anointing as a regular rite for healing.

5 See J. Roy Porter, 'Oil in the Old Testament', in Martin Dudley and Geoffrey Rowell (eds), *The Oil of Gladness: Anointing in the Christian Tradition*, London: SPCK, 1993, pp. 35–45, for a detailed analysis. For the meanings attached to oil in Scripture and Christian history, and its use in the Church of England's *Common Worship* services, see Simon Jones, 'Oil', in Christopher Irvine (ed.), *The Use of Symbols in Worship* (Alcuin Liturgy Guides 4), London: SPCK, 2007, pp. 39–56.

6 In *WURC*, the prayer before anointing connects explicitly with this meaning rather than others: 'I anoint you with the oil of gladness in the name of Jesus Christ,' p. 118.

But as well as these symbolic meanings, oil was also used as a medicinal ointment, as evidenced in the New Testament parable often called the parable of the good Samaritan, in which the man from Samaria uses oil in caring for the man who has been attacked ('He went to him and bandaged his wounds, having poured oil and wine on them.' Luke 10.34). Passages from the Hebrew Scriptures suggest a similar use for oil (for instance, 'From the sole of the foot even to the head, there is no soundness in it, but bruises and sores and bleeding wounds; they have not been drained, or bound up, or softened with oil.' Isa. 1.6).

Does this medicinal connection with oil suggest a possible modern parallel? Perhaps, rather than anointing with oil to accompany prayer for healing, we might encourage people to bring their antiseptic cream, or their tablets and medicines, and pray over those? This would give a very different focus for a healing service, but it might help people to keep their prayers for God's healing connected with God's work of healing through the medical profession.

Beyond the New Testament

Once we get beyond the New Testament the trail becomes harder to follow.[7] There is little evidence for the Church's practice in healing until we get to the third century. What seems to happen at that stage is that healing gets more formalized, and less spontaneous. This is partly due to the fall-out from the Montanist crisis, and the consequent suspicion of charismatic excesses. There is evidence of a shift from healing as something based on charismatic gifting, to something that is restricted to clergy by virtue of their office. We already saw the beginnings of that in the passage from James, which suggests that it is the elders that are called, not those who

---

7 For a good historical overview of healing in general, see Amanda Porterfield, *Healing in the History of Christianity*, Oxford: Oxford University Press, 2005. For more focused reflections on liturgical matters, see Bruce T. Morrill, *Divine Worship and Human Healing: Liturgical Theology at the Margins of Life and Death*, Collegeville, MN: Liturgical Press, 2009. For more detail on the early centuries, see Andrew Daunton-Fear, *Healing in the Early Church: The Church's Ministry of Healing and Exorcism from the First to the Fifth Century*, Milton Keynes: Paternoster, 2009.

are gifted in healing ministry. By the fifth century there is evidence that in some places the oil for anointing the sick was blessed by the local bishop, though it could still be administered by lay people, whether by self-application or to others. With Christianity's increasingly public and powerful position within the Roman Empire came a growth in the Church's involvement with the other side of healing ministry – medicine and nursing.

By the ninth century anointing had already become associated primarily with spiritual, rather than physical, healing. Now a tightening of clergy discipline meant that clergy were required (rather than 'could be called') to attend the dying to anoint them and give them Holy Communion. Perhaps in this we can see the beginnings of the unwelcome development which sees anointing becoming associated with dying rather than being healed. By the twelfth century, anointing with oil was seen as 'extreme unction' as part of the last rites. Even in a modern context, most ordained ministers who have visited a hospital ward wearing a clerical collar will probably have experienced the look of fear on the face of many patients because they associate the arrival of the clergy with impending death. In the Roman Catholic Church it was only in the 1960s that the ministry of anointing was affirmed once again as a rite of healing and not a part of dying.

Healing survived in the Church in the medieval period, associated primarily with the saints and their shrines and relics – special miracles for the few, rather than a normal part of the Church's ministry for all. For most ordinary Christians the expectation was limited to spiritual healing – forgiveness and salvation – rather than extended to include the possibility of physical healing.

The Reformation in Europe squashed the appeal to the saints in the Protestant Churches, though this aspect of healing remained strong in the Roman Catholic Church. However, it did not do anything to restore the idea or practice of healing into the Church's regular worship. Instead, prayer with laying on of hands and anointing died out and prayer with the sick, while *allowing* that God might mercifully grant recovery, was focused on preparation for possible death and the importance of confessing sin in order to guarantee eternal salvation.[8]

IN PRACTICE – Giving shape to prayer for wholeness and healing

The fourfold shape which was outlined in Chapter 3 makes a good framework not just for a healing service, but for more informal occasions for prayer for healing and wholeness, whether this is in a home or hospital or as part of prayer ministry offered during or after Sunday services.

Gathering – Tell your story. What is the problem, what has happened, why have you asked for prayer?

Word – Read a passage from Scripture to put alongside that human story. Perhaps something about God's faithfulness, an account of Jesus healing someone, or a faith-building passage or a passage of comfort.

Response – Offer prayer, perhaps with laying on of hands and/or anointing. It will be particularly good if the prayer for the individual is connected also with prayer beyond that individual, for the wholeness of the world.

Sending – Give encouragement to live out the trust and faith and wholeness which has been prayed for. Great care is needed with this phase of healing ministry to make sure that pressure is not put on the person who is ill. This must be, 'Go in faith and trust,' rather than, 'Go, and if you aren't healed you didn't have enough faith.'

Pastoral and theological issues in healing services

Despite the growth in popularity of healing services and other forms of healing ministry, there are many Christians who are nervous about this growing focus on healing. There are several reasons for this:

- For some there is a basic belief that healing in a 'miraculous' sense was for the New Testament context, and that the modern western context calls for a different understanding

---

8 See, for instance, 'The Visitation of the Sick' in the *Book of Common Prayer*.

of healing, focused on the work of medical professionals. This can arise from two possible perspectives. Some believe that healing miracles were never truly miraculous in the first place, but were the way that people in a pre-scientific age talked about and understood what was happening. Others are happy to believe that healing was miraculous then, but also believe that this was just for the early centuries before medicine had developed. (This latter view raises questions about what we are to expect in the many parts of the world where western medicine is not easily available today.)

- Some simply do not believe that healing ever happens (in the sense of divine intervention which changes outcomes), and therefore, any claims to healing are either bogus and falsified or could be explained by other, natural, means.

- Some have felt that the healing miracles in the New Testament are primarily about ending social exclusion, which illness often brought in Jesus' day. The healing is therefore not a permanent sign of God's desire to make us physically well, but a sign of God's desire to bring in those who are on the margins of society. Therefore, where there are other ways to end exclusion and marginalization, healing ministry is not needed.

- Some have seen pastoral damage caused by inappropriate use of healing ministry and do not feel confident that it can be done in such a way as to avoid this. For these people, the dangers outweigh any possible benefit. Such damage might be 'healers' projecting onto the sick the responsibility for their healing, so that a failure to be healed is due to a lack of faith. There can also be ongoing pastoral fallout in the wider congregation.

CASE STUDY – The healing prayer that doesn't 'work'

Zoey was a member of the youth group at St Matthew's Church, when she was diagnosed with leukaemia. Immediately the church swung into action: there was practical help for Zoey and her family with hospital visits, treatment, and recovery. Zoey was also encouraged by several members of the congregation to come to the monthly healing service. Here she was anointed with oil and prayed for with laying on of hands by the clergy and by other members of the church. After prayer, one of the members of the healing team said that he had a very clear sense, which he believed to be from God, that God was going to heal Zoey. This led to a great sense of faith and responsibility on the part of the church. Special vigils of prayer were set up to pray for Zoey regularly, and she was often anointed and prayed for at hospital, in her home, and when she was able to come to church.

After several months the treatment was continuing, but there was little sign of improvement. Zoey began to stay away from church. She herself was happy to leave her healing in God's hands, but she felt awkward coming to church and being so visibly 'not better' when so many people were praying and believing she would be healed. She felt that she was letting people down by continuing to be ill.

Some in the congregation were unsettled too. After such a clear indication from God that Zoey would be healed, her continuing illness seemed to undermine their faith. Were they praying wrongly? Had they mis-heard God? Perhaps they needed more faith, or perhaps Zoey did. When Zoey came to healing services, her presence seemed to inhibit others from giving testimony about the healing they had received, and numbers at the service began to drop off. Some said that in the light of Zoey's serious illness, their own seeking of prayer for ear infections and aching hips seemed too trivial to mention, and they had stopped asking for prayer and laying on of hands.

Some began to suggest that there might be some sin in Zoey that was blocking her healing, and they suggested that she needed to come to a healing service and confess that sin publicly so she could be forgiven and receive her healing. When this was suggested to Zoey's parents they absolutely refused to let her come to a healing service again.

Her condition deteriorated. When the minister came to see her in hospital, Zoey asked him to anoint her with oil, but not use any words. She herself seemed ready to speak about death and eternal life, but few in the church seemed able to speak to her in that way – it felt like a betrayal of their faith in God's healing power.

When Zoey died, the church was left traumatized. Not only had they lost a very dear and much loved church member, but they had also lost their confidence in God. The minister felt that he had failed to help Zoey to prepare for her death. Some of the healing team asked to come off the rota, and it was many months before attendance at the healing service picked up again. Some suggested that it be called a Service of Prayer for Wholeness rather than a Healing Service . . .

There are many pastoral and theological reasons for pausing before setting up patterns of healing prayer or healing services. Some of the issues include:

- How to understand disability in a healing framework (and vice versa). Some people with disabilities resist the view that these are problems needing a cure, and prefer to see any problems as socially constructed – that is, blindness (for instance) is not the problem, the problem is a world which assumes sightedness is the norm and is set up to work that way.
- How to understand and handle chronic and long-term illness within a healing framework. A conversation with a healthcare chaplain would be a good place to start to gain some wisdom about how to handle some of the dilemmas that this issue raises.
- How to take seriously the fact that the ultimate healing comes only with death and our new resurrection bodies – that is, anyone who is cured of a physical illness is still destined to die one day. How can we confidently offer prayer for healing, while not repressing a healthy willingness to talk about death and eternal life? This is a constant danger for the contemporary Church, which has rediscovered both healing and resurrection, but has sometimes missed out the crucial stage in between – being ready to die.
- How to recognize and affirm the place of medicine within God's healing and wholeness, so that medical professionals

do not feel undervalued by the Church, and so that those who are ill are not tempted to abandon their medications or treatment.

• How to handle the delicate relationship between physical well-being and spiritual well-being, which in some contexts is unhelpfully characterized as 'if you want healing you need to confess your sin'. We have already seen that in the book of James, the connection between healing and confession is made, and the story of Jesus healing the man let down through the roof by his friends (Mark 2) can suggest a similar link. The man is brought because he is paralysed, and the upshot of the healing is that he is able to walk, but the first words spoken by Jesus are: 'Son, your sins are forgiven' (Mark 2.5). After the ensuing controversy, Jesus then says, 'I say to you, stand up, take your mat and go to your home' (Mark 2.11), but the point of the miracle and Jesus' approach to it is that he has power both to forgive and to heal, and the implication is that the two go together. It is easy to see how this link can be misused and applied in ways which are inappropriate, but the positive side is the holistic approach, which connects with what so much modern science is helping us to see, which is that our physical well-being is connected to our emotional, psychological and spiritual well-being. Happy people live longer and get better quicker; people under stress or who carry anger or resentment are more vulnerable to illness, less able to fight it off, and take longer to recover.

Underneath many of these issues is a fundamental question: what *is* healing? More particularly, is there a difference between healing and curing?[9] 'Healing' in a New Testament sense is holistic, connected linguistically to the idea of salvation (the Greek word *sozo* can be translated as healing or salvation, depending on the context). However, in popular usage healing is associated

---

9 For a careful analysis of the difference between biomedical curing and ethnomedical healing, see Morrill, *Divine Worship*, pp. 71–80 and 93–9.

most directly with receiving a physical cure – and, indeed, in many church contexts this is what is intended. But being cured is not always what is needed or desired, or appropriate. Being made whole is a way of speaking which makes much clearer connections with the richness of the idea of salvation in Christian tradition – it recognizes that all physical healing is, at best, only temporary, and allows for death to be the means of receiving that wholeness. It also makes room for understandings which go beyond the physical and recognize the importance of wholeness which includes emotional and psychological 'salvation' and knowing the forgiveness and love of God.

Perhaps because of these theological issues (with their pastoral and practical implications) some churches are moving to a pattern of referring to a ministry or service of *wholeness* and healing, rather than simply talking about healing services or prayer for healing.[10] The intention is to keep the focus broad, allowing for a holistic approach which moves beyond physical cure, while not ruling out the healing power of God to work in every area of a person's life.

TO THINK ABOUT – Wholeness on the streets?

Anytown Baptist Church has a ministry called 'Healing on the Streets'. Every month, a small team sets up on the High Street, outside a charity shop which is run by a church member. Chairs are placed on the street, and a large banner proclaims 'Healing'. Church members give out leaflets explaining to passers-by that if they would like to receive prayer for healing, they should come and sit on one of the chairs, and team members will come and pray for them.

- How do you feel about this idea?
- Would it feel different (and in what way) if the banner and leaflets proclaimed 'Wholeness' rather than 'Healing'?

---

10 *CWPS* has a service for Wholeness and Healing; *MWB* has a form of service for Healing and Wholeness.

Practical considerations

Healing ministry in church brings with it many of the standard concerns which apply to any forms of pastoral care, and it is good to be mindful of the issues and to include them in any training about healing.

Confidentiality

Confidentiality is a major concern in all forms of prayer for healing, including prayer request books, telephone or email prayer chains, prayer trees, and so on. Whenever prayer for healing is offered it should be made clear what the boundaries of confidentiality are:

- How much am I going to be expected to reveal? Do I have to give specific details of what I want healing for, or can I speak more generally, or simply come forward for a generic prayer for wholeness?
- Who will hear what I say? Will I be speaking to just one person (or to a pair of persons), and will that person be an ordained minister or a lay person? Whoever I speak to, will they have had training? – that is, can I trust that they will treat the information I give them with appropriate confidentiality? Is it likely that I will be overheard by others (for instance, others in a queue to receive prayer, or kneeling near me at a communion rail, or others praying with other people)?
- How much and how far will the information be shared? If I tell the person praying for me that I have a hospital appointment later in the week, will that information be passed on to the ministers of the church? (Sometimes people will feel cross if the information is passed on; others may feel let down if the information is *not* passed on.) Will I discover that this information has been included in the intercessions in next Sunday's service?

It will be important not only that any healing team receive proper training for this role, including training in confidentiality, but that the wider church are aware of that training and are involved in the preparation of any policies relating to confidentiality. This will help to ensure that there is a general awareness and confidence in the congregation that the ministry will be 'safe'.

The use of touch

At one level, the use of touch, via the laying on of hands, is a basic symbol of human oneness, support and friendship. It carries some of the same meaning as shaking hands or holding hands.

For Christians, however, there is a further level of meaning. The use of touch in prayer for healing goes back to Jesus himself. Many services in which it is used pick up this connection with the touch of Jesus and apply it to the hands now being laid:

> In the name of God and trusting in his might alone,
> *receive Christ's healing touch* to make you whole.
> May Christ bring you wholeness of body, mind and spirit,
> deliver you from every evil, and give you his peace. **Amen.**[11]

As well as its use in healing, the laying on of hands is often used in other contexts as a sign of the Holy Spirit (for instance, in a confirmation service or ordination service). Laying on hands in healing can therefore carry echoes of those other uses, and be symbolic of prayer for the Spirit to come and bring God's wholeness and healing. The worship resources from the United Reformed Church explicitly pick up this symbolism of the Spirit and apply it to the laying on of hands in healing. The words offered at the laying on of hands are these:

> Healing Spirit of God, at work in Jesus, present here and now,
> fill your whole being, free you of all harm, and give you peace.
> **Amen.**[12]

---

11 *CWPS*, p. 21 (emphasis added).
12 *WURC*, p. 117.

In the *Methodist Worship Book*, three texts are given as options either for anointing or laying on of hands. Two of them specifically pick up the connection with the Spirit:

> Father, *send your Spirit of life and health* on your servant, N; in the name of Christ. Amen.

> May the *Spirit of the living God*, present with us now, heal you of all that harms you, in body, mind or spirit; in the name of Jesus Christ. Amen.[13]

Notice, incidentally, in all these examples, how the prayers are phrased to stress the holistic nature of the healing being sought.

The formal laying on of hands is a normal part of prayer for healing in many churches. However, there are important issues about the use of touch which apply here as in other contexts. In both church and beyond, we are much more aware of how touch can be used in appropriate and inappropriate ways, and how it can be used to reinforce unhelpful power dynamics. On the other hand, touch is also a basic human means of connecting with another person, and churches will do well to tread a careful course between obsessive avoidance of touch, and a careless approach which can cause harm.

Training for those who administer laying on of hands in the context of pastoral ministry should include questions about who touches whom, and where on the body it is appropriate to touch. Those being prayed for should always be asked specifically for permission before touch is used. In some church contexts it is fashionable to lay hands (or to place hands near) the person's heart, or on the part of the body being prayed for, and this needs to be used with great caution. In general, a hand laid gently on a shoulder or on the head should be the default. *Methodist Worship Book*, for instance, specifies that if laying on of hands is offered, the hands should be laid on the head, and that if the person is anointed with oil, the anointing should be applied to the forehead.[14]

---

13 *MWB*, p. 413 (emphasis added).
14 *MWB*, p. 408.

Where the healing prayer is for someone who has been abused, particular care should be taken, and the use of touch will often be inappropriate. Where those who are praying do not, for whatever reason, lay on hands, the person being prayed for might be invited to lay their own hand on the part of the body being prayed for.[15]

Words of knowledge

In charismatic and Pentecostal Churches it is often common for those who pray with people to ask God to guide them in their praying, perhaps asking for wisdom about how to focus their prayers, and sometimes seeking 'words' or pictures from God which might encourage or reassure or boost the faith of the person being prayed for. These words are usually associated with the New Testament spiritual gift which is sometimes translated as 'words of knowledge' (1 Cor. 12.8), or are referred to as 'prophetic words'.

Such words, coming directly for the person being prayed for, can be pastorally helpful where they open up faith and assure the person of God's love for them. Equally, they can be very damaging if they are applied in forceful or oppressive ways, and if they are delivered as the definite word of God to that person. Christians who have been damaged or hurt by inappropriate healing ministry in churches will often point to an occasion where a 'word' was badly handled as the source of their unease.

Therefore, the key to the use of these spiritual gifts and insights is to make sure that those who will be offering prayer have been carefully trained. That training will include how to listen and give attention to what God may be saying, but it will also need to cover how such insights can be delivered to the person being prayed for.

---

15 Richard Deadman, Jeremy Fletcher, Janet Henderson and Stephen Oliver (eds), *Pastoral Prayers: A Resource for Pastoral Occasions*, London: Mowbray, 1996, has a service for adults who have been abused as children, and for whom laying on hands or anointing with oil might not be appropriate, and gives wise advice for how to symbolize the corporate care being shown in prayer: 'A jug of oil and a small pot may be passed around for each person to put a drop of oil into. Oil from the pot is used to anoint the survivor and is symbolic of the affirmation of the group' (p. 71).

There is a world of difference between, 'God has just told me that you will be healed if you repent of that sin of pride that you have,' and, 'I think God might be saying that he wants to bring you spiritual wholeness as well as helping you with this illness.' In general, those who pray for others need to be taught to phrase things cautiously, to own what they are saying as their own impressions, rather than ascribing it to God, to use phrases like 'I think', 'I feel', 'I wonder', and 'God might be saying', 'God could be showing me', and so on. The temptation to demonstrate 'faith' by phrasing things in unequivocal ways should be avoided.

For Anglicans, there is some good brief guidance about incorporating prayer for individuals into public worship in *Common Worship: Pastoral Services*, which would be important to take account of in any training for a healing team or prayer ministry team.[16]

Exorcism

A combination of sensational horror films and high-profile television documentaries has given the ministry of deliverance (as most churches prefer to call exorcism) a reputation as something which can be abusive and forceful. In real life, things are (thankfully) often more dull, but any ministry which addresses spiritual oppression and connects with New Testament accounts of persons being 'demonized' (Mark 5.15; the phrase '*possessed* by a demon' does not occur in the New Testament) or 'having an unclean spirit' (Mark 5.2) needs to be handled with great care, wisdom and sensitivity.

In some Churches the ministry of deliverance is very much in the hands of the local leadership, but in Churches with wider lines of accountability (such as the Roman Catholic Church, the Church of England and the Methodist Church) there are clear guidelines which are designed to support and protect both local ministers and the persons receiving this ministry.

In the Church of England, every diocese has a bishop's officer for the ministry of deliverance, and any local minister who feels that this ministry may be needed has to contact that person.

---

16 *CWPS*, pp. 48f.

These special officers can make sure that good practice is followed in any ministry which results. Any proposed ministry has to receive specific permission from the bishop, and the form that it takes must also be agreed with the bishop.[17]

The Methodist Church does not focus the responsibility for overseeing this ministry so specifically, but has guidelines which stress that no minister should act independently (the Superintendent and any other Circuit Ministers should be consulted and the District Chair asked to suggest sources of help) and any ministry must include collaboration with those appropriately qualified in medical care, the social services and psychology.[18]

Sometimes a healing of 'spiritual disturbance' is needed or sought, which falls a long way short of the ministry of deliverance, but which overlaps with some of the same areas. The Church of England's *Common Worship* materials include a short section on Prayers for Protection and Peace, which are for use, 'where it would be pastorally helpful to pray with those suffering from a sense of disturbance or unrest'.[19] This section includes some psalms, the Indian prayer 'Christaraksha' (which can be used with a person or by the person on their own before sleep), a prayer for angels to watch over a place, St Patrick's breastplate (Christ be with you; Christ within you . . . Bind unto yourself the name . . .) and this prayer which carries that sense of Christ being in us and pushing out all evil:

Our Lord Jesus Christ,
present with us now in his risen power,
enter into your body and spirit,
take from you all that harms and hinders you,
and fill you with his healing and his peace.
Amen.[20]

---

17 In *CWPS*, see the Introductory Note to the Wholeness and Healing material on p. 12 and Notes 2 and 3 relating to 'Prayer for Protection and Peace' on p. 94.

18 Methodist practice is still governed by the 1976 Conference Statement on Exorcism: *Statements and Reports of the Methodist Church on Faith and Order, Volume One 1933–1983*, Peterborough: Methodist Publishing House, 1984, pp. 206–9.

19 *CWPS*, p. 94, Note 1.

20 *CWPS*, p. 95.

Self-care

In most situations, prayer with individuals for wholeness and healing is very different from counselling or other forms of therapy. However, as with these and other forms of pastoral care, those who share in it should be offered support and guidance about appropriate 'self-care'. That might mean being offered regular opportunities to 'de-brief' together (being mindful of confidentiality issues mentioned above), and to review how the ministry of healing is going. It also means helping those who pray to understand the importance of maintaining their own boundaries – making sure they don't overstep them and impinge on others, but also making sure they are clear about what their own responsibilities are and are not.

Praying with someone in deep distress, or hearing someone's story can leave the pray-er with their own issues and needs, and can also lead to the pray-er feeling a sense of responsibility to 'solve' the other person's problem. Establishing clear responsibilities, including a policy about referral, is important. Such referral might include having a list of professionals to whom people can be referred, knowing when a prayer team member needs to involve one of the ordained ministers or other church leaders, and making sure that those being prayed for are not discouraged, either explicitly or implicitly, from taking medication, and maintaining contact with their healthcare professional.

Using the pastoral liturgy toolkit in healing services

Telling the God story – Scripture

The theological issues and questions surrounding healing should make us aware that the way we tell the God story in a service of wholeness and healing will be key. One of the ways of telling that story will be through the Scripture readings which are used in specific healing services.

These can be categorized as follows:

- **Narratives of healing miracles** – If you ask Christians in most churches to suggest Bible passages for a healing service the likely first 'off the top of their heads' answers will include some of the healing miracles of Jesus: blind people made to see, lame people enabled to walk, those who are deaf allowed to hear. We have already noted some of the issues about healing and disability which this sort of healing raises today, but these passages are only one strand within the biblical record.

- **Passages reflecting on life and suffering** – Readings from the book of Job would give a very different feel to a healing service. In short sections (out of context) they could easily reinforce an unhelpful link with the idea that suffering comes from God and is caused by our sin or failure, or is part of God testing us. However, something from Ecclesiastes 3 (there is a time for everything) might offer opportunity to reflect on what this time means in this particular life.

- **Eschatological material** – This might include passages such as Romans 8.18–end, 'we, with creation, groaning as we wait for the future glory', or the prophecy of Isaiah 53, 'Surely he has borne our infirmities and carried our diseases . . . by his bruises we are healed', and its application in the New Testament to both physical healing (Matt. 8.17) and the forgiveness of sins (1 Pet. 2.24). A passage such as Revelation 22.1–5, 'The leaves of the trees are for the healing of the nations', puts prayer for individual healing in the bigger context of the ultimate renewal of creation.

- **Material focusing on the spiritual gift of healing** – 1 Corinthians 12.1–11 mentions healing among the gifts, but also mentions other gifts which are associated with this ministry in some churches, such as working miracles, word of knowledge, word of wisdom, and prophecy.

- **More general material about salvation** – Isaiah 61.1–4, 'The Spirit of the Lord God is upon me . . . he has sent me to bring good news . . . to bind up the broken-hearted . . .', paints a much broader picture of the freedom and release that the messiah brings, which could encompass, but is not restricted to, physical healing. (Note that in Luke's account of Jesus' reading of this passage at the synagogue at Capernaum – Luke 4.18 – the version quoted inserts 'recovery of sight to the blind' into the prophecy.) Other passages with a wide compass might include Matthew 11.28–30, 'Come to me, all you that are weary and are carrying heavy burdens, and I will give you rest . . .', or John 10.10, 'I have come that they may have life, and have it abundantly.'

Any one of these readings, or the many other possibilities,[21] will give a particular 'spin' to the understanding of what a service of healing and wholeness is for, or what prayer ministry is all about. However, often it will be the *juxtaposing* of readings which will make the most creative space in which to pray for wholeness. For instance, a healing service might include a passage recounting a healing miracle from the Hebrew Bible or from Jesus' ministry, paired with Paul's agonizing over his thorn in the flesh (2 Cor. 12.1–10). The combination would be very powerful, and one can see the possibilities, and indeed, the necessity, of providing similar combinations of readings, if services of prayer for wholeness are not to become skewed to one particular perspective on God's desire for us and what we can expect from prayer.

Telling the God story – forms of prayer

Although the Bible readings will be a key feature in shaping the God story, an understanding of what God has to say about wholeness will also be shaped in other ways, notably in the words which are used in prayer itself. The words used in prayer and any accompanying actions or symbols act as the liminal moment in a healing service – this is the point at which God is invoked in response to the human story, and it is important that any words used are

---

21 See, for instance, the long list of possible readings in *CWPS*, pp. 44–5, and the slightly smaller selection in *MWB*, pp. 410f.

congruent with the God story which has been established through the chosen Bible readings. Training of those involved in this ministry will be vital, so that they are aware of some of the theological and pastoral issues that we have explored above.

In churches in which the ministry of prayer and laying on of hands is fairly formalized, everyone gets the same, whoever is offering the prayer and whatever the need is. Though persons seeking prayer may be asked to indicate their particular need, the actual prayer will use fixed words, and the form of anointing or handlaying will be standardized. For some this is too impersonal and can seem mechanistic – a more personalized and spontaneous format is preferred. This can communicate the personal and individual care that God has for us, but it can also have a downside: too much can depend on who is praying, and their experience and wisdom.

Extempore and spontaneous prayer for healing is particularly susceptible to particular 'fashions' within church practice. Particular ways of praying or forms of words tend to come in and out of fashion. Often fashion triumphs over theology. If you pushed someone, they would acknowledge that if healing is down to God, then it doesn't matter what we say or how we say it – what matters is a willingness to bring a person or situation before God with hope and trust. In practice, though, people tend to copy patterns of prayer that they have experienced or heard about in a big conference or a 'powerful' time of worship, or on the internet or TV.

One of the ways to help those who minister primarily through extempore prayer to be more theologically aware is encourage them to study the fixed forms of words which some Churches provide for this ministry. These have often been carefully thought through and carry some of the breadth of the God story in a concise way, which takes account of some of the common pastoral issues. Take these examples from *Common Worship: Pastoral Services*:

The laying on of hands is administered, using these or other suitable words
In the name of God and trusting in his might alone,
receive Christ's healing touch to make you whole.
May Christ bring you wholeness

of body, mind and spirit,
deliver you from every evil,
and give you his peace.
Amen.

Anointing may be administered. The minister says
N, I anoint you in the name of God who gives you life.
Receive Christ's forgiveness, his healing and his love.
May the Father of our Lord Jesus Christ
grant you the riches of his grace,
his wholeness and his peace. **Amen.**[22]

Note the careful structuring and phrasing of these forms of prayer:

- They make clear that any healing comes from God, and not from the pray-er ('trusting in his might alone');
- They reinforce this by connecting with the narratives of Jesus' healing ministry, making clear that what is being offered is an extension of Christ's ministry, not something new or disconnected from it ('Christ's healing touch')
- They are explicitly holistic in focus ('wholeness of body, mind and spirit'; 'his wholeness and his peace'), mentioning forgiveness, deliverance, peace and wholeness as well as healing.

These words from *Methodist Worship Book*, for use at anointing or hand laying, are explicitly Trinitarian in pattern:

Father, send your Spirit of life and health on your servant, N; in the name of Christ. **Amen.**[23]

A similar Trinitarian pattern is observable in this prayer for use before the laying on of hands from the United Reformed Church resources:

---

22 *CWPS*, p. 21.
23 *MWB*, p. 413.

Compassionate God, encircle us as we reach out in love.
Wounded Christ, touch us in our weakness and our strength.
Life-giving Spirit, breathe through us, channels of your peace.[24]

In this prayer, notice also the careful way of addressing God
which avoids some of the usual emphasis on force, power and
strength, and emphasizes instead the immanence of a God who
is compassionate and alongside us in suffering and pain, as well
as able to give life by the Spirit. The expectation of change is still
present, but the underlying understanding of how God works to
bring that change is gentle rather than forceful. There are some
key principles here which could inform more informal and extempore patterns of prayer.

The ministry of reconciliation

There was a time when the ministry of reconciliation (sometimes
called sacramental confession) would have been something for
Roman Catholics and Anglicans of a more Catholic sort. The last few
decades, however, have seen some significant changes. Of course, it
is not that every Protestant Christian is now rushing off to confession every week, but there has been a significant shift in the understanding of this ministry and a growing recognition among those
who have previously been suspicious of it that it can be of value.

Some traditional arguments against

Protestant, and especially evangelical Christians, have typically
had a series of questions about the ministry of individual reconciliation, usually claiming that it is:

- unnecessary
- without extra benefit and
- potentially dangerous.

---

24 *WURC*, p. 117.

The case has generally been that there is no need for formal or sacramental confession to be made to a priest or to anyone else, because each and every Christian has direct access to God and can make a confession directly to God through Jesus Christ with the assurance of forgiveness. A special confession to another person is therefore of no extra benefit – all the benefit that can be received can be received through personal and direct prayer to God, either on one's own or in the context of corporate confession in church. Finally, some Christians have seen potential dangers in the role of the priest in Catholic forms of reconciliation, and the requirement to come to confession. They worry that this can lead to the priest being seen as someone who can control God's forgiveness, declaring it or withholding it.

The particular focus of Protestant and evangelical concern was the form of absolution in the Catholic form, which followed the Latin phrase *ego te absolvo* – 'I absolve you'. This seemed to suggest powers for the priest which Protestants had traditionally resisted. The practice of queuing up to enter the confessional booth, and the practice of penance in the form of saying the Lord's Prayer or the Hail Mary, have further reinforced the Protestant instinct that this ministry is being used in a mechanistic and even magical way.[25]

What has changed?

Recent years have seen a significant change in thinking about reconciliation and in its practice. Some of those changes have come from the Catholic side: 'making your confession' no longer needs to mean sitting in a confessional booth talking to an anonymous priest. Catholic practice increasingly encourages face to face modes of confession and a more pastoral approach, with a focus on careful listening and wise advice being given. This has

---

25 For a clear and succinct summary of some arguments for caution in the use of reconciliation, see Andrew Atherstone, 'Some Concerns', in Phillip Tovey, David Kennedy and Andrew Atherstone, *Common Worship Reconciliation and Restoration: A Commentary* (Grove Worship Series 187), Cambridge: Grove Books, 2006, pp. 12–18.

made it harder for Protestants to caricature and stereotype the ministry.

From the Protestant side there has also been a change. While still recognizing the potential for misuse, Christians who have traditionally seen no need for this ministry are beginning to recognize that it can bring benefits above and beyond those received from corporate confession in church or private confession on one's own. Though forgiveness is not made any more available, the sense of 'getting things off your chest' and 'feeling' the forgiveness can be greater when the sins have been spoken out, put in the outer world and acknowledged, and the words of forgiveness perceived and received through the senses. As Westerhoff and Willimon put it:

> . . . it is important to note that repentance and forgiveness may or may not coincide with the sacramental action of reconciliation. What the sacramental action does is make real for us what is indeed already true.[26]

Cicely Berry, director of voice for the Royal Shakespeare Company, and someone who understands about the power of words, reflects on this in her book about how to use the voice:

> To talk about something you have done wrong actually helps to cleanse you, the more difficult it is to talk about, the more cleansed you feel afterwards – you 'get it off your chest', or you 'get it out of your system', or it is a 'weight off your mind' – all those marvellously organic phrases which show just how closely the mind and the body are interrelated. This is why the act of confession must be a releasing experience, something which releases you physically as well as mentally. Words can heal.[27]

---

26 John H. Westerhoff III and William H. Willimon, *Liturgy and Learning Through the Life Cycle*, Akron, OH: OSL Publications, revised ed. 1994, p. 140.

27 Cicely Berry, *Your Voice and How to Use it Successfully*, London: Harrap, 1975, p. 44.

> ### CASE STUDY – The importance of telling someone else
>
> In March 2011, my local commercial radio station ran an item called the 'Apology Amnesty', in which they invited people to phone in with apologies and confessions. You might think that the response would be small, as people would be too embarrassed or even ashamed to admit these things over the radio. On the contrary, the phone lines were buzzing with people unburdening themselves and sharing their apologies publicly. The radio station made the connection with Christian ideas of confession explicit by choosing to play ecclesiastical-sounding music in the background. This was not exactly confessing to a priest (!), but it clearly mattered to people that they were making their apology publicly and to someone else (in this case to the DJ and the listening public). Does this help us to understand why formalized ways of saying sorry (not just to the person we have hurt but more generally) are often popular when they are offered in church?

When this ministry is accepted as useful *sometimes*, but not required all the time, then it becomes easier for evangelical Christians to accept its validity and value. This is all the more so when care is taken to ensure that the person declaring God's forgiveness does so in ways that make it explicit that the forgiveness is God's and not theirs. Theological work was done which helped to explore the *ego te absolvo* problem and to see ways in which it could be appropriate for a minister, speaking for the Church, to declare God's forgiveness. Scholars noticed again the passages in the Bible which Catholics had used in support for the ministry of reconciliation, the key text being the words of the resurrected Jesus to the disciples: 'Receive the Holy Spirit. If you forgive the sins of any, they are forgiven them; if you retain the sins of any, they are retained' (John 20.23). It was this passage which originally led Luther to keep Absolution as a sacrament alongside baptism and the Eucharist. While interpretations differed, it was increasingly recognized that there was a significant role for the Church in proclaiming God's forgiveness. Crucial in this was the work of Max Thurian, Protestant theologian and brother of the ecumenical community at Taizé in France.[28]

Changes in practice

A quick look in the *Methodist Worship Book* reveals the rather surprising fact that there is a section in it containing a Service of Repentance and Reconciliation. This is new territory for Methodists, and though it is unlikely to be heavily used, its inclusion in the book at all would have been unthinkable even 30 years ago.[29] What has changed? Evangelicals within Methodism (as within the Church of England) are feeling more confident and less defensive, and this allows for a fresh look at things which may have seemed like shibboleths and proofs of identity in previous generations. The ecumenical movement generally has engendered an atmosphere in which Christians are more willing to listen to one another and to see the best in one another, rather than to build stereotypes based on the worst interpretation of one another. The acceptance of the value of the formal ministry of reconciliation is part of the fruit of these changes. And, of course, in Methodism, no one has to use the *Methodist Worship Book*, so those who are unhappy can simply ignore it. This takes some of the heat out of the discussions – heat which often lingers in the Church of England, in which liturgical books are seen as a place in which doctrine is given shape.

In part, the inclusion of this form of service is a connection back to an early part of Methodist heritage. Though individual confession to an ordained minister was not part of Methodist practice, the early Methodist class and band system, in which Christians met together in small groups each week, included the mutual confession of sins to one another and a sense of spiritual

---

28 His book, *Confession*, London: SCM, 1958 has been very influential.

29 See Neil Dixon, *Wonder, Love and Praise*, Peterborough: Epworth, 2003, pp. 159f., for an account of the thinking which led to the inclusion of this service in *MWB*. It is followed by the equally surprising Prayer with the Dying.

accountability. John Wesley's rules for the Band Societies, drawn up in 1738, make this very clear:

> The design of our meeting is, to obey that command of God, 'Confess your faults one to another, and pray one for another, that ye may be healed.'
> To this end, we intend: -
> . . .
> 4. To speak each of us in order, freely and plainly, the true state of our souls, with the faults we have committed in thought, word, or deed, and the temptations we have felt, since our last meeting.[30]

What the *Methodist Worship Book* service provides is another mode in which that mutuality and accountability may be given shape in the church today. Crucially, the key part of the service, in which forgiveness is declared, is carefully phrased:

> God, the Father of all mercies,
> through Jesus Christ his Son,
> forgives all who truly repent and believe in him.
> By the ministry of reconciliation
> given by Christ to his Church,
> I declare that your sins are forgiven,
> in the name of the Father, and of the Son,
> and of the Holy Spirit. **Amen.**[31]

First, the context is set: it is God who forgives, through Christ, and this forgiveness is not mechanical, but is received by repentance and faith. Second, the ministry of reconciliation is given to the Church, and it is as a representative of the Church, and not as an individual with special powers, that the forgiveness is

---

30 Quoted in Rupert Davies, A. Raymond George and Gordon Rupp (eds), *A History of the Methodist Church in Great Britain, Volume 4*, Peterborough: Epworth, 1988, p. 23.

31 *MWB*, p. 425.

offered. Third, the 'I absolve you' phrase is avoided, and instead the minister 'declares' God's forgiveness.

There is no specific instruction about who may offer this ministry, other than the rubric immediately before the declaration of forgiveness: 'The minister may place her/his hand on the penitent's head or trace the sign of the cross on the penitent's forehead . . .' Dixon suggests that even this may have been an accident in the publishing process, and that the intention was that there should be no restriction on who could be the person giving assurance of forgiveness.[32]

After many decades of resisting any formalization of this ministry, the Church of England now has optional forms in its *Common Worship* resources – not in the Pastoral Services volume, but with the initiation material.[33] The ministry of reconciliation has long been offered in many Anglo-Catholic parishes of the Church of England, largely using forms borrowed from other Churches. The stumbling block was whether this practice should be formalized and Church of England forms provided.

The classic summary: 'None must; all can; some should', had long been standard advice about individual confession among Anglo-Catholics. Evangelicals, however, were more cautious, and wanted to resist anything that might suggest that confession was becoming 'expected' for Anglicans, or that the priest's role was becoming heightened. One of the key shifts has been a change in the overall framework for understanding Church of England services which allows for a category of 'commended' services.[34] A commended service is one that does not need to be authorized because it is not an alternative to a service in the *Book of Common Prayer*. Commended services do not have to be agreed by the General Synod of the Church of England and, crucially, they are not the only forms which are allowed. They are official in the sense that they are centrally produced,

---

32 Dixon, *Wonder*, pp. 159f.

33 *CWCI*, pp. 266–89.

34 For more on the categories of services, see Mark Earey, *Finding Your Way Around Common Worship*, London: Church House Publishing, 2011, pp. 14–16.

'commended' by the House of Bishops, and published along-side authorized services, but the crucial difference is that they are not compulsory. Other forms which are 'reverent and seemly', and 'neither contrary to, nor indicative of any departure from, the doctrine of the Church of England in any essential matter', may be used instead.[35] This means that we can have our cake and eat it: here are some carefully thought out forms of service, which Anglicans can use and feel are 'Anglican' and not Roman, and yet they are not compulsory, so that those who still feel uncomfortable do not have to feel any pressure to use them. The result? So far it seems to have worked. There has been no wholesale move to regular sacramental confession in Anglican parishes, but churches which have wanted to explore this form of ministry can do so without having to look to Roman Catholic resources. For some, that matters a lot.

TO THINK ABOUT – Where do these services belong?

Historically, the practice of reconciliation was linked to Christians who, because of serious sin, had been excluded from the fellowship of the church (excommunicated). During Lent, alongside those preparing for baptism, they would fast and prepare themselves for Easter, when they would be re-admitted to the church's fellowship in parallel with those who were joining it for the first time in baptism. The ministry of reconciliation was public, and was seen as a recovery or re-appropriation of the salvation received in baptism.

Partly for this reason, the services of reconciliation in the Church of England appear in the volume of initiation services, in the section called 'Reconciliation and Restoration: Recovering Baptism'.[36] The Methodist service of Repentance and Reconciliation follows the service of Healing and Wholeness, in a section called Healing and Reconciliation Services.[37]

---

35 The quoted phrases are from Canon B5 of the Canons of the Church of England.

36 CWCI, starting on p. 227.

37 Section 11 in MWB.

It is possible to see this ministry in both ways: theologically there is much to be said for recognizing it as connected with baptism, part of the journey of living out and entering into all that baptism means and does. In pastoral practice, however, this ministry often feels more like a form of healing, a means of receiving a wholeness which is spiritual as well as physical, and which may have implications for other emotional and physical aspects of someone's life.

Reconciliation in practice – using the toolkit

The basic framework of a rite of passage is easy to see:

- **Separation** – acknowledging what has happened.
- **Liminality** – confession and absolution.
- **Incorporation** – dismissal as a forgiven person who has responsibility to pray for others.

If we place this into the fourfold shape then we get this:

- **Gathering** – Why are we here? Because people sin, and the world is spoiled.
- **Word** – What does God have to say about this? That God longs to forgive and calls us to turn around in repentance.
- **Response** – How can we receive this? By confessing and receiving the assurance of forgiveness.
- **Sending** – What difference does this make to our lives? As forgiven people we offer prayer and forgiveness to others and become agents of reconciliation between them.

Gathering

The gathering will set the scene. The service in *Methodist Worship Book* uses the Lord's Prayer to do this – a prayer which belongs to all, which penitent and minister can say together, and which establishes the context: we need to forgive others as we wish to be forgiven ourselves; we all need God's help to resist temptation and to avoid the time of trial (a sort of, 'there, but for the grace of God, go I,' moment).

Word

The liturgy of the word will establish the God story. As with healing services, a careful choice of reading or readings will be important.[38]

Response

The key liminal moment is when the penitent is able to apply this to himself or herself and can make the move to cease to see himself or herself as a sinner, and instead be able to see herself or himself as a forgiven person. In this the act of absolution will be the key. Words are obviously at the heart of the Churches' debates and controversies over this rite. Churches in the Reformation traditions are keen to avoid some of the dangers (as they see it) of the *ego te absolvo* formula, but need to retain some element of performative action in the wording. An absolution which says, 'If you are truly repentant then I declare to you that you are forgiven, but if you aren't repentant then it doesn't apply,' will not do the job.

Here is where the wisdom of a pre-prepared form of words can be seen. It is important at this point not to get it wrong by accident. If prayer is to be extempore, it will be best if it has been informed by careful study of different forms used by churches which take a more formal approach. As with any use of performative language, less is often more: keep it short and focused. Longer and more expansive prayer for the person seeking forgiveness should come either before (for instance prayer that the penitent will be shown all that needs to be brought to God, and

---

38 *MWB* (pp. 423f.) has a good selection, giving 1 John 1.8–9, 'If we confess our sins, he who is faithful and just will forgive us our sins . . .', as the norm, to be supplemented by one other. A significantly different list of suggestions can be found in *CWCI*, p. 275.

given humility and honesty to confess) or after absolution (for strength to live a forgiven life and to avoid temptation).

However, important as the words are, one of the keys for an effective rite of reconciliation is using symbol and action at the liminal moment. The laying of a hand on the penitent's head and the tracing of the sign of the cross on her or his forehead are traditional actions. Anointing with oil would be another possibility (for joy and blessing and acceptance), but there may be other actions which would be appropriate or more helpful in different traditions. It is worth giving attention to other actions, on the part of the penitent and the minister – kneeling, sitting, standing. The minister is taking different roles during the service – at one point, alongside the penitent, the minister is a brother or sister, giving advice and hearing the story; later the minister takes the role of Christ, offering forgiveness and assuring the penitent of God's love. At this point it may be more appropriate for the minister to stand, or to take a different position from that used earlier in the listening phase.

It is worth thinking about where to offer this ministry. If it is to be in church there may be particularly appropriate places to use – kneeling in front of the holy table? In a side chapel? Near a cross or crucifix? By the lectern and an open Bible? Or, for churches which 'reserve' consecrated bread, perhaps before the blessed sacrament as a sign of Christ's presence. For churches which have 'altar calls' or a sinners' bench, that might be the place to use for this ministry.

IN PRACTICE – What shall I wear?

If an ordained minister is offering this ministry it is worth giving attention to what to wear. For this ministry it is important that the minister is seen as a representative of the wider Church and is ministering with that authority, and not as an individual in their own right. Sometimes clothing which symbolizes that wider authority may be helpful in this ministry, even if it is being offered in more informal contexts.

In traditions in which clerical collars, or stoles, or other robes or vestments are sometimes worn (even if not regularly in worship in this particular local church) one or more of these may help to signal the nature of what is being offered. The key is to make clear that it is in your 'office' that you offer this ministry, not as yourself.

If robes or other forms of special clothing are not normal in your tradition, then other signals, such as where the ministry takes place, may need be used instead. Where lay people offer this ministry, either individually or in the context of mutual confession in a small group, it is important that they don't try to mimic the role of the ordained, but they might also wish to include something which connects with the wider Church, such as using some fixed forms of words or traditional symbols drawn from Christian tradition.

Another factor in considering how to mark this ministry off from other forms of pastoral help, such as counselling, spiritual direction or simple pastoral conversations, is the importance of being clear about the limits of confidentiality. We have already noted how important this is, but it has particular bearing where the person seeking reconciliation discloses information about abuse of some sort (which they have either perpetrated or survived). In this case it is vital that both minister and penitent are clear whether the situation is a formal 'making a confession', because this may well influence the expectations of those involved.

In Churches where confession to a priest is part of the tradition, there is usually an expectation that anything revealed is completely confidential. This is sometimes called 'the seal of the confessional' and it has required some clarity in recent years, as issues of abuse and disclosure of abuse have become more public. The Church of England gives guidance about this which suggests that the confidentiality of formal confession to a priest should be retained, but reminds clergy that absolution can be withheld in that context, for instance, until there is evidence that a penitent who has disclosed some form of abuse has revealed their behaviour to the appropriate authorities.[39] The guidelines also point out that there is no clear evidence that the law will uphold the traditional absolute confidentiality of sacramental confession.

Though this may not impact on other traditions so obviously, it is important for all Christian ministers to be aware of these issues. Particularly outside the Churches, few people are aware of the differences between Catholic priests and Baptist ministers, and it can be possible for the folk memory of the 'seal of the confessional' to affect the expectations of anyone who speaks privately with someone who is wearing a clerical collar.

Sending

One traditional way to end the ministry of reconciliation is for the minister to say something like:

Go in peace,
pray for me, a sinner,
and remember the mercy of God.[40]

This very clearly puts the penitent in a new category – a Christian who knows God's forgiveness themselves and can pray for others. This clear placing of the minister alongside the forgiven penitent (perhaps symbolized by the minister kneeling beside the penitent again, or inviting the penitent to stand) is important both for reinforcing the fact that the minister operates not as a perfect individual Christian but as a representative of the Church, with their own need for forgiveness, and for showing that the forgiven penitent is now fully reconciled and treated as a valued member of the church.

---

39 See *Guidelines for the Professional Conduct of the Clergy*, London: Church House Publishing, 2003, pp. 7f. There is further acknowledgement of the importance of clarity about what is and what is not a formal confession in *Responding to Domestic Abuse: Guidelines for Those with Pastoral Responsibility*, London: Church House Publishing, 2006, p. 29.

40 This particular form of words is from *MWB*, p. 425.

CASE STUDY – Offering a fresh start

After the service one Sunday just before Easter, Vanessa and Leroy asked their minister, Vera, very hesitantly if they could see her about getting married. Vanessa had been a member of the church for some time, but Leroy had only recently come to faith following an Alpha course. Vera expressed delight, but the couple were clearly troubled by something. When they came to see her later that week, they told her that Leroy had been married before and divorced. Vera began asking some of the pastoral questions which are normal in these circumstances, and it emerged that the divorce was instigated by Leroy's former wife on the grounds of his adultery. Leroy acknowledged that this was the cause of the breakdown of the marriage. During the Alpha course on the Holy Spirit day, he felt God challenge him about this, and he had been confessing it to God since then, asking for forgiveness. However, he was struggling to believe that he really could be forgiven, and was worried that his marriage service to Vanessa would be over-shadowed by his feelings of guilt.

Vera suggested that something that might help him would be to make a formal confession and receive the ministry of reconciliation. She arranged to meet Leroy to talk further, and suggested that he stayed behind after the service on Good Friday evening, to receive the ministry of reconciliation. When she met with him, after listening carefully to the whole story, she suggested that he write a letter to his former wife, expressing his sorrow for what happened and accepting his part of the blame for it. He brought the letter with him on Good Friday. After the service, when everyone else had left, Vera knelt next to Leroy and led him through a simple act of confession, in which he expressed out loud what he had done, and laid his letter at the foot of the cross as a symbol of wanting that sin to be wiped away. He agreed to send the letter to his former wife, whatever her reaction might be. Vera then stood in front of Leroy, laid a hand on his head and assured him of God's forgive-ness for all who truly repent, and made the sign of the cross on his forehead. She then picked the letter up and gave it to him saying: 'The Lord has forgiven: go in peace and learn to forgive yourself.'

Summary

In this chapter we have focused on the connections between liturgy and doctrine, and how pastoral liturgy needs to build on careful theological reflection. In the next chapter we will look at an even more complex example in which pastoral liturgy not only reflects people's beliefs but also shapes them significantly.

7

Funerals

What is a 'Christian funeral'?

When we considered Christian wedding services, we asked the question, what makes a Christian wedding? We concluded that some of the things that might help to indicate a Christian wedding were:

- A Christian leader or ordained minister presiding over the service.
- The wedding taking place in a place of Christian worship.
- Christian expectations and assumptions of what marriage is about and of God's interest in the marriage.
- The words of the service pointing towards the Christian story.

At the bottom of the list was a question: is the faith of the couple themselves important in making a wedding 'Christian'? Our tentative conclusion was that while the Christian faith of one or both of the persons being married is likely to affect whether the *marriage* is Christian, this was not essential in order for the service itself (the wedding) to be a Christian pastoral rite. Instead, the wedding can be seen as an invitation to put the human story of this particular relationship alongside the God story of how Christians understand marriage and what God hopes for from committed relationships.

Can we then ask the same question of a Christian funeral? Can we apply the same model, in which the Christian nature of a funeral is determined by things such as:

- A Christian minister leading the service.
- A place of Christian worship being used for the service (there are then implications if the service takes place entirely at a 'secular' crematorium).
- A form of service which articulates Christian assumptions about life, death, and life beyond death, for this person who has died and more generally.
- A service in which the wider story being told also draws on Christian assumptions about the nature of God and the world.

Some Christians might instinctively want to add a further point: that the person who has died, or key members of their family, are practising Christians. But is that necessary? Can a Christian funeral be determined by the other criteria, and offered, like a Christian wedding, as an invitation to a family to see the life and death of their loved one in a Christian framework and through the lens of Christian hope and in a context of Christian prayer?

This is an important question, because in Britain this is how it still happens in the vast majority of cases. When a death occurs, a majority of families who do not have a strong affiliation to any Christian church, but who would not count themselves as atheists or members of another faith, will turn to the Christian Church, or, at least, to a Christian minister,[1] to perform the funeral service for their loved one. This may be because of the echo of a fading Christendom, in which many people consider themselves to be 'in' the Church (and not just the Church of England) unless they have consciously and deliberately opted out. Or it may be due to a 'just in case' insurance policy approach ('We'd better get the church involved, just in case the God stuff is true'). Or perhaps it is simply a recognition that Christian ministers are those who have the skills for dealing with these sorts of formal rituals, and a desire to make sure it is 'done right'. Perhaps,

---

1 A significant current trend is the number of 'freelance' ministers, who may or may not have been ordained in any mainstream Christian Church, who are taking funerals without connection to any Christian congregation.

most significantly, people are simply not aware of (or do not trust) other options, such as humanist funerals, or funerals led by trained non-religious 'celebrants' or even by the funeral director herself or himself.

Whatever the reason, many a family is steered in the direction of a Christian minister by the funeral director. The funeral director may ask a general question about involving a minister, but there will be no intensive questioning about the faith either of the deceased or of the next of kin. Once the minister is involved, the commitment is already part-made, and the phone call to make an appointment to visit the family and make arrangements for the funeral is not a time to ask inquisitorial questions about faith or churchgoing. The reality is that most ministers, lay or ordained, are taking funerals for people who did not profess a Christian faith.

Funerals on the basis of 'charitable assumption'

For some, the idea of a Christian funeral for someone who was not a practising Christian might seem like hypocrisy, but that depends on who you think ultimately receives eternal life. Some Christians believe that God's love is irresistible and salvation is universal, and therefore confident statements about eternal life are easy and appropriate at any funeral. For them there is no hypocrisy in proclaiming salvation for every individual, whether or not the person professed a Christian faith. Of course, not every Christian believes that. If, on the other hand, you believe that only professing Christians receive eternal life, full stop, then it would clearly be odd to offer a Christian funeral to someone who did not profess that faith. But most Christians in Britain are not nearly so clear about that. They may not believe everyone is necessarily saved automatically, but neither are they ready to restrict eternal life so radically. They work on 'charitable assumption' – commend the deceased to God in the general context of Christian hope in a loving God, and let God worry about the detail. For these Christians, the model of a Christian funeral as gift and invitation is a good starting point.

In Britain these questions have been matters of controversy since the Reformation. The Puritans were very nervous about how 'sure and certain' the hope could be for those who were notorious sinners and were keen that the Burial service (and Baptism too) should not assume that all of those for whom it was used were regenerate and 'in an actual state of grace'.[2]

The Puritan qualms were ultimately rejected when the revised Prayer Book was published in 1662, and 'charitable assumption' has generally reigned since then. However, it should also be remembered that, as with weddings, the further the actual human story is from the God story which the service assumes, the harder it is for the rite to retain integrity and to do its job. Charitable assumption must not be allowed to trump someone's free choice not to associate themselves with the Christian Church, and the Church must be careful not to be over-possessive about funerals for those who clearly articulated that they did not believe in God, Christ or eternal life. In practice, a desire to offer a Christian funeral to all as a gift can be heard as the Church claiming funerals as theirs by right. What is more, we need to be careful that in the text of services, or in well-intentioned 'tributes' or prayers, we do not put words into the mouths of either the deceased or the congregation which do not ring true.

TO THINK ABOUT – One funeral service or two?

One way to solve the dilemma for some Christians about whether you can have a Christian funeral for those who are not practising Christians would be to provide two funerals: a full-on confident proclamation of the resurrection and of salvation for this particular person for the funeral of a practising Christian; and a funeral-lite service which is more cautious and talks of the Christian hope more generally (and tentatively) for someone whose own faith was not expressed in this life.

Put like this it does not feel like a gracious or appealing proposition, but it is nonetheless true that the funeral of a practising

---

2 See Colin Buchanan, *The Savoy Conference Revisited* (Alcuin/GROW Joint Liturgical Studies 54), Cambridge: Grove Books, 2002, p. 25.

Christian always feels different – there is a different level of confidence and hope and even joy which comes from knowing that the person who died not only is heading for eternal life, but *knew it themselves*, and that this faith is shared confidently by those who now grieve for them.

Some Churches have chosen to provide different forms of service. Both The Episcopal Church in the United States of America and The Anglican Church of Canada, for instance, have services for someone who did not profess the Christian faith.[3] The Canadian service is designed for someone 'of another faith community, or a non-believer'. The emphasis is on 'keeping in mind the integrity of the person who has died'.[4] However, this is not a full form of service, but a selection of prayers which are intended to be used with an 'adapted' form of the standard funeral rites. The special prayers are addressed to God, but avoid reference to Christ and focus on the needs of the bereaved. No instructions are given about how to integrate these with the normal funeral service, which is Christ-centred and confident about the hope of resurrection. The American provision has a selection of possible readings and is less cagey about mentioning Christ in the general prayers, though it avoids referring to him in the committal prayer which is included.[5]

However, most Churches which produce forms of service centrally have taken the view that there can only be one basic Christian funeral for all. That funeral may come in different theological 'flavours' depending on your denomination or tradition, but it is not determined by the faith, or otherwise, of the deceased or the bereaved family. It is possible, however, by producing alternative texts within that one service, to allow for something of the two-track

---

3 'Burial of One Who Does Not Profess the Christian Faith', *The Book of Occasional Services*, New York: The Church Hymnal Corporation, 2nd ed. 1988, pp. 171–4; and 'Burial of One Who Did Not Profess the Christian Faith', *Occasional Celebrations of the Anglican Church of Canada*, Toronto: Anglican Book Centre, 1992, pp. 74–8.

4 *Occasional Celebrations*, p. 75, opening rubric.

5 The prayer is addressed to, 'Holy God, Holy and Mighty, Holy Immortal One', and stays focused on returning the body to the ground (*Occasional Services*, p. 174). There is also a prayer of commendation, though it is called instead a Prayer for the Deceased. It is a prayer for God to 'work in *him* the merciful purpose of your perfect will, through Jesus Christ our Lord'.

policy which has been resisted at the level of the service as a whole. Those who take funerals are invited to reflect on their own practice and the ways in which they might do this either deliberately or subconsciously.

So, if a Christian funeral can be offered to all, as a gift and invitation from the Church, does it make any difference if the deceased was a practising Christian? In practice, of course, it makes all the difference. The key is to recognize that the difference it makes is not necessarily because the whole rite is changed, but because the human story is different – it already includes God and the hope of eternal life. That, in turn, means that the way the God story and the human story are *connected* is changed, and it is this which can make the funeral of a Christian believer such a profoundly hopeful, and often joyful, experience.

Funerals as places of public theology

A funeral is not only an invitation to consider our stories alongside the God story of Jesus and his resurrection, but also the place where the Church articulates its theology of death, salvation, resurrection, eternal life, the communion of saints, and more. In other words, a funeral is the place where the God story of life and death is given shape. This in turn means that it is the place where many Christians, and others who are not practising Christians, will hear that story, so it is important that we get it as right and as clear as we can. As Ronald Grimes puts it:

> However we put it, or avoid putting it, death raises questions about the nature of reality and the constitution of the self, and death rites are predicated on the answers we give to such questions. It also works the other way around: Rites teach us the expected answers to such questions.[6]

6 Ronald L. Grimes, *Deeply into the Bone: Re-inventing Rites of Passage*, Berkeley, CA: University of California Press, 2002, p. 251.

> ## CASE STUDY – A witness to the resurrection
>
> Some years ago I went to the funeral of one of my wife's relatives, which took place in a United Reformed Church. It was the first time I had been to a funeral in that tradition. When I was given the order of service, I was surprised to see that on the front it said, 'A Service of Witness to the Resurrection and Thanksgiving for the Life of N'.[7] I had never seen a funeral described in that way, but the more I thought about it the more I saw the strengths: it stressed that this was primarily an act of Christian worship; it placed that act of worship firmly in the context of the Christian hope of resurrection; it saw the thanksgiving for the particular person who had died in that bigger context.
>
> *There are lots of positives to this way of naming a funeral. Can you think of any negative implications?*

What is the God story at a funeral?

It is one thing to acknowledge a funeral as a place for the Church to express its theology (its God story) about life and death, but what is that story? Here we quickly get into the detail of some of the disagreements between Christians about what happens at and beyond death:

- Who is saved? Is it everyone, or only some, and if only some, who?
- Where do we go after death? This question connects with the first.
- How should or can we pray for and about those who have died?

As in other pastoral rites, the God story at a funeral will be given expression through the Scripture readings which are used, and the way they are preached on. But there are also other significant points at which Christian understandings of life and death will

---

7 The title is taken from 'Services for a Funeral – One' in *WURC*, p. 199.

explicitly or implicitly shape what is said and what happens at a funeral. These include:

- opening words which explain why we are here
- prayers
- the commendation and committal
- the concluding prayers at the dismissal.

It is at these points that some of the theological questions will come into sharp focus. So let us consider the questions and the implications for the funeral rite.

Who is saved?

Christian views about salvation range from those who believe that only those who repent and profess faith in Christ in this life can be saved, through to those who believe in some form of universalism, that God's love is so strong that ultimately all will be saved, either automatically, or following a period after death in which they will be given the chance to turn to God. Between these extremes lie other possible positions, and the controversies over this rage every now and then.[8] This is not some arcane theological debate – it has pastoral and liturgical implications, because the theological stance you take on this may influence the prayers and texts you choose for a funeral, the Bible passages you read at the service, and the way that you answer the child who asks, 'Has my granny gone to heaven?'

How can Christian rites place before people the call of Christ to repentance and discipleship, while also proclaiming the compassion and justice of God, and giving a strong flavour of hope and joy in the face of death? One way is to say strong things,

---

8 As I write this, evangelical Christians are going into print taking sides over Rob Bell's new book, *Love Wins*, London: Collins, 2011. Though not crystal clear where he stands on universalism, Bell is clearly suggesting a broader category of those who are saved than some evangelical Christians are comfortable with.

but not to connect them necessarily with this particular person.[9] Consider this prayer from the United Reformed Church:

> Holy God, by your mighty power you gave us life,
> and in your love you have given us new life in Jesus Christ.
> We now entrust N to your merciful keeping:
> in the faith of Jesus Christ, your Son our Lord,
> who died and rose again to save us,
> and is now alive and reigns with you
> and the Holy Spirit in glory for ever. **Amen.**[10]

and this from *Common Worship: Pastoral Services,*

> God our creator and redeemer,
> by your power Christ conquered death
> and entered into glory.
> Confident of his victory
> and claiming his promises,
> we entrust N to your mercy
> in the name of Jesus our Lord,
> who died and is alive
> and reigns with you,
> now and for ever.
> **Amen.**[11]

In both of these prayers there is a strong confidence and faith in Christ, but the confidence is held corporately – we (the Church) have confidence in God through Christ, and in that confidence we entrust our loved one to God. It does not depend on the faith

---

9 In the Church of England this careful treading of a middle way was instituted in the report that led to the revised services of Series Two in the 1960s. In its report to the Convocations the Liturgical Commission set out its aims, which included that 'the rite should not assume that the soul of the deceased is, at the time of the burial of the body, in any particular place or state', The Church of England Liturgical Commission, *Alternative Services: Second Series*, London: SPCK, 1965, p. 106.

10 *WURC*, p. 206. This prayer is adapted from the commendation prayer in the Church of England's *The Alternative Service Book 1980*.

11 *CWPS*, p. 267.

of the departed, but it does express a strong faith in Christ. Here is the Church expressing its faith, and inviting others to see it that way.

Now consider the commendation in the Methodist service:

Into your keeping, O merciful God,
we commend your servant N.
Receive *her/him* into the arms of your mercy,
into the joy of everlasting peace,
and into the glorious company of the saints in light;
through Christ our Lord. **Amen.**[12]

There are some assumptions here – the reference to the person who has died as 'your servant' could suggest that the deceased is being counted as a Christian, whether they themselves would wish to be counted in this way or not. Here is the key – too confident an assertion of salvation, at least in the 'everyone is a Christian' mould, can not only sound false to those who knew the deceased the best, but can also risk appropriating them for the Christian faith in a way that they would have resisted themselves. We must respect people's decisions about faith in this life, even if we believe that those decisions will not ultimately affect their eternal fate.

Perhaps because of some of these issues, there is an alternative commendation printed immediately after the first:

Loving God, we commend N to your perfect mercy and wisdom,
for in you alone we put our trust. **Amen.**[13]

This is warm enough about God ('Loving God') and about trust in God, but it does not move beyond trust to hope, and certainly contains no particular expectation. Is this helpfully broad, or does it sell-out to a sub-Christian (though not anti-Christian) perspective?

---

12 *MWB*, p. 456.
13 *MWB*, p. 456.

Where do we go after death?

There are two issues here. The first is connected back to the previ-ous question about who is saved. If not all are necessarily saved, then there must be more than one possible destiny. For good pas-toral reasons, few funeral services mention hell, even in churches in which the reality of hell is an important doctrine. But there are other ways. References to judgement and justice can leave room for the idea that not everyone is entering unhindered into eternal life.

The following prayer for readiness to live in the light of eter-nity is not heavy about judgement (and certainly not about hell), but it retains the idea that this life matters, and carries the hint that this might have consequences.

> Grant us, Lord,
> the wisdom and the grace
> to use aright the time that is left to us on earth.
> Lead us to repent of our sins,
> the evil we have done and the good we have not done;
> and strengthen us to follow the steps of your Son,
> in the way that leads to the fullness of eternal life;
> through Jesus Christ our Lord.
> Amen.[14]

Perhaps the fact that it is a prayer for us who are left, rather than about the deceased, helps?

There is a further aspect to this, which is to take account of the third possible venue – some form of purgatory. Purgatory has never been accepted in the Orthodox Churches, and was re-jected by the Reformers of the sixteenth century and therefore by Protestant Churches. Technically, purgatory is not a third des-tination, but a waiting room for entry to heaven – a place to be cleaned up and made ready to enter the presence of God.

However, a belief that after death your immediate destina-tion was not heaven itself, but a much more unpleasant place of

---

14 *CWPS*, p. 362.

purification, cleansing and discipline, had a big impact on how some Christians have understood the place and role of the funeral and its effect on those who have died. We will see its impact when we look, below, at how we may pray for and about those who have died.

And even if we focus on the saved (whether all or just some), what are they saved to? Where are they headed and what is it we are commending them to? The New Testament is complex on this matter, and offers not one simple answer but a range of metaphors and images which include being:

- in paradise (Luke 23.43)
- carried to Abraham's side (Luke 16.22f.)
- 'at home with the Lord' (2 Cor. 5.8)
- asleep (Acts 7.60; 1 Cor. 7.39, 15.6, 1; Thess. 4.13, in which 'fallen asleep' is often translated 'died')
- with Jesus in the Father's house (John 14.2–3)
- part of the great cloud of witnesses (Heb. 12.1, 23)
- at rest from labour (Rev. 14.13)
- gathered before the throne of God (Rev. 7.9).

It is not easy to construct a single coherent picture from all these snapshots. What is constant is the New Testament emphasis that the resurrection of Jesus is central. Tom Wright (among others) has reminded the Church that much of our talk of saving souls, and going to heaven when we die, has been borrowed from Platonic ways of thinking rather than from Hebrew and Christian ways of understanding death.[15] Wright does not deny the idea of going to heaven, but he reminds us that the true and ultimate Christian hope is in 'life after life after death'[16] – that is, that heaven is a temporary state before we are clothed on the Day of the Lord with new resurrection bodies.

---

15 See his *The Resurrection of the Son of God*, London: SPCK, 2003, for a thorough exploration; or his *Surprised by Hope*, London: SPCK, 2007; or his *New Heavens, New Earth: The Biblical Picture of Christian Hope* (Grove Biblical Series 11), Cambridge: Grove Books, 1999, for more concise expressions of the same themes.

16 Wright, *Resurrection*, p. 31.

How is this given expression in funeral services? Much funeral material is clear in affirming the resurrection of the body. Take this committal from the Church of England:

> We have entrusted our *brother/sister* N to God's mercy,
> and we now commit *his/her* body to the ground:
> earth to earth, ashes to ashes, dust to dust:
> in sure and certain hope of the resurrection to eternal life
> through our Lord Jesus Christ,
> who will transform our frail bodies
> that they may be conformed to his glorious body,
> who died, was buried, and rose again for us.
> To him be glory for ever.
> **Amen.**[17]

That seems pretty robust about the physicality of the resurrection rather than a hope for some disembodied existence for an immortal soul. But other prayers can be less clear:

> Almighty God,
> you judge us with infinite mercy and justice
> and love everything you have made.
> In your mercy
> turn the darkness of death into the dawn of new life,
> and the sorrow of parting into the joy of heaven;
> through our Saviour, Jesus Christ.
> **Amen.**[18]

Here the reference to the joy of heaven is more vague and is not connected explicitly to the resurrection. The Baptist liturgist, Paul Sheppy, has urged the Church to draw back from what he perceives to be an unhealthy dualism in the way we talk about the deceased at the funeral and to be bold in affirming the resurrection

---

17 *CWPS*, p. 269.
18 This is one of the two optional opening prayers, *CWPS*, p. 260.

of the body.[19] He suggests that the separation of the commendation from the committal in a funeral has the effect of reinforcing the idea that a human being is essentially an immortal soul
which is the part that survives death. This downgrades the body
to an unnecessary encumbrance, and in the process reinforces the
idea that our eternal destiny will be disembodied and marginalizes the Christian doctrine of the resurrection of the body. He
stresses a unitive anthropology, in which 'soul' means the whole
person in relationship with God and in which our eternal life is
dependent on our being kept in the memory and love of God.

In his own funeral texts, he has replaced the separate commendation and committal prayers with a single, unitive, 'Word of
Resurrection', in which the whole person is entrusted to God:

Lord, you renew the face of the earth;
gather to yourself N whom we have loved,
and grant to *her* those things
which eye has not seen, nor ear heard,
nor the human heart imagined.

*The following prayer may be used in addition as desired and
as appropriate.*

AT A GRAVESIDE
From the dust you made us, O God,
to the dust we return.
Here is your *daughter* N.
Awaken her from the sleep of death,
and feed her at the table of eternal life.[20]

Theologically there is much to be said for this approach, but pastorally it conflates the journey too much. There is a psychological

---

19 Paul Sheppy, *Death Liturgy and Ritual. Volume 1: A Pastoral and
Liturgical Theology*, Aldershot: Ashgate, 2003, pp. 39–42 and 62–4.

20 Paul Sheppy, *In Sure and Certain Hope: Liturgies, Prayers and Readings
for Funerals and Memorials*, Norwich: Canterbury Press, 2003, p. 59. There is
an alternative prayer for the second part for use at a crematorium.

need for the bereaved to be able to entrust the person they have loved to God before they are ready to commit the body to the ground or the cremator, and though the two can coincide, this part of the journey feels kinder if it is stretched just a little. Perhaps it is for this reason that when Sheppy's Word of Resurrection appears in the Baptist liturgical resources *Gathering for Worship*, it is preceded by a more traditional commendation (called a 'Prayer of Farewell'), in which the person is entrusted to God before the committal.[21]

Does all of this matter? The issues being tackled here are fairly detailed and technical, but they touch on key theological issues which have pastoral implications. In particular, the resurrection of the body as the hope for eternity has two important implications:

1. It affirms the essential goodness and importance of the physical. This has implications for how we treat the creation and other human beings in this life, as well as implications for what we hope for in eternity. The idea that our immortal soul is the only important part of us, and that perfection is about escaping the physical, has sanctioned a cavalier approach to the earth and the environment and some appalling treatment of other human beings.

2. It is a doctrine which requires God. Hope for an eternal existence on the basis of an immortal soul has allowed all manner of sloppy thinking about life after death to thrive (of the 'granny is a star in the sky' kind) which has

---

21 Baptist Union of Great Britain, Christopher Ellis and Myra Blyth (eds), *Gathering for Worship: Patterns and Prayers for the Community of Disciples*, Norwich: Canterbury Press, 2005, pp. 237–9. Cranmer's first Prayer Book of 1549 commends the deceased's soul to God and their body to the ground in one prayer. In the more Reformed 1552 book (retained almost identically in 1662) it is made clear that God has already taken the soul, and that all that remains is for the body to be committed to the ground. It was liturgical revision in the twentieth century which returned to the idea of a commendation as well as a committal, but this time the two were put into separate prayers and the commendation is of the person, rather than of the soul.

no need of God – the soul is thought to have its own intrinsic life, which goes on with or without God. It can be profoundly sub-Christian. By contrast, the resurrection of the body requires God both to keep us in his love and knowledge between death and resurrection, and to raise us to new life at the Day of the Lord. It is profoundly Christocentric.

In general, published or official texts tend to be carefully thought through on these matters. It is in the sermon or extempore prayer, or the use of prayers from other resources, that ministers and others can find themselves talking unreflectively about 'going to heaven' rather than using terms which are more rigorously Christian, such as eternal life, resurrection, God's eternal reign, and so on.

The truth is, however, that in popular culture, people have got so used to hearing about 'going to heaven' as a Christian view of life after death, that talk in a funeral about resurrection may go straight over people's heads or be heard as just another way of talking about heaven. The sermon, therefore, may have to do some work to interpret and express this central Christian idea that life beyond death is not just about the salvation of souls for a disembodied eternity, but is about looking for the renewal of the cosmos, in which we can participate, in God's good plan and time.

How may we pray for or about the departed?

It is possible to think about this question in terms of several possible 'levels' of prayer. At which level (if any) do you start to feel uncomfortable?

Level 1 – Praying about the departed
This might include giving thanks to God for them, or expressing sorrow to God about their death. For instance, 'Loving God, we thank you for Alice, who has meant so much to us.'

Level 2 – Praying for the departed

This might be as explicit as 'Please accept her into your loving arms' or more general, such as, 'Grant to N a place of light and joy . . .'[22] It might be prayer for peace, salvation, or 'rest eternal'. Generally the more general it is and the less explicitly about salvation, the greater the number of Christians who will be comfortable with it. It is important to remember that the medieval prayer for the departed which the Reformers found so offensive was not prayer for salvation as such, but prayer for the *faithful* departed. It was prayer that their time in purgatory would be reduced, not prayer to rescue them out of hell.

Level 3 – Addressing the departed in prayer

This is most commonly in the form of addressing the departed at the commendation, such as, 'N, we commend you now to God's loving care . . .'[23]

Level 4 – Praying to the departed (that is, to the saints)

Here we hit the other issue which the Reformers had with the idea of purgatory, which is that it tends to divide departed Christians into two categories: those who go straight to be with God (the official 'saints') and who we might ask to 'put in a good word for us'; and those who are stuck in purgatory, to whom we do not pray.

Most Catholic Christians would think nothing of praying to Mary, whereas most Protestants would not dream of doing so. At a funeral though, the issues are more subtle. In my own

---

22 This is from the vigil service in *MWB*, p. 447.

23 In *A New Zealand Prayer Book*, there is a form of commendation which addresses the departed on p. 836, '. . . we commend you N, to God's judgement and mercy, to God's forgiveness and love . . .', and then, more unusually, a form of committal which also does so, 'Now therefore, N, we commit your body to be *buried/cremated* . . .', p. 837. This seems unhelpfully to mix up the two stages on the journey. Once the person has been entrusted to God, it seems odd to then address them again as if they were still with us.

ministry, it has not been my normal practice to address the departed, but I can think of some funerals where it has felt appropriate to address the person who has died as I have laid a hand on the coffin in commendation.

The Reformers, however, were clear – addressing the departed suggested a permeable barrier between this life and the next which they did not accept. Hence in Thomas Cranmer's first *Book of Common Prayer* of 1549, his commendation retained the medieval Catholic pattern of addressing the departed:

I commend thy soul to God the Father Almighty,
and thy body to the ground . . .

By the time he produced his more Reformed book of 1552, this had disappeared. Now God has taken the departed, who can therefore no longer be addressed, and our job is simply to deal respectfully with the body:

Forasmuch as it hath pleased almighty God of his great mercy to take unto himself the soul of our dear brother here departed: we therefore commit his body to the ground . . .

Though these issues can feel very ancient, they are still controversial for some. Not every Christian, for instance, would be comfortable with the prayer of commendation we looked at above from the *Methodist Worship Book*:

Into your keeping, O merciful God,
we commend your servant N.
Receive *her/him* into the arms of your mercy,
into the joy of everlasting peace,
and into the glorious company of the saints in light;
through Christ our Lord. **Amen.**[24]

---

24 *MWB*, p. 456.

For some this goes too far. It is one thing to commend someone to God, for God to make the decisions, but it is not our place to tell God what that decision should be. 'Receive her/him into the arms of your mercy' might work as an expression of hope, but not as a prayer for God's action. What is more, if the person is destined for eternal life, it is an unnecessary prayer – why ask for what we know to be the case? But is that what is going on? Isn't a prayer like this really a talking about the deceased in the presence of God, an expression to God of what we long for this person, not an instruction or an assumption? So much depends on context when we come to interpret words in situations like this.

In a Church which does not insist on the use of centrally agreed prayers (such as the Methodist Church) these matters are interesting, but tend not to produce huge controversy, as no one is compelled to use them. In the Church of England it is more complicated, and there is a long history of controversy about the inclusion of prayers for the departed. The Reformation inheritance had outlawed these, but several factors brought them to the fore again in the last century:

- The Anglo-Catholic revival in the nineteenth century restored the idea of purgatory and prayer for the departed to liturgical practice in large parts of the Church of England.
- The scale of death in the First World War (and the following influenza epidemic) created a huge national pastoral need for comfort in corporate bereavement, and prayer relating to the departed was one way to meet that need. It was in the proposed (and rejected) 1928 Prayer Book that experimentation with prayer for the departed began.
- Both these factors contributed to a growth in the keeping of All Souls Day (still referred to in official texts as The Commemoration of the Faithful Departed) which reinforced the division of the departed into two categories, something the Reformers resisted vigorously. This was coupled with services at which the departed were named and candles lit

(a form of prayer for them?). Many churches which are not Anglo-Catholic have picked up this practice, either at this time of year or at other times, holding 'memorial services' to which the bereaved are invited.

Though the practice and insights of the Anglo-Catholic party fed into liturgical revision in the twentieth century as it grew in numbers and confidence, it was generally resisted by evangelicals.[25] It is only in more recent decades that evangelicals (themselves more confident now) have been able to receive some of the insights.[26] Nonetheless, in the official texts there is still great caution and a desire to produce texts which can be used by all, even if some might wish they said more. In the Methodist Church there has been a parallel influence exerted by more sacramental Methodists, which has made an impact on the services in *Methodist Worship Book*.

How then, should we understand prayer for the departed today? One of the key insights is from linguistic theory, which reminds us that words are not always doing what they appear to be doing at face value. So much depends on the 'language game' being played, and an awareness of the larger 'form of life' of which any use of language is part. These terms from Wittgenstein's work remind us that words need a context in order that we may understand what they are *doing* as well as what they mean.[27] Is 'Receive her into your arms of mercy' really a prayer of petition, or an expression of love and a desire for comfort?

---

25 For an account of some of the battles in the Church of England, see Colin Buchanan, *An Evangelical Among the Anglican Liturgists* (Alcuin Club Collections 84), London: SPCK, 2009, pp. 8–11, and Colin Buchanan, *Taking the Long View: Three and a Half Decades of General Synod*, London: Church House Publishing, 2006, pp. 85–7.

26 And not all have received the insights with gratitude. See N. T. Wright, *For All the Saints? – Remembering the Christian Departed*, London: SPCK, 2003.

27 See Wittgenstein's *Philosophical Investigations*, trans. G. E. M. Anscombe, Oxford: Blackwell, 1963. Anthony Thiselton reflects on similar issues in *Language, Liturgy and Meaning* (Grove Liturgical Studies 2), Nottingham: Grove Books, 1975, pp. 10–16.

Here are some principles which may help us to reflect on our practice of prayer for and about the departed.[28]

- First, when is it said in relation to the death of the person? Some things feel appropriate at the moment of death, but less appropriate later on. For instance, something which addresses the deceased, such as the prayer, 'Go forth upon your journey, Christian soul . . .',[29] may be uncontroversial at the time of death, but may raise questions for some if used at the funeral. On the other hand, the fact that it is seen by some as an appropriate prayer at the funeral reminds us that in some ways the funeral can be seen as a symbolic recapitulation of the moment of death itself.

- Second, who says it, and what was their relationship to the deceased? Graveside visits by close family often include a natural and unforced talking to the deceased. In the more formal setting of a funeral there are some things which feel natural when said by the spouse or child of the deceased, but which feel different if said by a minister. In a eulogy or tribute, for instance, the speaker often addresses the deceased. In this context it feels a natural way for someone to speak if they knew and loved the person who has died.

- Third, is the focus of the prayer individual or corporate? 'Rest eternal grant *them*,' feels different from, 'Rest eternal grant *her*.' A prayer such as, 'Bring us with her to the fullness of eternal life,' puts the prayer in a bigger and eschatalogical context and makes it a prayer as much for us as for the person who has died. The less individualized the prayer is, the more likely it is to find acceptance among a wide range of Christians.

---

28 For helpful reflections and principles, see Christopher Cocksworth, *Prayer and the Departed* (Grove Worship Series 142), Cambridge: Grove Books, 1997.

29 This traditional form of prayer can be found in Prayers with the Dying in *MWB*, p. 431. Two revised versions ('N, go forth from this world . . .' and 'N, go forth upon your journey from this world . . .') are provided for prayer at the time of death in *CWPS*, pp. 229 and 376.

What does the funeral do?

We have taken a long time to get here, but we now reach the crucial question: What does the funeral do? The Church of England Liturgical Commission considered this question back in the 1960s, and in its report on proposed Alternative Services (Series Two) gave the following summary of what a funeral ought to do:

(a) to secure the reverent disposal of the corpse
(b) to commend the deceased to the care of our heavenly Father
(c) to proclaim the glory of our risen life in Christ here and hereafter
(d) to remind us of the awful certainty of our own coming death and judgement
(e) to make plain the eternal unity of Christian people, living and departed, in the risen and ascended Christ.

It would, perhaps, be natural to add a sixth point, namely the consolation of the mourners; but the Commission believes that this object should be attained by means of the objects already included in its answer.[30]

That the consolation of the bereaved should be thought of as a secondary result of the five primary purposes, rather than being put at the top of the list, is a salutary reminder of how much the assumptions of what a funeral is for have changed in recent decades.

Much of the answer to the question, 'What should a funeral do?' depends on who we think the funeral is for. We have seen in the other rites we have looked at that the answer to this second question is almost always much bigger than it seems at first sight.

---

30 The Church of England Liturgical Commission, *Alternative Services: Second Series*, London: SPCK, 1965, pp. 105f.

Who is the funeral for?

In Christian history there have been different answers to the question, 'Who is the funeral for?' and these have impacted on what the funeral is expected to do. This in turn has impacted on the shape and content of the funeral service itself. Here are some of the historical answers.

- **Medieval** – the funeral is for the deceased (to pray for them and ease their journey through purgatory).
- **Reformation** – the funeral is for the living (to warn them to amend their own lives and be ready for their own death).
- **Modern** – the funeral is 'for' the deceased (to commend them into God's care) *and* it is for the living (to comfort them and help them to honour and remember their loved one).

It is often said today that 'the funeral is for the living'. If that is the case, then it is certainly also true that the funeral is for them in a very different way from the way the Reformers would have understood things. The pressure today for funerals 'not to be sad', to be 'thanksgivings' and 'celebrations' often comes from the desires of those who know they are dying and who want to make it easier for their loved ones after they have gone. It is well-meant, but often counter-productive, and it must never cause funerals to avoid the hard stuff about sorrow and guilt and questions about eternity.

Paul Sheppy encourages us to put the deceased back at the centre of the rite: 'The funeral is for the dead person, and the mourners meet to say farewell.'[31] Now, what does it mean to say that the funeral is 'for' the person who has died? It is not 'for' them in the same way that it was in the medieval pattern (though something of that understanding survives in the Roman Catholic Requiem Mass).

For most people today, the funeral is 'for' the deceased not in a causal sense, but in the sense that the deceased still matters

---

31 Sheppy, *Death*, Vol. 1, p. 59.

and has not yet been definitively handed over to God, hermetically sealed and separated already from those who live on. The funeral is 'for' the deceased in the sense that it ritualizes the journey of the deceased into the hands of God in a way that puts it back in synchronization with the journey of the bereaved. It does not 'make things happen' so much as it maps out what is happening.[32] Roger Grainger quotes a nine-year-old girl as saying, 'You have to have a funeral, so God knows you're coming.'[33] We might want to affirm the sentiment, but put it more cautiously: 'You have to have a funeral, so we know we've sent you.'

But it is bigger even than that. The funeral is for a whole range of people, and each of them needs it to do a different job. Those leading funeral services need to make sure that it does all the jobs required for all the people present.

IN PRACTICE – Who is the funeral for? Pastoral implications

The close family are often at the front of the mind of both funeral director and minister – it is for them that the service is often designed and they are the people who have most opportunity to shape what goes into the service. The increasing commercialization of the funeral industry and the 'client–provider' relationship between next of kin and the funeral director all reinforce this. When the person taking the funeral service has not known the deceased, it is even easier to get sucked into this pattern, because the close family are the only contact.

Sometimes this control by the next of kin can prevent the service doing what it needs to do for others, such as wider family and friends, church members, or even those who were very close to the deceased, but who do not have the legal right to control or influence the service. Most ministers will know of family situations where the next of kin have wanted to close down conversation or

---

32 Sheppy, *Death*, Vol. 1, pp. 78–83.

33 Roger Grainger, *The Message of the Rite: The Significance of Christian Rites of Passage*, Cambridge: Lutterworth Press, 1988, p. 31.

ignore certain parts of the life story of the person who has died. Perhaps the deceased was gay and their parents have not come to terms with this? Maybe the deceased had a former partner who is not welcome at the funeral and whose children have been air-brushed out of the story? Perhaps the next of kin simply has not known the person in recent years and is unaware of the impact of a recent conversion to Christian faith or of changed political allegiance. For all these reasons and more, it is important that those who take funeral services keep their horizons broad when hearing and recounting the story of someone's life and shaping a funeral service which connects with it, to make sure that the human story that is told has integrity with the actual life of the departed, and not just with someone's version of it.

In particular it is important to recognize that someone deserves to be remembered and honoured not just because they had a family which loved them, but simply because they lived. Our worth is proclaimed in the funeral service, and the death of anyone diminishes me and impacts on society – 'No man is an island . . .' and all that. Our declaration of God's love for those who have died is not just said to comfort the bereaved but as a statement to society: this person was a creature of God, whether their life was long or short, happy or tragic and whether they were kind or unkind. This is why it is important that the Christian funeral is not only 'life-focused' and backward looking. For those without a Christian hope, it is easy to see why life-centred funerals with a focus on joy and thanksgiving have become so popular. But that approach has little to say at the funeral of a baby, or when someone dies who no one liked, or for whom life held little for which to be thankful. But the Christian funeral still has something to say because it is not just life-centred, it is eternal-life centred and forward looking. It is the community's moment to hand the person from its care to God's care. It is 'for' the person who died, *and* for those who miss them, *and* for the wider community.

Modern services take account of this complex web of jobs which a funeral must do. The introduction to the *Common Worship* funeral service lists the purposes as follows:

We have come here today
to remember before God our *brother/sister* N;
to give thanks for *his/her* life;
to commend *him/her* to God our merciful redeemer and judge;
to commit *his/her* body to be *buried/cremated*,
and to comfort one another in our grief.[34]

The Methodist service makes clear that the first job is to worship God:

We meet in this solemn moment to worship God;
to give thanks for the life of our *sister/brother* N;
to commend her/him to God's loving and faithful care;
and to pray for all who mourn.[35]

Interestingly, each of these omits another crucial aspect, which is that we meet to be reminded of our own mortality, and the need to live our lives now in the light of eternity. We might also follow the United Reformed Church, and add 'to proclaim the resurrection'.

And what does a Christian funeral do for 'non-religious' people? I suggest that one of the things that it does (along with the things listed above) is that even if people are not *sure*, it keeps open the possibility of a future beyond death in the midst of a culture that has largely stopped expecting it, and it keeps alive the hope of an ongoing relationship with the departed in prayer, even if that is articulated more as 'talking to God about them' or even 'asking God to pass on a message' rather than praying directly to those who have died.

---

34 *CWPS*, p. 260. It is worth noting how much of the list of purposes of a funeral from the 1965 Liturgical Commission report on Series Two services has found its way into this introduction. Particularly noteworthy is that comforting the bereaved makes it onto the main list.

35 *MWB*, p. 449.

What 'makes' a funeral?

There are many aspects and elements that make up a 'funeral', and these include elements beyond the Christian service as well as those within it. In addition, cultural factors play a huge part, and so what feels 'proper' will vary from place to place, from one age to the next, and sometimes within a locality depending on the different social groups represented (for instance, gypsy or traveller funerals may be very different from other funerals in a given area, as may Caribbean funerals).

It is an interesting exercise to draw up a list of what some of the typical cultural norms might be. A typical list for a funeral in the UK context might include some of the following:

- Wearing black clothes (or token elements of black clothing) – this is breaking down as an expectation, especially among young people and also as people increasingly want a funeral to celebrate a life rather than acknowledge a death. 'We don't want people to be miserable' is a common sentiment, and wearing black is seen as unhelpfully sorrowful rather than thankful.
- A slow journey to the service by both the hearse and the close family. Though the requirements of modern traffic means that a hearse will not travel *too* slowly on main roads, it is not unusual for the funeral director to get out of the car and walk in front of the cortege as it approaches the church or crematorium, slowing everything down to a walking pace.
- Removing hats, bowing heads etc. as a funeral cortege passes. The decline in hat-wearing has made this a rare thing, and even a simple stopping and bowing of the head is unusual. In some places those in the street where the deceased lived might close their curtains on the day of the funeral as a mark of respect.
- Placing of flowers on the coffin, or throwing of flowers into the grave.
- Some sort of 'wake' or refreshments.

Where do these practices come from?

As with weddings, an examination of these practices shows a variety of origins. When we are 'in' them they can feel like universal practices, but this is an illusion. The wearing of black is, in the UK, most immediately associated with the Victorian era, which developed a complex system of mourning which controlled clothing and many other aspects of life. But in the longer view, the wearing of black was part of funeral practice in the pre-Christian Roman Empire, something which was reversed by the early Christians.

The sharing of refreshments after the funeral similarly is both basic hospitality, but also echoes the practice of meals held at graves in pagan Rome, a feeding of the departed which was meant to appease the dead and send them on their way. Again, the early Christians altered this, replacing it with the sharing of the Eucharist.

The practices come from a mixture of Church, wider culture, folk memory and long forgotten practice, but the key is that together they define what is 'proper'. They are not universal – they vary from place to place, person to person and time to time. But in their overall nature they show patterns that set expectations and define boundaries. They can and do change, but often slowly over time. Even when people want to deviate from the norm, they will often do so only a little, or in some aspects. There is usually a line over which they will not tread for fear that the effect will be to leave the ritual improper.

As with weddings, this inherently 'public' and corporate nature of funeral ritual and liturgy is very important for ministers to understand. One of the key implications is that funeral liturgy belongs to the wider community. It is not the property of the minister taking the service, nor even of the bereaved close family (though they may feel that it belongs to them). Rather, the expectations belong to the wider community, and therefore, so does the sense of whether it is 'proper'.

The journey through a funeral service

Having established who the service is for, let us consider the journey through the service.

Gathering

The gathering will need to establish the community which has gathered. This will include recognizing the many 'layers' of involvement of those present. Some will have known the person who has died very well indeed, while for others the loss will be more distant. This is the moment to be clear about the minister's own connection with the deceased – perhaps a family member or friend, or someone who the minister did not know in life, but has discovered through the testimony of friends and family in the recent days.

This part of the service will also need to recognize the particular context of the person's death – a life which ended by suicide at a young age presents a different context from a person in their 80s who died after a short illness, and different again from someone who died in a tragic accident.

The key part of the Gathering, however, will be the telling of the human story of this person's life. This is the point at which to tell the story which the family have shared with the minister, but it may also be the point at which to invite others to share in that story-telling – friends and family who will add personal memories to the minister's overall framework.

IN PRACTICE – Letting the story speak

The Church is sometimes tempted to move too quickly from the human story and all its mixed emotions to the God story and resurrection hope.

At an official level, the funeral service in the Church of England's *Alternative Service Book 1980* did this by putting a prayer about resurrection right at the beginning of the service:

Heavenly Father,
in your Son Jesus Christ
you have given us a true faith and a sure hope.
Strengthen this faith and hope in us all our days,
that we may live as those who believe in
the communion of saints,
the forgiveness of sins
and the resurrection to eternal life;
through Jesus Christ our Lord.
Amen.[36]

The prayer was right, but the place was wrong. It sounded like a prayer for a 'stiff upper lip' and had the effect of suppressing any sadness under a veneer of resurrection hope. This prayer survives in *Common Worship*, but is placed much later in the service, where it fits the flow much better. By contrast, the first of the two opening prayers in the *Common Worship* funeral service acts as a permission-giver for crying and grief, by pointing out that even Jesus cried at a funeral:

God of all consolation,
your Son Jesus Christ was moved to tears
at the grave of Lazarus his friend . . .[37]

The too-hasty move to resurrection hope can also happen at a more local level. The family choose a particular pop song or piece of music which reflects something of the human story of the person who has died. They ask for it to be played as the coffin is carried in, and then the minister leads the procession in booming, '"I am the resurrection and the life," says the Lord.' The tradition of reading sentences of Scripture as the coffin is brought in may be helpful to some, and may be better than entering in silence, but it is not always the best way to start, especially if it has the effect of silencing the human story before it has even started.

---

36 *CWPS*, p. 271.
37 *CWPS*, p. 260.

God's word

The human story needs to be followed by and then connected with the God story – the reading of Scripture and the preaching of the gospel in such a way that the human and divine stories can touch, even if the person who has died did not consciously make that connection in their life, and the family do not make that connection either.

The core of any funeral sermon should be the proclamation of the death and resurrection of Jesus Christ. The term 'eulogy' or 'tribute' is sometimes used for the part of the service which is directly to do with talking about the life of the deceased. This should never be allowed to replace or surpass the preaching of the gospel.[38]

The funeral of Princess Diana in 1997 seems to have been significant here: it's not that eulogies were unheard of before, but they were rare and tended to be expected more for 'special people' (local councillors, celebrities, local worthies, leaders of groups, school headteachers, etc.). Earl Spencer, at Diana's funeral, changed that. Because there was no other 'sermon' (in the sense of the preaching of the Christian gospel) what he said felt like the sermon slot, and that has subtly shaped expectations for a large number of people ever since.

Now, in many ways, this is simply the final stopping point of a pendulum swing which has been moving since the Prayer Book burial service omitted any mention of the deceased's name, making do instead with a generic 'our brother/sister'. No one is suggesting a return to that pattern. However, from a focus on warning the living with a generic reference to the departed, we have moved to a highly personalized focus on the dead, and a

---

38 The notes to the *Common Worship* funeral services make a particular point of noting the difference between the sermon and the tribute (*CWPS*, p. 291, Notes 4 and 5), and the Outline Order for Funerals makes clear that the two things are separate (p. 257), though in practice (as Note 4 on p. 291 acknowledges) the two may be joined more seamlessly. The third form of funeral service in *WURC* similarly separates the tribute from the sermon, and the second form stresses that the sermon is 'on the Christian Hope' (pp. 227 and 199). *MWB* makes no explicit mention of a tribute.

reticence to speak too confidently of the other story, the God story of Jesus' death and resurrection. The sermon is the key place to do that work, bringing the stories together and helping those present to see one in the light of the other.

That is why, although the usual place to look for a Bible passage for a funeral will be among the New Testament passages which reflect directly on resurrection and eternal life,[39] it might be that once you know something of the story of the deceased, some other passage is a more natural starting point for linking that story to the story of God and Jesus Christ.

CASE STUDY – Jenny's funeral

Jenny was well known in the town. She was of indeterminate age, probably older than she looked, and lived alone. She could be seen every day walking from her bungalow to the parade of shops with her two shopping bags. If you passed her, she would harangue you with any topic which took her fancy that day – once started she was impossible to stop, meaning that most people would cross the road to avoid her. When it was the minister from the church that she harangued, it was always about the same thing: the church was full of hypocrites, and you wouldn't get her inside that church until she went in feet first in a box. Sadly, her prediction was accurate.

Her funeral was packed with those who had tried to avoid her in life, a sign of affection for someone who had been a significant figure in the community. At the funeral, the Bible passage chosen was Matthew 6.1–18, in which Jesus criticizes the hypocrisy of those who make their religion a show. The sermon took this as a starting point: Jenny might not have been a church person, but she shared something in common with Jesus: a dislike of hypocrisy. From this starting point, the links were made, connecting and illuminating the stories of Jenny and Jesus.

---

39 There are good lists of suggested passages in: *CWPS*, pp. 390f; *MWB*, pp. 501f.; *WURC*, pp. 237–50; Sheppy, *In Sure and Certain Hope*, pp. 28–41.

Response

In response to the telling of the stories and the connecting of
them each to the other, come the prayers. These will need to do
several jobs, and it is important to get those in the right order, to
fit the overall journey:

- Prayers of thanksgiving will acknowledge the image of God
  in the person who has died, and allow for the articulation of
  some of the particular memories and reasons for thankfulness of those who knew the deceased best.
- Prayer for those who mourn will naturally follow. These
  prayers will begin with those closest to the deceased, but
  need to stretch out to those on the margins of the service,
  whose connection was less strong – these might include
  neighbours, those who have cared for the deceased in hospital, hospice or home. These carers (or representatives) are
  often present at a funeral and their own grieving, as well as
  their care, needs to be acknowledged.
- There may be a need to pray about the specific context of
  this death and any particular circumstances or emotions
  which relate to it. There may be guilt, or shame, or even
  joy at the death of some persons, and the minister who has
  listened carefully at the funeral visit will look to name these
  in sensitive ways in the service itself, possibly in the prayers
  which remember, or those which look to the future.
- There will then be a need for prayers for all who are present.
  This takes the focus off the deceased and recognizes the role
  of the funeral in placing before us our own mortality and
  our need to be ready to see God face to face. A prayer which
  asks for help to live our lives in the light of eternity begins
  that forward-facing phase of the service.

The key liminal moment will be the act of commendation, in
which the deceased is commended into God's care. There may
be further liminal moments in the committal, whether this takes
place immediately (for instance, in a service at a crematorium) or

fairly soon (for instance, at a graveside after a short journey to the cemetery) or after a longer period (for instance, at the committal of cremated remains the following week, or the disposal of remains after medical research).

The formal 'handing over of care' at the commendation is a key moment in both the symbolic journey of the deceased and the journey of the bereaved. Churches have often taken great care over the phrasing of these moments, and the particular handing over will depend to some extent on different Christian understandings of what happens beyond death (for instance, is this person on their way to purgatory, or are they now 'sleeping' until the day of judgement?). Tempting as it is to be creative at this point, there is much to be said for being cautious and checking on expectations. If most of those present will be expecting to hear some variation on, 'Earth to earth, ashes to ashes, dust to dust,' at the committal, the minister needs to make sure that these words are present, otherwise the congregation may be left feeling that the service has not done the job properly.

Symbol and action are also important at these liminal moments. Where the minister stands in relation to the coffin, the use of touch (perhaps the minister touching the coffin as the commendation prayer is said), and gesture (many will be used to seeing the sign of the cross made over or towards the coffin at the words of committal), will all be important parts of making the liminal moments make sense and stand out. Asking the congregation to stand, for instance, is another way of signalling that a key moment has arrived. We are used to using music to highlight key moments in services, but it is good to remember the other senses: for instance, incense is used powerfully in some traditions to accompany the prayer of commendation, engaging both sight and smell.

The response section is especially complicated when it is interrupted by a move from church to crematorium or cemetery. In this case it is important that when everyone has gathered again, the service picks up at the point in the journey where it left off, and does not end up feeling as if it is starting all over again.

IN PRACTICE – To close the curtains or leave them open?

In a crematorium service one of the essential questions to get clear is whether or not the curtains around or in front of the coffin are to be closed at the point of committal. This is not only practical but also pastoral, and can be an important part of the conversation at a funeral visit.

For some, the closure of the curtains marks too sharp and sudden a division between them and their loved one, and the most common choice these days seems to be to leave them open. Is this about a fear of 'closure' – both literal and figurative? It can be seen that way.

There is, however, another way of seeing it: at a burial, although the coffin is interred (and in some cultures, the grave filled in there and then) the mourners are able to move away in their own time. The parting is more gentle and is about the mourners leaving the departed. When the curtains are closed at the crematorium (or, worse, the coffin descends into the bowels of the building, or slides away horizontally) it feels more like the departed is being taken away from the mourners, and they are disempowered. Leaving the curtains open can allow for a more gentle parting, more like that of a graveside, in which the mourners make the first move. If the layout of the crematorium makes it possible for the mourners to file past the coffin on the way out to make their own private farewell, even better.[40] Of course, in practice the time constraints at crematoria make this more measured parting much harder to achieve.

Dismissal

This is the phase in which to help those present to look to the future, both for themselves and for the deceased. Having commended their loved one to God, they need help to begin to remember in a different way. A prayer that asks God's help to follow in the footsteps of the departed 'in all that was good in their life'

---

40 For more reflection on this, see Tony Walter, 'Committal in the Crematorium: Theology, Death and Architecture', in Peter C. Jupp and Tony Rogers (eds), *Interpreting Death: Christian Theology and Pastoral Practice*, London: Cassell, 1997, pp. 204–6.

is one way to do that. For those of faith, the prayer may include remembering them safe in God's eternal care. For all of us it will be important that the prayer acknowledges the process of grieving which will now move into a different phase – lives being re-shaped, learning to live without the person who has died.

This will also be the part of the service in which to gather all present by inviting them to remember before God not only the person whose funeral this is, but others whom they have known and loved but see no more. For the closely bereaved this may enable some connections to be made with other family members who have died (at a cemetery or churchyard burial, those relatives may be buried nearby, and so the physical place itself becomes a trigger for making those connections). But for all who are present, this is the place to acknowledge those personal griefs that the funeral may have re-ignited or brought to the surface. The integration of this death into the bigger human story of life and death will often be an especially important moment for those whose connection to the deceased was more distant.

This connecting (which, in Christian theological terms, is part of the recognition of the communion of saints) is also a way of saying to those who are most closely bereaved: there is hope – others have trodden this path (you may have trodden it yourself already) and have come through it, hard as it was. Bereavement is part of life and there are others who can support you through this phase of your life.

IN PRACTICE – Practical announcements

Towards the end of this section, but before any final prayer, blessing or dismissal, can be a good point at which to make practical announcements. Is there a collection and if so, who is it in aid of? Is there an invitation to refreshments and a further informal sharing of memories? Are there practical notices about how and when to leave the church or chapel?

These too, are part of the journey of the funeral service. They are pastoral as well as practical because they signal: life goes on, we go on.

Checking that the journey makes sense

Increasingly, people wish to include items which personalize and contextualize the funeral service, and this is surely a generally good thing. Perhaps a grandchild wishes to play a piece of music on the violin which meant a lot to her late grandfather? Maybe one of the children of the deceased wishes to read a poem about their mum. Or maybe a family friend wants to read a non-biblical reading that they found on the internet. At the funeral of a teacher, children from her class may wish to share memories or to read a prayer they have written.

An understanding of the journey will help the service leader to make wise decisions about how, and especially where, to incorporate these items. They need to be placed to serve the journey, and not for reasons of mere convenience. So if someone wishes to read a poem, the key question is, 'What sort of poem?' A poem which primarily shares memories of the deceased is best placed with the rest of the telling of the human story. A piece of music which meant a lot to the person might be played as a time for recalling our own personal memories. On the other hand, a poem which is essentially about entrusting the person to God might fit more appropriately later in the service, perhaps before the commendation.

Issues in contemporary funerals

In recent revisions of funeral services in many Churches there have been some common factors.

Restoring resurrection joy

One of those common factors has been an attempt to reclaim something of resurrection joy in a Christian funeral. At the Reformation, the heavy emphasis on penitence and the fear of purgatory was in theory removed, replaced by a confident assurance of salvation and eternal life. In practice, however, though purgatory had gone, in its place was a stern tone of warning:

now there were only two possible destinations: heaven or hell, and the purpose of the funeral was to warn the living against ending up in the latter. Hence, though the theory was confidence in salvation through faith, the mood remained sombre and heavy.

The seriousness with which the Victorians took mourning seems to have added to this. More recent services have sought to recover something of the confident hope and joy of eternal life. However, the more you recover the confident joy, the harder you may make it to use with those who have no professed faith and who therefore may not have that sense of confidence in themselves. Hope, yes; but confidence?

The funeral of a child

A second issue has been the recognized pastoral need to provide more appropriate resources for the funeral of a child. Most denominations that produce funeral materials now make sure there is appropriate and fuller provision.[41] Ironically, this is not because child funerals are on the increase, but because infant mortality has reduced. The funeral of a child is therefore seen as a much rarer and therefore more significant event than in the era when childhood death was expected and much more normal. The resources are generally more tender and gentle in tone, and capture something of the special pain caused by the death of a child. In terms of the funeral journey, the key aspect for service leaders to be aware of is that when a life has been short (and sometimes very short) the human story has to be told in different ways, and many of the skills which ministers use in listening to

---

41 For instance, see *CWPS*, pp. 297–315 (an outline order and a range of resources for the funeral of a child – these have been brought together into a service in *Funeral Services of the Christian Churches in England*, pp. 42–7); *MWB*, pp. 478–96 (services for the funeral of a child and for a stillborn child); *Gathering for Worship*, pp. 252–5; *Order of Christian Funerals* (RC), pp. 220–363 (includes some different prayers for baptized and unbaptized children); *Book of Common Order* (Church of Scotland), pp. 305–25. In addition, there is a wealth of material which is available independently of denominational resources.

and then telling the human story in adult funerals do not transfer in straightforward ways. In this, as in so many other areas, healthcare chaplains are an important resource and support to those whose ministry is focused in the local church. Much of the reflection and resources in this area have arisen from chaplaincy contexts, where what is rare in parish or circuit is part of regular ministry.[42]

There are three other particular issues in contemporary funerals, each brought about in one way or another by cremation.

It isn't over till it's over

In the last hundred years, cremation has moved from being a marginal form of disposal to being the most common form of disposal in the UK.[43] Cremation was initially resisted by the Christian Churches, for a variety of reasons:

- Burial was seen as the 'proper' form of disposal for Christians because of the precedent set by Jesus – 'If it was good enough for Jesus, it's good enough for me.'
- Cremation was associated with 'pagan' practice and non-Christian religions. In the Roman Empire, when Christianity became the dominant religion cremation was pushed out in favour of burial.
- The Christian focus on the resurrection of the body led to a feeling that having a place of burial was important – a place from which to be resurrected. Even though careful theological thought showed that God was able to resurrect, whatever the mode of death and disposal, the popular sentiment remained that a body in a grave somehow made it easier.

---

42 For wise and practical guidance, see Paul Nash, *Supporting Dying Children and their Families: A Handbook for Christian Ministry*, London: SPCK, 2011, 'Services, rituals and blessings', pp. 125–48.

43 In 2010, cremations accounted for over 73 per cent of all funerals in the United Kingdom. Source: The Cremation Society of Great Britain, www.srgw. demon.co.uk/CremSoc4/Stats/National/ProgressF.html, accessed 21 December 2011.

The Church of England prevaricated for decades, at first acknowledging the practice of cremation and justifying it on the grounds that it was not a means of disposal in itself, but a form of preparation for burial, essentially speeding up what nature would do in a grave over many decades. Only in 1944 did it make a clear statement accepting the appropriateness of cremation for Christians.[44] The Roman Catholic Church did not accept cremation for Catholics until 1964, and many Churches still do not see it as appropriate for Christians.

After the initial controversies, cremation quickly became an alternative means of disposal on its own, as well as being something done in preparation for burial, scattering, or strewing of the cremated remains.[45] It is that choice about how to dispose of the remains which presents the liturgical problem: in a nutshell, when is it over? When is the committal? There are now two main options:

1. The committal is seen as what takes place at the crematorium and is a committal to be cremated.
2. The committal is seen as what takes place at the final burial, scattering or strewing of the ashes,[46] and is a committal to the ground (or, potentially, the river, sea, or whatever).

In the latter case, there is a further question: What do you say at the crematorium if the burial of ashes is the committal? In theory you cannot have two committals. The Church of England's *Common Worship* resources recognize this dilemma and provide two different patterns.[47]

---

44 For a thorough history of cremation and its acceptance in Britain, see Peter C. Jupp, *From Dust to Ashes: Cremation and the British Way of Death*, Basingstoke: Palgrave Macmillan, 2006. For a more brief exploration of cremation and its acceptance by the Christian Churches, see John S. Lampard, *Theology in Ashes: How the Churches Have Gone Wrong over Cremation*, Methodist Sacramental Fellowship, 2007.

45 Strewing is the technical term for lifting a piece of turf, placing the cremated remains underneath and then replacing the turf.

46 'Ashes' will be used here, as it often is colloquially and in service books, though 'cremated remains' is the more accurate technical term.

47 This is laid out in a table in Mark Earey, *Finding Your Way Around Common Worship: A Simple Guide*, London: Church House Publishing, 2011, p. 103.

In the first, the 'earth to earth, ashes to ashes' words are saved for the final committal (the burial of the ashes), and at the crematorium these words are used instead:

> We have entrusted our *brother/sister* N to God's mercy,
> and now, in preparation for burial,
> we give *his/her* body to be cremated.
> We look for the fullness of the resurrection
> when Christ shall gather all his saints
> to reign with him in glory for ever. **Amen.**[48]

In the second pattern, the cremation itself is seen as the primary committal, and the 'earth to earth, ashes to ashes' words are used at the crematorium.

But what happens if the family then decide that they will have the ashes buried? What is left to say? In this case there is an alternative form of committal at the burial of ashes, which could be used:

> God our Father,
> in loving care your hand has created us,
> and as the potter fashions the clay
> you have formed us in your image . . .
> We claim your love today,
> as we return these ashes to the ground
> in sure and certain hope of the resurrection to eternal life.[49]

There is no avoiding it though – it still looks and feels like two committals. Perhaps there is no way to avoid this, and perhaps it doesn't actually matter that much to the bereaved. After all, those who gather for a burial of ashes are likely to be a smaller group than those at the funeral, so perhaps it is important that at each gathering, there is a committal. However, for the minister it is good to get a feel for the overall journey, and to make sure that

---

48 *CWPS*, p. 269 – the key line is the second.
49 *CWPS*, p. 328.

any committal at the burial of ashes does not seem to 'undo' any committal that has already taken place at the crematorium.

IN PRACTICE – Asking the question

The problem here is that, at the point when the minister visits to plan the funeral, the family does not always know what they want to do with the remains. Often there is disagreement. There is no way to avoid this, but it does mean that the wise minister will make sure to ask the question on a funeral visit – Have you thought about what you will do with the cremated remains? Just asking the question can be helpful pastorally, as it can be the first time that the family together have had to think about it. Having a sense of what the family intend, can then help with the planning of the service.

Words of committal at a cremation

In all of the above we have assumed that a primary text at committal is the traditional 'earth to earth, ashes to ashes, dust to dust', which derives from the *Book of Common Prayer*. In the Church of England and the Methodist Church services, this basic text is still the norm, slightly amended, whether the committal is a burial or a cremation.

However, in its original Prayer Book context it was the committal for a burial service, as there was no other option. Though it mentions ashes, the assumption is clearly that what is happening is that the remains are being laid to rest, where all that we are (dust, ashes, earth) is once more what we become.

IN PRACTICE – Cremation dressed up as burial

This deep-rooted sense that burial is the default mode of disposal is evident in some crematoria, where the layout of the building is designed to allow the coffin to descend at the moment of committal, mimicking the descent of a coffin into a grave.

Some have suggested that in an era when cremation is the dominant mode of disposal, the Church should provide texts which reflect that, and which draw on different imagery, notably the imagery of fire. One of the key writers in this area is J. Douglas Davies. He has encouraged the Church to think differently and recognize the different dynamic and imagery needed where a cremation is seen not as preparation for burial but as the primary mode of disposal. Here is his suggestion for a form of committal:

> O Lord, . . . receive now the mortal remains of this your servant
> Departed this earthly life.
> Dutifully we give her (his) body for cremation,
> As ashes to ashes and dust to dust,
> In the hope of life eternal,
> Through Christ our Risen Lord.
>
> *During these last words the coffin is removed and the Minister*
> *continues with minimum pause*
> That as the flames of earth end our mortality
> So in the fullness of time the flame of your love
> May remake us eternally in the
> Glory and stature of Christ.
> He alone is the light of the world, the light no darkness can end,
> Who with you and the Holy Spirit,
> Is God for ever and ever, Amen.[50]

In this committal he draws on the idea of the flame of God's love (Song of Songs 8.6). He picks up slightly different connections, of fire as a purifying element, in this general prayer for use in a cremation service:

> O God, whose fire renders things of earth
> to their frail dust,
> so refine us by your mercy that we may attain
> to your everlasting purposes.[51]

---

50 J. Douglas Davies, *Cremation Today and Tomorrow* (Alcuin/GROW Joint Liturgical Studies 16), Nottingham: Grove Books, 1990, p. 44.

51 Douglas Davies, 'Theologies of Disposal', in Jupp and Rogers, *Interpreting Death*, p. 77.

The United Reformed Church resources take a different approach again, this time drawing on the New Testament associations of fire with the flame of the Holy Spirit for a committal at a cremation:

> All fire and heat, bless the LORD,
> praise him and magnify him for ever.
> The earthly life of *A* has come to an end,
> we have released *him* into God's merciful keeping.
> We now assign *his* body to the flames.
> Formed of the earth, to dust it shall return.
> Breathe on us, breath of God;
> in the refining fire of your holy Spirit,
> may we be brought with *A* to everlasting life. Amen.[52]

Each of these texts attempts to use the imagery of fire in positive ways at a cremation, to take seriously that this is not a preparation for burial, or a derivative from burial, but a valid means of disposal in its own right.

So, do they work? I want to suggest that despite valiant efforts to find positive images of fire in the Bible, each of these attempts falls short. This is not because they are, in themselves, inadequate, but because in the popular imagination, the strongest association of fire is with hell, and nothing that writers do to show that they are drawing on different associations can avoid that. In some cultures this would not be the case, but in British culture, which still carries such strong echoes of Christendom, it is unavoidable, and explains why at crematoria, everything possible is done to avoid confronting the mourners with the reality of fire. There is something unavoidably aggressive and violent about the act of burning a body which British culture largely finds distasteful. We recognize that the end result is much the same as for burial, but something about the violent intentionality of cremation means that though we value it for its speed, hygiene, and relative economy (not to mention the way it puts paid

---

52 *WURC* – additional material on CD Rom.

to the irrational, but common, fear of being buried alive), we do not wish to have the reality of its practicalities forced upon us, least of all at the highly emotional moment of committal.[53]

Committal first

Traditionally, when burial was the norm, a funeral would take place in church, followed immediately by interment in the churchyard or a cemetery. The growth of large municipal cemeteries on the edges of towns extended the time between church service and burial, and sometimes for convenience the whole service would be held in a cemetery chapel.

When crematoria started to be built, a new factor emerged. Crematoria are not as common as churchyards and cemeteries, so they are not as local. The journey to the crematorium can take a significant amount of time. In a big town or city with its own crematorium the journey can easily take 45 minutes, and in the countryside over an hour. There are pastoral implications to this: those who travel to the crematorium for the committal are often close family and friends. Everyone else who has come to the funeral might stay at the church (or a nearby hall or hotel) for refreshments. From the end of the service to the return of the close family might take two hours or more. Not everyone can stay that long, and so when the close family return they find many people have already left and others are getting ready to leave. The opportunity to tell stories and share jokes, to remember more informally, has been lost, and this is a loss indeed, for this low key community story-telling is an important part of what a funeral should facilitate.

---

53 In the light of this, it is interesting to note the different ways Churches choose to phrase a cremation committal. One way is to commit the body 'to be cremated' (Church of England, Methodist, Roman Catholic, Baptist, Church of Scotland all use this form). An alternative is to commit 'to the elements'. *WURC* uses this (p. 209), as does the 1979 *Book of Common Prayer* of The Episcopal Church in the USA (p. 501). *MWB* gives it as an alternative (pp. 457f.). The Anglican Church of Canada offers the more bold, 'to be consumed by fire' (*The Book of Alternative Services*, p. 587) and *A New Zealand Prayer Book* goes with, 'turned to ashes' (p. 837).

To solve the problem, various options have been tried. One is to have the committal at the church and then send the body to the crematorium unaccompanied. Effectively this is 'committal into the hearse'. It can be convenient both for the family and for the funeral director (because those long journeys to the crematorium can be hard to time accurately, and they tie up staff and cars for a long time). However, though it can solve one pastoral problem, it can create another: the family can feel that they have abandoned their loved one for the final part of the journey. Everyone knows that this happens anyway at the crematorium. Few families are present when the coffin actually enters the cremator (though in Hindu funerals a family representative usually does witness this). But somehow it feels different sending your loved one off on a long journey without the closest family members. It can be helped by sending one representative to the crematorium to accompany the body. This could be the minister, or one of the relatives of the deceased. But it is still not the same, and some can be left feeling uneasy about it. It is worth helping a family to talk through how they feel about the implications to make sure they have thought it through.

Another option is to turn the traditional order round: have the committal first, for closest family and friends, followed by a memorial or thanksgiving service later for a larger number of people. This change, too, has largely been driven by cremation, though it can be applied to burial as well. Typically the committal might take place in the morning, followed by the bigger service later that afternoon. Alternatively, the larger service could take place the next day, or a day or two later. Back in 1985, Wesley Carr noted this trend, but felt that it was unlikely to take off:

It has been proposed by some that cremation should precede the funeral, but there seems little enthusiasm for this and the image of a funeral service around an urn, rather than the corpse, seems strange. It is, however, important that, whatever arrangements are made, the bereaved family should, as a general rule, watch the disposal of the body through burial or its reception to the crematorium. Any ritual which does not include this formal separation from mortal remains, is deficient.[54]

How wrong he proved to be about the level of enthusiasm for this change.

This is a pattern which was already common for the funerals of those with a high public profile, such as local councillors, school headteachers and celebrities, where time was needed to organize a very large service but it was important not to delay the funeral for close friends and family.[55] What has changed is that this is now becoming a more popular option for 'ordinary' people, and the time between committal and the bigger service is getting smaller.

Methodist Worship Book, for instance, sets out two basic options for a funeral. The first (Funeral Service leading to Committal)[56] follows the traditional pattern, whereas the second (Funeral Service followed by Thanksgiving)[57] follows this alternative

---

54 Wesley Carr, *Brief Encounters: Pastoral Ministry Through the Occasional Offices*, London: SPCK, 1985, pp. 118f. For a more positive view of the alternative pattern, see Herbert Anderson and Edward Foley, *Mighty Stories, Dangerous Rituals: Weaving Together the Human and the Divine*, San Francisco: Jossey-Bass, 2001, pp. 119f.

55 See Donald Gray, *Memorial Services* (Alcuin Liturgy Guides 1), London: SPCK, 2002, for advice on planning this sort of service.

56 *MWB*, pp. 448–60.

57 *MWB*, pp. 461–77. WURC and *Gathering for Worship* also provide for these two options. In the case of *WURC*, the second pattern for a funeral allows for a committal without a formal commendation, followed later by a service of Thanksgiving and Release, which does include a commendation. In this case the body could be committed to be cremated (or buried) before the person has been commended into God's safekeeping – an odd, and potentially disturbing, symbolic journey. (In fact, the service includes in the general prayers before the committal, a bidding, 'Let us commit N to God's sure keeping,' but this is not labelled as a commendation, and is a bidding followed by silence, rather than an actual prayer – *WURC*, p. 212.) *Common Worship* does not give two options, though it provides an outline and sample service for a Memorial Service which is designed to be used 'several weeks' after the funeral (*CWPS*, pp. 331–44) and which includes a form of commendation (though this is different from those provided for the funeral itself). A note states that if a memorial service is to take place on the same day as the funeral (that is, committal first), then the funeral service is to be used again, but without the committal (Note 2, p. 334).

pattern.The instructions say that after the funeral part, 'The service continues in church either on the same day or at a later date.'[58]

Does it matter? In one sense, no, especially if it solves some of the pastoral problems outlined above. However, it does raise some liturgical issues, which have pastoral implications. What does this pattern do to the liturgical and pastoral journey? For some, perhaps most, of those at the Thanksgiving service, this *is* the funeral. They need to do the commending work which normally takes place at the funeral, and may also need to feel that they have been part of the committal. But neither can happen, because both have already taken place. How is the service to provide a liminal moment, to turn it from a service that means something into a service that does something?

There is a risk that rather than being a pastoral rite which does something, the Thanksgiving becomes a service whose 'theme' is the person who has died and thanksgiving for their life. This is an important part of a funeral, but as we have already seen it is only part of a Christian understanding of what the funeral does.[59]

In addition, what is the focus of the service? At a funeral, there is normally a very clear focus, provided by the coffin. The coffin marks the tangible absence of the deceased – it makes it unavoidably clear that they cannot walk into the room. There is no escaping the reality of the death, and that itself can be part of the grieving process for those present. At the Thanksgiving what is the focus? The Methodist Thanksgiving service begins with a note which says,

---

58 *MWB*, p. 472.

59 It should be noted that Quaker practice has long included this possibility of a burial or committal followed by a worship meeting. However, the difference is that for Quakers, both the committal and the worship meeting follow their normal practice of having no formal liturgy and consist of silence and the contributions which participants feel moved to add. For this reason, the 'journey' of commendation and committal is not articulated in the same way as in other Christian traditions. See Josephine Adams, 'Quaker Burials: How Much did the Non-Conformist Quaker Conform to the Quaker Ideal?', *Anaphora*, Vol. 3, Part 2, 2009, pp. 7–10.

If the urn or casket containing the ashes is brought into church, it should be placed on a table which has been covered with a white cloth, in front of the communion table.[60]

Clearly, if the ashes are to be present, then a reasonable time must have elapsed between the committal at the crematorium and the later service. Even more clearly, this is not an option if the earlier funeral was a burial. And an urn or casket of ashes may help, but it cannot represent the person who has died in the same way that a clearly body-shaped and body-sized coffin does. There are some similar issues when someone dies and leaves their body for medical research, but there feels a world of difference between an extreme situation and a regular norm.

Without the focus of the coffin, and without the key liminal moments of commendation and committal, there are real dangers that the service can be seriously weakened. It is tempting to avoid the messy reminder of our mortality which a coffin represents, and which is part of the job of a funeral. And while a service which is life-centred is a good and positive thing, it misses out on something central to the Christian faith, which is that a Christian funeral is forward looking, not just backward looking.[61] That forward focus is given shape in a Christian funeral primarily at the commendation. The service does not stop at the sharing of memories from the person's life. Nor does it just talk powerfully of resurrection in the sermon. It gives shape to the hope of resurrection by confidently commending the person into the future care of God. For these reasons, ministers who lead services of thanksgiving after an earlier committal need to think hard about how to make the service 'work'.

---

60 *MWB*, p. 473.

61 There is a lengthy description of the funeral of a young woman, followed by an instructive analysis of the 'celebration of life' approach, in Bruce T. Morrill, *Divine Worship and Human Healing: Liturgical Theology at the Margins of Life and Death*, Collegeville, MN: Liturgical Press, 2009, pp. 208–31 (esp. pp. 222–5).

- How can symbol and action be used?[62]
- How can a liminal moment be provided, which makes the service *do* something – and how can that happen in a way that does not 'undo' or subvert what has been done already at the funeral?
- How can the service be resurrection focused, and not merely backward looking and thanksgiving focused?[63]

Summary

In looking at funerals we have seen how pastoral liturgy can also be a place for pastoral *theology*. We have suggested again that a good model for pastoral services is that they are a gift from the Church, offered generously to all.

In the final chapter we will return to the key principles and begin to explore how to apply them in new contexts and for a wider range of pastoral needs than the traditional services we have looked at thus far.

---

62 *WURC*, for instance, includes the option of lighting thanksgiving candles in the Service of Thanksgiving and Release (p. 219).

63 *Gathering for Worship* (p. 246) suggests that at the Thanksgiving service, the prayers might include concerns that were close to the heart of the deceased. This is not forward-looking in the way that a commendation prayer is, but it does point ahead and begins the process of 'remembering the deceased differently' (in this case, in a way that affects how we pray).

8

Moving On and Out

In this chapter we will go back to the principles that we have identified (the toolkit) and then see how we can apply them to three different contexts: first, to individual contexts where there is no established form of service; second, to corporate pastoral situations; third, to situations beyond the Church and to what has been called 'apt liturgy' in the community.[1]

Summing up the principles

Most of the principles which can be applied to pastoral services are principles which need to apply in all worship contexts; hence, ministers need not to forget the skills which they use all the time in constructing Sunday worship when they come to plan pastoral services. However, some of those principles apply in particular ways to pastoral services. We considered some of them when we thought about Sunday worship, and in Chapter 3 we explored others in greater depth. Now it is time to bring them together and give a reminder of the key principles for pastoral liturgy:

1 Know your basic tools

These are the basic tools of any act of worship, but they may be applied differently in pastoral rites from the way they are applied in regular worship.

---

1 The term 'apt liturgy' was coined by Ann Morisy in her book, *Beyond the Good Samaritan: Community Ministry and Mission*, London: Mowbray, 1997. See later for more information.

- Words, music, song, gesture, symbols and action ('ritual'). In pastoral rites there may be expectations or rules which determine some of these, though in some situations it will be necessary for the minister to help to choose, adapt or create them.
- Resources from the Christian tradition, and specifically the books and other resources provided by your own Church.
- The human story and the God story and the way that they connect. The God story will come especially from Scripture, but will be reflected in other ways in the service. The human story needs to be told with integrity and made individual in pastoral rites, and it may be that the Bible reading will be chosen to fit either the need or the person.
- The particular tools of liminality: performative words, powerful but clear symbols, coherent actions.

2   Understand shape and journey

This is about how the tools are applied, so as to achieve what needs to be done.

- Any act of worship should be dynamic, not static (think 'aim', not 'theme') – 'What does this service need to *do*, or to help us to do?', not just, 'What does it mean?' In any service, including pastoral services, the primary thing that needs to be 'done' is to worship God, but there are always secondary aims and in pastoral services the need to 'do' something is more clearly expected and more closely focused.
- Identify the liminal moment (or moments) and make sure it is in the right place in the journey through the service.
- Know and use the fourfold shape: Gather (the human story); Word (the God story); Response (bringing the two together and making space for transformation); Sending (to live in the light of the change).
- Think about beginnings, flow, transitions, high points, endings.

- Use juxtaposition to allow new meanings to emerge – remember the difference between Explanation, Reinforcement and Subversion.

3 Mind your language (and assumptions)

- Remember that language impacts on issues of inclusion and exclusion (who is 'us'?).
- Consider how your language about God and addressed to God will shape images of God. In pastoral services, many in the congregation may rarely engage in corporate worship at other times, so the impact of our ways of talking to and about God will be proportionally greater.

4 Think long term and big picture

- Let people tell their full human story (not just the nice bits) and tell the full Christian gospel (not just the easy bits).
- Remember that pastoral services are for everyone who is present, and not just for the person or family who have requested the service. The needs of the wider congregation need to be balanced with the needs of those immediately concerned with the pastoral situation which has triggered the service.

5 Know your level of authority

- A pastoral service is not just for those who have asked for it. The question, 'Who does this service belong to?' has a more complex answer than sometimes at first appears.
- Be clear about the expectations (and sometimes laws) that shape norms. It may be important to 'do it right' so it feels as if it has 'worked'.

Considering a trajectory

Having established and reminded ourselves of those principles, I want now to suggest a trajectory for pastoral rites, which moves

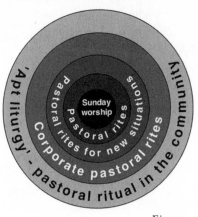

Figure 4

beyond those familiar contexts of Sunday worship and established pastoral services, to consider new layers of contexts in which these principles may apply. If we imagine Sunday services at the core, leading to individual pastoral services, I want to add three more layers:

- Individual pastoral rites for new needs and contexts – that is, things that are not in much evidence in the official books.
- Corporate pastoral rites, when the need is still pastoral, but the situation is corporately felt, rather than individually.
- The use of the principles of pastoral rites out in the wider community – what has sometimes been called 'apt liturgy'.

Pastoral rites for new needs

Re-working existing rites

Sometimes existing rites are dying. Perhaps they do not ring true any more, or do not connect with current realities, or the stories they tell, both human and divine, are now contested. Perhaps they have become tools of control rather than transformation. Harvey Cox was reflecting on the danger of this back in 1969:

Ritual becomes *ideology* when it is used to throttle creativity, to channel religion or fantasy into safely accepted molds. Organized religion in periods of decline, nations anxious to enforce patriotism and obedience, individuals who feel they may be losing a grip on themselves – all become self-conscious and meticulous about ritual proprieties. Enforced ritual, handed down from above, chokes off spontaneity and petrifies the spirit.[2]

When this happens, existing rites may need a significant make-over, or more a fundamental re-think. This is why books of creative rituals and services often contain a lot of 'new takes' on existing services (funerals, weddings, baby blessings) as well as services for life's hidden events or more unusual situations.

Creating new rites for new situations

Sometimes we need new rites. As we saw in Chapter 2, this may be because important life transitions have been ignored or sidelined by the Church, and so there are no existing patterns. In this case, the problem is simply lack of precedent – it just is not part of the existing repertoire in most churches. A form of prayer and worship for someone who has retired would fit this category. For some services, however, the problem is not just lack of precedent, but the presence of controversy or a particular need for sensitivity. Services in this category might include same-sex relationship blessings or prayers for someone who has just come out of prison.

Alternatively, we may need new rites because life patterns have changed, or technological or medical advances or other changes have created new situations which a previous generation never had to negotiate. Effectively, the terrain has changed and we need

---

2 Harvey Cox, *The Feast of Fools: A Theological Essay on Festivity and Fantasy*, Cambridge, MA: Harvard University Press, 1969, p. 71 (emphasis in original).

new maps to help us negotiate the new situation.[3] Increasingly, these new or creative rites are finding their way into print.[4]

IN PRACTICE – Finding resources

The problem is, when these resources exist, they are often highly personal or particular to one situation, rather than generic to a range of similar situations. Books like *Human Rites*[5] are often structured around several basic areas. For instance, the section headings in *Human Rites* include 'Beginnings and namings', 'A celebration of relationships'. 'Healing our wounds', 'Separations and goodbyes' and so on. However, within each section there are then a series of very particular services created for people or situations, rather than one service for, say, moving house, which can be adapted. This means that they make good places to search for creative ideas, but not to find ready-to-use resources.

Can rites be too personal?

Harvey Cox warned of a second danger for ritual. At the other end of the scale from ritual that becomes ideological is ritual that becomes idiosyncratic:

> Ritual becomes *idiosyncratic* when it ceases to be shared by a group or to emerge from historical experience, when it becomes the property of just one, or of just a few people.[6]

---

3 See Herbert Anderson and Edward Foley, *Mighty Stories, Dangerous Rituals: Weaving Together the Human and the Divine*, San Francisco: Jossey-Bass, 2001, pp. 125–48 for a helpful analysis of why we might need new rites and how we can create them.

4 For instance, Hannah Ward and Jennifer Wild, *Human Rites: Worship Resources for an Age of Change*, London: Mowbray, 1995; Diann L. Neu, *Women's Rites: Feminist Liturgies for Life's Journey*, Cleveland, OH: Pilgrim Press, 2003; Jim Clarke, *Creating Rituals: A New Way of Healing for Everyday Life*, Malwah, NJ: Paulist Press, 2011; and Dorothy McRae-McMahon's books, including *Liturgies for the Journey of Life*, London SPCK, 2000 and *Prayers for Life's Particular Moments*, London: SPCK, 2001.

5 Ward and Wild, *Human Rites*.

6 Cox, *Feast*, p. 73 (emphasis in original).

This idea of 'creating' rituals, then, raises some key issues about the nature of pastoral rites. Back in Chapter 3, I assumed that pastoral rites are corporate repeated events, but this is not universally acknowledged. Very early in his book *Creating Rituals*, Jim Clarke states, as a fundamental assumption: 'Rituals are meant to be unique for each person, group, or situation.'[7] Are they? Some Christians, among others, are producing extremely personalized and one-off pastoral rites. They often point out that the creativity and the connection with the context seem to be the key points which make the rites work, and not any sense that they are repeated or belong more widely. Feminist groups have been particularly notable in this move, and Jan Berry gives a helpful summary of the arguments and issues around this.[8] The creativity is clearly proving pastorally helpful for lots of people, and is rescuing pastoral liturgy from a potentially unhelpful control by the Church. It reminds us that the existing standard rites are 'models of ritual wisdom',[9] and should not become liturgical straitjackets. But there are some questions to ask too.

Is there anything new under the sun?

First, it is important to recognize that 'created' rites often draw on models and shapes which are familiar from other more established services. For instance, a rite for leaving a home might follow a shape which echoes that of a funeral, acknowledging loss, letting go, moving on. It is often the content and symbolism which is contextual, creative and unique to the individual or situation, rather than the structure or shape of the rite, which may borrow from other forms or services. The fourfold pattern we noted above, and the basic pattern of separation, liminality and incorporation, are often found.

---

7 Clarke, *Creating Rituals*, p. 6.

8 Jan Berry, *Ritual Making Women: Shaping Rites for Changing Lives*, London: Equinox, 2009, especially pp. 5 and 101–29.

9 Anderson and Foley, *Mighty Stories*, p. 133.

Often the uniqueness of the rites is because of the sheer fact that the life events being recognized are those which have not yet made it into column 1 of the table in Chapter 2. But will that sense of individuality still be needed or valued if and when they become more mainstream and common? If a rite to acknowledge the onset of the menopause (for instance) became a common pastoral rite, with lots of people asking for it, and even more people having been part of the rite, would its form be shaped by commonalities of experience and would those who asked for it want it to be 'like the other one I went to last year', rather than something newly created just for them?

As more and more 'unique' rites become more widely known, either through publication in print or through the internet, they start to look less unique as certain sorts of rite appear in more than one place and as people start to borrow ideas from one another. As in other areas of liturgy, the good ideas tend to get copied and those that either do not seem so appropriate, or seem very specific to a particular situation, do not. It is possible that commonalities will harden into expectations, and that creative ideas which *work* will become regular patterns or symbols, sought and used by others.

The importance of the process of ritual creation

An important insight of feminist and other ritualizers is that the process of creating the rites can be almost as significant as the rite itself. This could be a group working collaboratively to produce a rite for themselves or for one of their group. Alternatively, a ritual may have been devised for one person, perhaps with the help of a 'ritual specialist' who has worked with them. In this case, too, the process of devising the ritual may have been extremely important.[10]

---

10 The term 'ritual specialist' is from Jim Clarke, *Creating Rituals*. Clarke stresses the value and importance of the process of producing the ritual, pp. 73ff.

When groups produce rites for their own members, or a specialist works with an individual, the process is clearly powerful and creative. But pastoral rites often reach beyond, to larger groups of people. This means that it is hard to invent pastoral rites generically, because if a rite is to 'work' for all who are present, the symbols must speak very clearly (and therefore operate at a very instinctive level) or they must connect with symbols which are familiar from other contexts. Without this, the rite risks becoming exclusive, because it only speaks to and works for those who were part of its creation.

TO THINK ABOUT – Personal rituals and corporate rites

What happens then, when a rite (including rituals) is created or planned by one group of people, but experienced by many others? Building on Victor Turner's work, Jim Clarke draws a distinction between a ritual and a ceremony. Rituals, he states, are transformative and have only participants and no audience, whereas ceremonies are not transformative and often involve a large audience who take part but are not transformed.[11] He recognizes that an event may be transformative ritual for some and non-transformative ceremony for others.

I agree with him about the importance of transformation, but think that he draws the line too tightly around ritual, and distinguishes it too starkly from ceremony. He fails to make room between them for the rite – the larger context in which the liminal ritual takes place. Pastoral rites often involve quite large numbers of people, though only some of them are the central figures. Often a pastoral rite has different levels of transformative power, and those furthest from the centre of it may nonetheless experience transformation, even if it is at a much less intense level than those at the centre of the event. For them, it is not an intense ritual experience, but neither is it 'mere ceremony'.

Aidan Kavanagh reminds us that, '. . . symbols are carried in the vital pulses and structures of a social group. They may be

---

11 Clarke, *Creating Rituals*, pp. 22 and 116f.

discovered: they may mutate. But they can never be confected by a committee out of whole cloth.'[12] His target was Churches trying to invent new generic pastoral rites. The current growth area, however, is not church committees, but groups and individuals effectively ignoring the Church and creating rituals for particular situations and individuals. In these cases it sometimes does feel more like starting from scratch, but his point about rituals being discovered rather than invented may still be an important corrective and a helpful guide for those who are doing this creative work. Whether we see the work as being creative or exploratory, what is clear is that there is much scope for working with particular people to make particular rites work better, and this may be an area where the Church needs to work harder, rather than offering pastoral rites on a 'take it or leave it' basis.

CASE STUDY – A rite of adolescence

Elaine Ramshaw describes a church trying to create a rite of passage to mark the transition from childhood to adulthood.[13] To work, she suggests, it cannot be created from nothing or without reference to the existing cultural signs and symbols of that transition, which include being able to drive a car, to vote, to buy alcohol and so on. As an example of how a church could connect in that way, she suggests a rite in which the teenager is presented with the car keys accompanied by a prayer for safety – as she puts it, 'solemnizing a reality'.

The challenges of the new ritualizers

Though I have raised some questions about the creation of new and unique pastoral rites, I also want to note the value of this

---

12 Aidan Kavanagh, 'Life-Cycle Events, Civil Ritual and the Christian', in David Power and Luis Maldonado (eds), *Liturgy and Human Passage* (*Concilium* 112), New York: Seabury Press, 1979, p. 21.

13 Elaine Ramshaw, *Ritual and Pastoral Care*, Philadelphia: Fortress Press, 1987, p. 43.

work. Those who are at the forefront of some of this work are opening up new possibilities, and in particular are breaking out of unhelpful stereotypes and showing new models of process. As well as modelling the powerful use of fresh symbols and actions, they offer several challenges to the Churches and to existing patterns of pastoral rites:

- They raise the question of who controls the rite and who it belongs to, particularly challenging the idea that the rite belongs to the Church and is simply delivered to you more or less ready-formed. The sacramental model is particularly prone to this danger, and feminist writers have rightly pointed out that in Churches where the sacraments have been the preserve of male priests, this has perpetuated a patriarchal model where the Church (a male Church) does something to or for you, rather than working with you to help you mark your transition.
- They offer models of collaborative working, particularly working with the person or group for whom the rite is being produced.
- They remind us of the need for careful listening, so that rites (especially new ones) draw on the right mix of traditional connections. For instance, a house blessing could be an occasion for focusing on grieving and acknowledging loss or for celebrating a fresh start, or both – and the balance between the two which is right for this service is not necessarily the same as for a service for someone else moving to a new home.
- Above all, in an increasingly fragmenting cultural context, they perhaps show us that the creation of ritual is one way of creating a ritual community, when that community cannot be assumed already to exist.

Time will tell

Only time will tell how these unique rituals will look in 50 years' time. Already, some are noting how symbolic actions which at first looked creative and fresh can begin to look tired and predictable, but not yet stable and a sign of continuity.[14] Perhaps it is possible to discern a process:

- **Stage 1** – A symbol or action is truly fresh and new for that context.
- **Stage 2** – The same symbol gets repeated or copied, but in contexts where people are still trying to be creative and unique. The symbol therefore starts to feel clichéd, and is avoided.
- **Stage 3** – The rite becomes established strongly enough that people want and expect the symbol: it has become traditional, and though there might be problems with that, it no longer feels like failed creativity, and for some might feel like safe continuity and a sense of belonging to something bigger than oneself.

None of this negates the value of the individual ritual for the unique context and person for whom it was first devised. But it reminds us that for pastoral rites which will not just express one person or group's journey but also provide a map to help a wider community, evolution not revolution is probably what to expect.

IN PRACTICE – Testing resources

When you find a service in a book of creative resources, or perhaps on the internet, which seems to connect with your particular need, it can be tempting to see that as the answer to your prayers. Beware! Here are some tips for proceeding with caution with 'new' resources.

– Check that it works as 'liturgy' as well as 'poetry'. Many creative rites are produced by people who are good with words. Often they are 'poetic', even if not poems in the normal sense. But liturgy is not the same as poetry. Liturgy has to work in a corporate context. Its imagery must be evocative, but not so eccentric (in the technical sense of 'off centre') that it only connects with some of

---

14 See, for instance, Berry, *Ritual Making Women*, p. 104.

those present. Poetry is written from a personal perspective and often intended to be heard like that: 'Here's my way of imagining this reality.' Liturgy, on the other hand, has to speak to and for a congregation, and to come from 'the Church' in the broadest sense, not from one person (whether minister or writer).

– Check especially what you are putting into the mouths of others. Words spoken or actions performed by the leader of a service need to take account of the points made above, but for words or actions which are given to the congregation there is a further test: can they say it with integrity? Not everyone needs to be able to say everything and mean every word (if they did, there would be a lot of silence in a lot of places in many churches when we said the creed, or sang some songs or hymns), but congregational material needs to be able to carry most of the congregation and work as an expression of what they need to say or to do for the service to do its work.

– Finally, check how it might sit with the expectations of those who will be present. Corporate worship does not always have to conform to expectations; sometimes it will be most effective where it challenges them. But challenging expectations generally works most effectively within a basically supportive framework – if not, the congregation spend too much time working out whether they believe this, or can do this, etc. to be able to engage properly in doing it. If you are going to challenge expectations, make sure that you realize you will do so and have plans for how to warn the congregation or to handle that clash of expectations in a constructive, rather than destructive, way.

Guidance for the less confident

All this creativity which is 'out there' gives plenty of encouragement to 'have a go' oneself. However, for those who are less confident it can lead to confusion, or to people taking services from one particular context and trying to use them in a context which is much less appropriate. In these cases, it may be better to go back to first principles and to apply the tools we have established here:

- Use the fourfold shape as a structure.
- Establish what the human story is.
- Consider what the God story might be, and how to connect it to the human story.
- Consider what the service needs to do. This will help you to think what the liminal moment needs to be, when the service does what it needs to do.
- Use tools of liminality to establish that liminal moment: performative words, movement, symbols and actions.

Once that basic structure is established, it becomes possible to look at the creative resources already available in books and on the internet and to see whether ideas from those sources will fit.

Then there are the other questions. Whose service is this? Who are the stakeholders, and who are those who will be present but on the margins? How will the service address them and, through them, the wider community? What are the precedents for this service? What will need to happen to make it feel 'proper'? Where expectations are not established, the minister has to proceed cautiously. Are there connections with services which are familiar?

Corporate pastoral rites

We began this book by considering the ways that regular corporate worship (what we called 'Sunday worship') can care for people. We saw that such care was usually non-specific, and we quickly moved on to consider services which care for people in particular circumstances, where Sunday worship's care would be too generic, even though it might help. Most of the contexts we considered are those in which the pastoral need is primarily individual – it might involve one person, one couple or one family. Though the ripples will stretch further (and we have seen that this is a key factor to bear in mind) the primary focus is one particular need of one small unit of people.

Sometimes, however, the pastoral situation is particular or specific, but those affected form a bigger group than just one individual or family unit. Examples that spring to mind include situations such as the murders in Soham in 2002, or the Hillsborough Stadium disaster in 1989, or the Birmingham Pub bombings in 1974. When events like these take place, whole communities are affected and have a need for pastoral care. That pastoral care can include the church offering pastoral rites ('caring rituals'). Typically these include making the church building available for private prayer (perhaps including the chance to write a prayer or light a candle or leave a message), special vigil services and memorial services.[15]

There are other sorts of corporate pastoral rites too – ones which are not one-offs in response to a particular situation, but ones which occur regularly. In a fishing village the annual blessing of the fishing boats might be a pastoral rite, because through it the whole community is assured of God's concern and care for something which is of supreme importance to that community. A very different example might be an annual service to remember victims of road traffic accidents, which gathers a 'community' of those touched by that particular tragedy.

Remembrance Sunday as a corporate pastoral rite

Remembrance Sunday, whether celebrated in a church service or as a civic commemoration, may not feel like a pastoral rite, but that is part of what it does. Armistice Day commemorations emerged out of the corporate and national trauma of the First World War. After this was compounded by the Second World War, Remembrance Sunday began to take over, with services which could encompass more than one conflict. Since then, the scope has been further widened to a remembrance for all conflicts and all those affected by them. Indeed, as more

---

15 Liturgical resources for times of remembrance, including following on from traumatic community events, can be found in Jean Mayland (ed.), *Beyond our Tears: Resources for Times of Remembrance*, London: CTBI, 2004. See also Donald Gray, *Memorial Services* (Alcuin Liturgy Guides 1), London: SPCK, 2002.

recent conflicts have claimed significant numbers of British lives, Remembrance Sunday events, which seemed to be on the wane, seem now to have captured the national imagination once again, as has Armistice Day itself. Of course, there is a lot of difference between a civic service at a war memorial, perhaps in the open air, and a local church's smaller-scale remembrance of war, and those killed or injured by it, but some of the same issues arise. Certainly after the World Wars, the services were not just collective remembrances; rather, they connected with the actual experience of loss and trauma which had affected every family – they were pastoral, not just commemorative.

More recent conflicts too, and the international terrorist atrocities, though not on the same scale, seem to have reached and touched more people. Though we may not have been personally affected by injury or bereavement, we know, or know of, those who have been affected in that way. Or we simply know of those who are 'in harm's way', and so our pastoral need is connected not just with grief but with fear. This has been heightened by television reporting which records and names those who have been killed and informs us all. There has been some analysis and critique of some aspects of Remembrance Day commemorations, and particularly the way that the interpretive story from two World Wars (of sacrifice for the sake of our nation and its freedoms) has been projected onto more recent conflicts whose aims and achievements are less clear.[16] We will recognize those questions, but focus on the celebrations as they currently are, with all their strengths and weaknesses.

What does this service need to do?

The service must do what it says on the tin: it must enable us to remember. However, this is not a simple answer. There are important questions about *how*, *what* and *whom* we remember.

---

16 See, Kate Guthrie, *Reimagining Remembrance*, a report published by the Christian thinktank Ekklesia (www.ekklesia.co.uk) in 2009.

- Whom do we remember? Do we remember all those who fought, or only those who fought and died? Is there room to remember others who did not fight but were injured or killed, and are we remembering only 'our' losses or all those who suffered and suffer still?
- What do we remember? Which conflicts get consciously re-membered and which do not? Is it easier to remember ones which 'we won'?
- How do we remember? Do we remember the so-called glory of war (as war memorials tend to: 'The glorious dead') or the waste of human life? Do we suggest that war is a neces-sary evil, or do we remember it as something which is never an appropriate solution? Do we remember with thanksgiv-ing or with shame or lament?

There may also be a need for an element of grieving, though it will be felt differently by different persons present. There is certainly a need for an expressed commitment to live differently in the light of what we have remembered, for us individually, for our nation and for the world. All of this reminds us that a Remembrance Sunday service is not just a service with a remem-brance theme – it is a service that has many jobs to do, several of which connect with pastoral care.

What is the God story?

The God story which is told at a Remembrance service often depends on which of the human stories dominates. Sometimes, it is a God story about heroism or sacrifice, sometimes it is a God story of comfort and strength in difficult times or in bereavement. Sadly, it has sometimes become a God story of nationalism and patriotism, which at its worst can suggest that loyalty to one's country is equal to loyalty to God. The Scripture readings which are used at Remembrance services will be important in determining the God story which is told, but equally important will be the choice of hymnody and the content of prayers.

What are the key symbols or actions?

Traditionally these include any or all of the following: individual poppies; poppy crosses (a poppy on a small wooden cross – an interesting juxtaposition of symbols); poppy wreaths being placed at memorials; the sounding of the Last Post (and possibly Reveille); standards being dipped as a sign of respect; the keeping of silence; the reading of the Exhortation (from the words of Laurence Binyon, 'They shall grow not old as we that are left grow old . . . We will remember them') and the Kohima Epitaph ('When you go home tell them of us and say, for your tomorrow we gave our today'); the reading of names of those who have been killed.

In a Remembrance Sunday service in a local church these symbols and actions may happen in more informal or less fixed ways, and there may be particular local customs. The important thing is to make sure that things happen in an order which supports the journey through the service.

What are the liminal moments? Where does transition happen?

Normally there is a point at which we move from remembering to committing ourselves to doing differently. That may come at the silence. The two key texts often make that journey for us. The Exhortation calls us back to remember; the Kohima Epitaph points us forward to the purpose of our remembering, that in remembering we might value our freedoms and (implicitly) live in a way that is worthy of the sacrifices made. Some understanding of the principles of pastoral rites can help to make sure that elements of these services are in the right order and may suggest ways of helping to make the journey more effective.

For instance, the placing of wreaths as part of the remembrance phase (separation, in van Gennep's model) is often a very moving and powerful moment. It belongs most naturally in the first part of the service, but sometimes gets moved to the end of the service for the sake of convenience (perhaps because we need to move outside to a war memorial).

The silence marks the key liminal moment as we each apply the remembrance to our own situation. The use of silence is crucial. It is the absence of words in this liminal moment which enables this pastoral rite to work for such a large group of people, because it allows for the wide range of pastoral work which the service needs to do. The silence allows for a multitude of individual human stories to be put alongside the overarching story. For some that will be about remembering a grandparent with thanks, or recalling the sights on the television screen, but for others it will be the moment for much stronger feelings of grief from a close and recent bereavement to be given their space.

IN PRACTICE – Making Remembrance forward looking

Often the weakest part of a Remembrance service is the final part where we move from remembering to looking forward. Some services include a formal commitment to work for peace, but is there some symbol or action that we can use at this point, something to take home, something to do? The white poppy (produced by the Peace Pledge Union) is used by some to emphasize not only remembrance and support for the armed forces, but active working for peace and reconciliation.

In one church, people were invited to lay down their red poppies under a cross at the front of church at the end of the service as a sign of their remembering, and then to pick up and take home a white poppy, as a reminder and sign of commitment to pray and work for peace and reconciliation in their own lives and in the world. This is not an action that would work in all contexts (particularly because the white poppy is not universally understood, and is sometimes misunderstood as showing disrespect for those who have died), but it shows what might be possible.

Other corporate pastoral rites

Remembrance rites are regular and repeated and have developed their own patterns and expectations. Another, very different, example is the national service to commemorate the bicentenary of the Abolition of the Slave Trade in 2007. Although this anniversary was also marked in many small-scale ways by local churches, most attention was focused on the national commemoration in Westminster Abbey. Some national or large-scale services and commemorations have the potential to be pastoral, and this was one of them. For some, both individuals and groups, this commemoration connected with very personal and perhaps very painful aspects of their current identity and self-understanding, as well as their experience of life within this nation. Let us do some similar analysis.

- What did this service need to do? It needed to give thanks, to commemorate, but it also needed to include lament. The story had to be told, both of slavery and its trade and of the abolition of that trade. Thanks needed to be given, individuals remembered, and there needed to be some commitment to continue in all that was good about the movement which led to this event. The ongoing traffic in human beings today was part of the backdrop to the commemorations, and this needed to be articulated and acknowledged.
- What were the key symbols and actions? The presence of the Queen as head of state, and other national leaders was itself a key symbol that this was something being recognized nationally and corporately. Among the many elements of music, prayer and words, the key moment was a silence for remembrance.

Did the service 'work'? The service is remembered now, some years on, primarily for the interruption by Toyin Agbetu, who brought the event to a halt when he left his seat and began shouting out that the service was an insult. His main point was that the crown, the government and the Church, who were all implicated in the slave trade, were busy 'patting themselves on the back' when they should have been saying sorry.

The service needed to be a pastoral rite as well as a national commemoration. To do that, it needed to acknowledge the story of those for whom those events are not academic or historical, but part of their lives today. For many, it needed to include an apology. A proper one: one that said 'sorry', not just one that expressed regret. An expression of regret is not a performative use of language (as politicians know so well): apology is, because it changes things. That would have been the key liminal moment, and its absence meant that whatever the merits of the service, it was limited as a pastoral rite.

CASE STUDY – Making a service do something

Not all corporate pastoral services need to be concerned with trauma, grief or difficulty. Like individual rites of passage, corporate pastoral rites can sometimes be about celebrating new beginnings or new phases.

When I was a vicar in a town in West Yorkshire, there was an annual 'Mayor's Sunday' service. The service was an opportunity for the community to celebrate with their newly chosen mayor. One year it was the turn of our church to host it. The service tended to follow a standard pattern, amended from year to year by the choice of hymns and readings. It was a chance to get uniformed organizations in a parade, to sing some rousing hymns and generally to feel good about our town and community. There was just one thing missing – it was not clear what it did. The addition of a simple act of commitment made a big difference. The new mayor was invited to come forward and to commit himself or herself to service of the community, and those present were asked to commit themselves to support and pray for the mayor for the duration of his or her time in office. This was followed by a simple prayer, with laying on of hands, for the mayor and her or his work in the year to come. A simple change introduced a liminal moment (by use of words, movement and action) and turned a mayor-themed service into a corporate rite of passage, effecting a change in relationship between mayor and community, and doing so in the context of Christian worship and an articulation of the God story.

Other examples of corporate pastoral rites might include things like:

- The closing of a church building (or a school, or other community facility).
- An annual memorial service for those who have been bereaved. Here the connections with funeral rites are obvious, but this is not a funeral: the context is a corporate one, with many people sharing similar but not identical experiences.
- The departure or retirement of a minister in a church (or the arrival of a new one). Here there are often rites, particularly about the arrival of a new minister, but they are not always thought of in terms of pastoral care and therefore not as pastoral rites. This means that some of the grief or the sense of responsibility is not dealt with, either on the part of the minister or the part of the congregation.

Sometimes services which are not primarily pastoral rites can become so because of particular circumstances. For instance, during a time of crisis for the farming community, such as the widespread outbreak of foot and mouth disease, Harvest Thanksgiving services could become corporate pastoral rites which express and symbolize God's care and the care of the church for those most severely affected. During a time of uncertainty or distress at a local school, a service on Education Sunday could, similarly, become a pastoral liturgy. The key is to make sure the service has an aim, not just a theme, and to ensure that suitable symbols, words and actions mark a liminal moment that helps make it feel as if the aim has been achieved and something has happened.

These pastoral liturgies provide good opportunities for mission in its broadest sense – a chance to invite a group of people to put their human story (in this case, a professional as well as personal story) next to the God story and to see the connections.

Pastoral liturgy and the wider community

In her book, *Beyond the Good Samaritan*, Ann Morisy coins the phrase 'apt liturgy' for occasions where the church uses its skills and experience with prayer, ritual and symbol to help change to happen.[17] The distinctive aspect of apt liturgy is that it does so out in the community, rather than in the church's own preferred context.

What is 'apt liturgy'?

Apt liturgy is sometimes hard for people to get their heads round. In order to help, Morisy gives the example of a senior citizens' day centre minibus trip to the places they were evacuated during the Second World War, and the opportunity for a minister to lead a short time of reflection when they returned in which connections were made between their wartime experience and the experiences of those in parts of the world affected by war today. She goes on to suggest that apt liturgy 'in relation to a project providing debt advice might link the personal debt of those seeking advice with the debt faced by the poor nations of the world'.[18]

Here is the secret of apt liturgy's missional potential: it connects. Yes, it connects people with God – we would hope that this would be good news. But even if that connection with God is not explicit, it connects people with *others* – other people, places and times – the first step to recognizing that we are not alone, that there is something beyond us and our experience. 'Apt liturgy invites people to lift their eyes above the horizon and respond to that aspect of our humanity which is beyond our creatureliness.'[19] The hope is that this connection with others

---

17 Morisy, *Beyond*, pp. 48ff.

18 Ann Morisy, *Journeying Out: A New Approach to Christian Mission*, London: Morehouse, 2004, p. 157. The minibus trip is described in Morisy, *Beyond*, pp. 55f., and summarized in Morisy, *Journeying*, p. 156.

19 Ann Morisy and Ann Jeffries, 'Apt Liturgy: To lift eyes above the horizon', in Tim Stratford (ed.), *Worship, Window of the Urban Church*, London: SPCK, 2006, p. 60.

might be a first step in connecting with The Other, with God. Apt liturgy, then, is a short symbolic act connecting people with God, the experience of others, the wider world, their emotions and stories of Jesus.

Here we see the connections with pastoral liturgy – this is the Church using its ritual skills to serve the world. However, though the Church is using its skills, it is not doing so on its terms or its territory. 'Apt liturgy is about the churches doing what only they can do,' writes Morisy, but it 'does not require people to cross the threshold of the church'.[20] Apt liturgy draws on the *tradition* of the Church, without the *culture* of the Church (that is, venue, language, style, constraints, and so on). It requires a good deal of faith and a willingness to take risks, to leave things fuzzy and not spelt out, to let the Spirit do some of the interpretation and not to turn the event into an excuse for a sermon. This is the Church working in what Morisy calls the 'foundational domain', the world where the expectations, traditions and communal codes of the Church are foreign territory and much of its symbolism is opaque and alien. It is important that we are clear what is being suggested: it is not that the Church is bringing God to the situation, for we will find that God is already at work there, though not necessarily recognized or named. What the Church brings is its skills in symbolism, ritual and big stories, which help people to make sense of what is going on and hopefully to begin to recognize the God who is active in every place and time.

Only distress?

In the glossary of *Journeying Out* Morisy gives this definition: apt liturgy is,

> a specific liturgy which aims at including people with little faith and Christian knowledge and often focuses on a particular distress that has arisen within a community.[21]

---

20 Morisy, *Journeying*, p. 156.
21 Morisy, *Journeying*, p. 237.

The importance of the word 'distress' in this definition is that it helps us to recognize why Morisy prefers the term 'apt liturgy' to 'contextual liturgy'.[22] Apt liturgy is indeed contextual, but in a specific rather than a general sense. The point is that, like pastoral rites, apt liturgy arises out of a specific need, event, or stage in life. Unlike most pastoral rites, that need, event or stage is in the life of a *community*, rather than an individual or family.

In practice apt liturgies will often develop out of situations of distress, but they don't have to, and Morisy acknowledges this.[23] For instance, I heard about a situation where a Christian who had been involved in the planning and organization of a new community shop in a village was invited, in quite a spontaneous way, to 'say a few words' at the cutting of the ribbon. What was invited was not a sermon, but a chance to make connections and perhaps to point to the God story and to consider how to enhance and share the liminality of the moment.

Typical content of apt liturgy

Apt liturgy will, by its very nature, be very specific to the particular context, community and event. However, here are some common themes which come through in apt liturgy which may help us:

- The use of a **Bible** story that resonates with the particular situation or struggle.
- **Prayer** or a reflection which 'names' fears, struggles, sorrows etc.
- **Putting this situation into a larger (global) context** to give a sense of **shared** struggle and not being alone.
- An expression of trust in a God who **shares** our griefs, hopes and struggles.
- A simple **symbolic** act.

---

22 Morisy and Jeffries, 'Apt Liturgy', pp. 61f.
23 Morisy, *Journeying*, p. 180, n. 19.

CASE STUDY – Lament on the streets

In March 2009, staff and students from the Queen's Foundation in Birmingham organized an act of lament in Birmingham City Centre on the sixth anniversary of the beginning of the Iraq war. The aim was to try to engage with feelings of confusion and frustration among some in the wider community about this long-running war which many felt ambivalent about, and which was claiming many lives month by month.

A drumbeat was maintained throughout, as the names of some of the dead were read out, both British and Iraqi. Readings from the book of Lamentations were used, as much for their mood as their content, and anyone present was invited to be marked on the head with ash as a sign of lament and grief. For Christians there were connections with Ash Wednesday but the symbolism was not made explicitly Christian, and some came forward to receive the ash who were not associated with any church. The reading of names had echoes of Remembrance Sunday patterns, but the Lamentations reading and the drumbeat gave a very different feel from the nationalistic mood which sometimes associates itself with Remembrance events. One of those who took part described it as, 'an implicit challenge to the inertia and powerlessness to which we have as a nation succumbed'. Another said, 'It was good to be doing something on that sad and shameful anniversary.' The sense that something was being 'done' is a key connection with other pastoral rites.

This was different from the apt liturgies which develop out of a community group or activity. However, it shares some things in common with apt liturgy, in that it took a God story out of the church building and offered ritual and Christian symbolism in a simple, hospitable way in a public space. In doing so it met a pastoral need for at least some people.

How is apt liturgy different from 'regular' pastoral liturgy?

Let us return to the analogy with the channels of a sound system, which we explored in Chapter 2. There we said that in Sunday

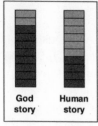

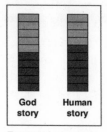

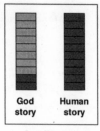

God story	Human story		God story	Human story		God story	Human story
Regular corporate worship			**Pastoral services**			**Apt liturgy**	

Figure 5

worship, the God story is the loudest, with human stories being heard, but normally in a generalized way.

In pastoral services, by contrast, the human story and the God story will often be equally 'loud'. Both will be explicitly and clearly articulated, and then brought together.

In apt liturgy the human story is definitely dominant and clearly articulated. The God story will be present, but it may or may not be explicit, and it may well be much more tentative, because the Church comes to this event, this context, as guest rather than as host. (See Figure 5.)

Here are some other differences which mark out apt liturgy from normal pastoral liturgy.

- It is always *corporate*, not focused on the need of one individual or family.[24]
- There is usually *no existing precedent or expectation* to shape what 'should' happen (or if there is, it is more vague).
- Christian content is therefore more *tentative* – you have to 'earn the right' to speak of Christ.

By definition, there won't be 'ready to use' material in resource books . . . even the more creative books.

---

24 Morisy and Jeffries, 'Apt Liturgy', pp. 61f.

Is it really liturgy?

There is a real question about whether 'apt liturgy' is the right or best term for what is being described. Morisy states: 'Apt liturgy should not be confused with worship.'[25] This feels, at first sight, like an odd statement, because the term liturgy is one that does normally imply worship. However, I think that the point Morisy is making is that though the outward form may be liturgical in the sense that it includes words, symbols and actions, it is not necessarily required that everyone present is offering these to God as an act of worship. The liturgy can be on the outside (as it were) without worship necessarily happening on the inside. The liturgy is a framework which invites worship and makes it possible, but which does not require it.

I think that what she is describing is Christian pastoral ritual in the community, or rather, Christians using ritual and connecting with the Christian story, in the community. The ritual may well be of a low-key and creative sort. There will be some connection with God, though it may also be low-key and even implicit rather than explicit. But it will only be worship in the most general of senses for most of those who take part.

In fact this is not very far from the model of pastoral rites as the Church's gift which I have been offering throughout this book. In a Christian funeral (for instance) the Church offers worship to God in the form of a liturgy. That liturgy provides a framework for understanding a particular pastoral event and invites those involved to connect with that framework and therefore to join the offering of worship: but the liturgy does not depend upon the active worship 'in Spirit and truth' of every participant.

CASE STUDY – Break-up of a team

There is a small team of specialist nurses in an NHS hospital. The team is about to be broken up due to funding issues and staff changes. You, as a Christian (a member of the team? a Minister in Secular Employment? a chaplain?) get the opportunity to help

---

25 Morisy, *Journeying*, p. 157.

the team to mark this change. Other members of the team are not Christians (some may belong to other faith communities). You are not being asked to do a Christian 'service' as such. What 'apt liturgy' might you use?

Think about:

- how to help the team to 'tell their story'
- possible appropriate passages of Scripture (the God story)
- possible symbols/actions/rituals of separation or incorporation
- what will be the liminal moment? What will it do, and how will you mark it?

A starting point here is to spot the parallel with a funeral. This is the closest connection to 'normal' pastoral liturgy, and it is likely that in marking the 'loss' of the team, this will be the model and the expectation most likely to be uppermost in the minds of those taking part.

Telling the human story in a situation like this could be very creative and informal. It might include a sharing of memories verbally, but it might also mean producing a photo-board, or collecting the thank-you cards that have been sent by grateful patients over the years.

Scripture passages might connect with endings, or with being sent out (the disciples heading out to different places?) or the uncertainty about the future (Abraham setting out without knowing where he was going?). Part of the key here is to give attention to what the dominant emotions are likely to be and to make sure that the chosen God story connects with these, rather than choosing something on a more cerebral thematic basis. These passages would not be introduced as 'Bible readings' but the leader might simply say, 'There's a story in the Bible about a man called Abraham, who has to leave the city and way of life he is familiar with and go somewhere new, without knowing where that new place was. I wonder if some of the feelings he had were like the feelings we are experiencing at this time of uncertainty.'

> The liminal moment needs to represent the breaking up of the team, and yet the continuation of their skills and work. The simple act of cutting a cake and everyone sharing a slice (or taking a slice away) might be one way to show this, or a photo-montage could be cut into a jigsaw puzzle with everyone taking a piece.

From Sunday to Monday

We began this book by considering the caring which may take place through Sunday worship. We then recognized that sometimes this is not enough, that caring, to be more effective, needs to be channelled through special services which are in addition to Sunday worship. We took some time exploring some of those more specific services, which we called pastoral rites. I suggested that a good way to view them is as a generous gift and open invitation from the Church.

Finally we have launched out beyond Sunday worship to the world of work and leisure and neighbourliness and to those who are not at all familiar with Sunday worship but who may gain from the Church's experience in handling change in life. We have worked outwards from the core of Sunday worship to the layers of new contexts and forms of pastoral care through ritual and rite. But the journey can work the other way for those we serve. This is what makes this part of the *missio Dei*. Through connecting with others beyond them, people may be helped to connect with the Other beyond us all. By being served in their particular pastoral need, they may come to see how the roadmap of worship may equip them for other contexts in their lives.

If the Church is to be truly missional the focus must always be on the God who reaches out to us, and not simply on getting more people to come to church. But we must never lose sight of the fact that the worship of the Church (and not just in traditional parish or circuit mode), with its regular focus on the living and self-giving God, is itself the surest way to strengthen human persons for all that life throws at them as we await the renewal of all creation when God will be all in all.

Further Reading

General

Herbert Anderson and Edward Foley, *Mighty Stories, Dangerous Rituals: Weaving Together the Human and the Divine*, San Francisco: Jossey-Bass, 2001.

J. L. Austin, *How to Do Things with Words*, Oxford: Clarendon Press, 1962.

Jan Berry, *Ritual Making Women: Shaping Rites for Changing Lives*, London: Equinox, 2009.

Alan Billings, *Secular Lives, Sacred Hearts: The Role of the Church in a Time of No Religion*, London: SPCK, 2004.

Paul Bradbury, *Sowing in Tears: How to Lament in a Church of Praise* (Grove Worship Series 193), Cambridge: Grove Books, 2007.

Paul Bradshaw (ed.), *A Companion to Common Worship*, Vol. 2, London: SPCK, 2006.

Paul F. Bradshaw and Lawrence A. Hoffman (eds), *Life Cycles in Jewish and Christian Worship*, Notre Dame, IN: University of Notre Dame Press, 1996.

Paul Bradshaw and Paul Melloh (eds), *Foundations in Ritual Studies: A Reader for Students of Christian Worship*, London: SPCK, 2007.

Stephen Burns, *SCM Studyguide to Liturgy*, London: SCM Press, 2006.

Stephen Burns, Nicola Slee and Michael N. Jagessar (eds), *The Edge of God: New Liturgical Texts and Contexts in Conversation*, London: Epworth, 2008.

Wesley Carr, *Brief Encounters: Pastoral Ministry Through the Occasional Offices*, London: SPCK, 1985 (2nd ed. 1994).

Neville Clark, *Pastoral Care in Context: An Essay in Pastoral Theology*, Bury St Edmunds: Kevin Mayhew, 1992.

Jim Clarke, *Creating Rituals: A New Way of Healing for Everyday Life*, Malwah, NJ: Paulist Press, 2011.

Neil Dixon, *Wonder, Love and Praise: A Companion to the Methodist Worship Book*, Peterborough: Epworth Press, 2003.

Mary Douglas, *Natural Symbols: Explorations in Cosmology*, London: Routledge, 1996.

Mark Earey, *Finding Your Way Around Common Worship: A Simple Guide*, London: Church House Publishing, 2011.

Mark Earey, *How to Choose Songs and Hymns for Worship* (Grove Worship Series 201), Cambridge: Grove Books, 2009.

Mark Earey, *Leading Worship* (Grove Worship Series 152), Cambridge: Grove Books, 1999.

Mark Earey and Carolyn Headley, *Mission and Liturgical Worship* (Grove Worship Series 170), Cambridge: Grove Books, 2002.

Mark Earey and Gilly Myers (eds), *Common Worship Today: Study Edition*, Nottingham: St John's Extension Studies, 2007.

Arnold van Gennep, translated by Monika B. Vizedom and Gabrielle L. Caffee, *The Rites of Passage*, London: Routledge, 1977.

Elaine Graham and Margaret Halsey (eds), *Life Cycles: Women and Pastoral Care*, London: SPCK, 1993.

Roger Grainger, *The Language of the Rite*, London: Darton, Longman and Todd, 1974.

Roger Grainger, *The Message of the Rite: The Significance of Christian Rites of Passage*, Cambridge: Lutterworth Press, 1988.

Robin Green, *Only Connect: Worship and Liturgy from the Perspective of Pastoral Care*, London: Darton, Longman and Todd, 1987.

Ronald L. Grimes, *Deeply into the Bone: Re-inventing Rites of Passage*, Berkeley, CA: University of California Press, 2002.

Christopher Irvine (ed.), *The Use of Symbols in Worship* (Alcuin Liturgy Guides 4), London: SPCK, 2007.

Liam Kelly, *Sacraments Revisited: What Do They Mean Today?*, London: Darton, Longman and Todd, 1998.

Gordon Lathrop, *Holy Things: A Liturgical Theology*, Minneapolis: Fortress Press, 1998.

Joseph Martos, *Doors to the Sacred: A Historical Guide to the Sacraments of the Christian Church*, London: SCM Press, 1980.

Edwin Muir, *Ritual in Early Modern Europe*, Cambridge: Cambridge University Press, 2nd ed. 2005.

Neil Pembroke, *Pastoral Care in Worship: Liturgy and Psychology in Dialogue*, London: T&T Clark, 2010.

Michael Perham, *The New Handbook of Pastoral Liturgy*, London: SPCK, 2000.

David Power and Luis Maldonado (eds), *Liturgy and Human Passage* (*Concilium* 112), New York: Seabury Press, 1979.

Elaine Ramshaw, *Ritual and Pastoral Care*, Philadelphia: Fortress Press, 1987.

Frank C. Senn, *The People's Work: A Social History of the Liturgy*, Minneapolis: Fortress Press, 2006.

David Stancliffe, *God's Pattern: Shaping our Worship, Ministry and Life*, London: SPCK, 2003.

A. C. Thiselton, *Language, Liturgy and Meaning* (Grove Liturgical Studies 2), Nottingham: Grove Books, 1975.

Ross Thompson, *SCM Studyguide to the Sacraments*, London: SCM Press, 2006.

Victor Turner, *The Ritual Process: Structure and Anti-structure*, London: Routledge, 1969.

Leslie Virgo (ed.), *First Aid in Pastoral Care*, Edinburgh: T&T Clark, 1987.

Janet R. Walton, *Feminist Liturgy: A Matter of Justice*, Collegeville, MN: Liturgical Press, 2000.

Fraser Watts and Liz Gulliford (eds), *Forgiveness in Context: Theology and Psychology in Creative Dialogue*, London: T&T Clark, 2004.

John H. Westerhoff III and William H. Willimon, *Liturgy and Learning Through the Life Cycle*, Akron, OH: OSL Publications, revised ed. 1994.

William H. Willimon, *Worship as Pastoral Care*, Nashville: Abingdon, 1979.

Service books and liturgical resources (general)

For liturgical resources relating to specific services, see also below under the particular chapter headings

Anglican Church of Canada, *The Book of Alternative Services of The Anglican Church of Canada*, Toronto: Anglican Book Centre, 1985.

Anglican Church of Canada, *Occasional Celebrations of the Anglican Church of Canada*, Toronto: Anglican Book Centre, 1992.

Baptist Union of Great Britain, Christopher Ellis and Myra Blyth (eds), *Gathering for Worship: Patterns and Prayers for the Community of Disciples*, Norwich: Canterbury Press, 2005.

Jan Brind and Tessa Wilkinson in the series, *Creative Ideas for Pastoral Liturgy*, Norwich: Canterbury Press, from 2008 onwards.

Ruth Burgess, *A Book of Blessings and How to Write Your Own*, Glasgow: Wild Goose Publications, 2001.

Raymond Chapman, *A Pastoral Prayer Book: Prayers and Readings for Times of Change, Concern and Celebration*, Norwich: Canterbury Press, 1998.

Church of England, *The Book of Common Prayer*, 1662.

Church of England, *Common Worship: Christian Initiation*, London: Church House Publishing, 2006.

Church of England, *Common Worship: Pastoral Ministry Companion*, London: Church House Publishing, 2012.

Church of England, *Common Worship: Pastoral Services*, London: Church House Publishing, 2nd ed. 2005.

Church of England, *Common Worship: Services and Prayers for the Church of England*, London: Church House Publishing, 2000.

Church of Scotland, *Book of Common Order of the Church of Scotland*, Edinburgh: St Andrew Press, 1994.

Church of the Province of New Zealand, *A New Zealand Prayer Book; He Karakia Mihinare o Aotearoa*, Auckland, London: Collins, Collins Liturgical, 1989.

Richard Deadman, Jeremy Fletcher, Janet Henderson and Stephen Oliver (eds), *Pastoral Prayers: A Resource for Pastoral Occasions*, London: Mowbray, 1996.

Roger Grainger, *Staging Posts: Rites of Passage for Contemporary Christians*, Braunton, Devon: Merlin Books, 1987.

John Leach and Liz Simpson, *'Bless this House'* (Grove Worship Series 204), Cambridge: Grove Books, 2010.

Andrew Linzey, *Animal Rites: Liturgies of Animal Care*, London: SCM Press, 1999.

Dorothy McRae-McMahon, *Liturgies for the Journey of Life*, London: SPCK, 2000.

Dorothy McRae-McMahon, *Prayers for Life's Particular Moments*, London: SPCK, 2001.

Methodist Church, *Methodist Worship Book*, Peterborough: Methodist Publishing House, 1999.

Diann L. Neu, *Women's Rites: Feminist Liturgies for Life's Journey*, Cleveland, OH: Pilgrim Press, 2003.

Roman Catholic Church, *The Rites of the Catholic Church: The Roman Ritual, Revised by Decree of the Second Vatican Ecumenical Council and Published by Authority of Pope Paul VI*, New York: Pueblo, 1976.

Rosemary Radford Ruether, *Women-Church: Theology and Practice of Feminist Liturgical Communities*, San Francisco: Harper and Row, 1985.

The Episcopal Church of the USA, *The Book of Occasional Services*, New York: The Church Hymnal Corporation, 2nd ed. 1988.

United Reformed Church, *Worship from the United Reformed Church*, London: United Reformed Church, Part 1–2003 & Part 2–2004.

Hannah Ward and Jennifer Wild, *Human Rites: Worship Resources for an Age of Change*, London: Mowbray, 1995.

Hannah Ward, Jennifer Wild and Janet Morley (eds), *Celebrating Women*, London: SPCK, 2nd ed. 1995.

Birth rites

Mark Earey, Trevor Lloyd and Ian Tarrant (eds), *Connecting with Baptism: A Practical Guide to Christian Initiation Today*, London: Church House Publishing, 2007.

Ron Grove, 'Baby dedication in traditional Christianity: Eastern Orthodox "churching" of forty-day-olds', *Journal of Ecumenical Studies*, 27, No. 1, Winter 1990, pp. 101–7.

Natalie Knödel, 'Reconsidering an obsolete rite: The Churching of Women and feminist liturgical theology', *Feminist Theology*, 14, Jan. 1997, pp. 106–25.

Trevor Lloyd, *Thanksgiving for the Gift of a Child: A Commentary on the Common Worship Service* (Grove Worship Series 165), Cambridge: Grove Books, 2001.

Joanne M. Pierce, '"Green Women" and blood pollution: Some medieval rituals for the churching of women after childbirth', *Studia Liturgica*, 29, 1999, pp. 191–215.

Marriage

Jan Brind and Tessa Wilkinson, *Creative Ideas for Pastoral Liturgy: Marriage Services, Wedding Blessings and Anniversary Thanksgivings*, Norwich: Canterbury Press, 2009.

Church of England, *Marriage: A Teaching Document from the House of Bishops*, London: Church House Publishing, 1999.

Church of England, *Marriage in Church after Divorce: A Discussion Document from a Working Party Commissioned by the House of Bishops* (GS 1361), London: Church House Publishing, 2000.

Bufford Coe, *John Wesley and Marriage*, London: Associated University Presses, 1996.

Susan Durber (ed.), *As Man and Woman Made: Theological Reflections on Marriage*, London: URC, 1994.

Joint Liturgical Group, *An Order of Marriage for Christians from Different Churches*, Norwich: Canterbury Press, 1999.

Mark Jordan (ed.), *Authorizing Marriage: Canon, Tradition, and Critique in the Blessing of Same-sex Unions*, Princeton, NJ: Princeton University Press, 2006.

Stephen Lake, *Using Common Worship: Marriage*, London: Church House Publishing, 2000.

Stephen Lake, *Welcoming Marriage: A Practical and Pastoral Guide to the New Legislation*, London: Church House Publishing, 2009.

Trevor Lloyd, 'The Church's Mission and Contemporary Culture in the Making of the *Common Worship* Marriage Liturgy', *Anaphora*, Vol. 2, Part 2, 2010, pp. 55–68.

German Martinez, *Worship: Wedding to Marriage*, Washington, DC: Pastoral Press, 1993.

Methodist Church, *Vows and Partings: Services for the Reaffirmation of Marriage Vows and Suggestions of How to Pray When Relationships Change or End*, Peterborough: Methodist Publishing House, 2001.

Charles Read, *Revising Weddings* (Grove Worship Series 128), Nottingham: Grove Books, 1994.

Charles Read and Anna de Lange, *Common Worship Marriage* (Grove Worship Series 162), Cambridge: Grove Books, 2001.

Kenneth Stevenson, *Nuptial Blessing: A Study of Christian Marriage Rites* (Alcuin Club Collections 64), London: SPCK, 1982.

Kenneth Stevenson, *To Join Together: The Rite of Marriage*, New York: Pueblo, 1987.

Kenneth Stevenson, *Worship: Wonderful and Sacred Mystery*, Washington, DC: Pastoral Press, 1992.

Kenneth Stevenson (ed.), *Anglican Marriage Rites: A Symposium* (Alcuin/GROW Joint Liturgical Studies 71), Norwich: Hymns Ancient and Modern, 2011.

Adrian Thatcher, *Marriage after Modernity: Christian Marriage in Postmodern Times*, Sheffield: Sheffield Academic Press, 1999.

Healing and wholeness

David Atkinson, 'The Christian Church and the Ministry of Healing', *Anvil*, 10, No. 1, 1993, pp. 25–42.

David Atkinson, *The Church's Healing Ministry: Practical and Pastoral Reflections*, Norwich: Canterbury Press, 2011.

Colin Buchanan, *Services for Wholeness and Healing: The Common Worship Orders* (Grove Worship Series 161), Cambridge: Grove Books, 2000.

Church of England, *A Time to Heal: A Report by the House of Bishops on the Healing Ministry*, London: Church House Publishing, 2000.

Ian Cowie, *Prayers and Ideas for Healing Services*, Glasgow: Wild Goose Publications, 1995.

Andrew Daunton-Fear, *Healing in the Early Church: The Church's Ministry of Healing and Exorcism from the First to the Fifth Century*, Milton Keynes: Paternoster, 2009.

Martin Dudley and Geoffrey Rowell (eds), *Confession and Absolution*, London: SPCK, 1990.

Martin Dudley and Geoffrey Rowell (eds), *The Oil of Gladness: Anointing in the Christian Tradition*, London: SPCK, 1993.

Peter E. Fink (ed.), *Alternative Futures for Worship Vol. 7 – Anointing of the Sick*, Collegeville, MN: Liturgical Press, 1987.

Christopher Gower, *Sacraments of Healing*, London: SPCK, 2007.

David Gregg, *Ministry to the Sick: An Introduction* (Grove Ministry and Worship Series 58), Bramcote: Grove Books, 1978.

David Gregg, *Penance* (Grove Ministry and Worship Series 53), Bramcote: Grove Books, 1977.

John Gunstone, *Healed, Restored, Forgiven: Liturgies, Prayers and Readings for the Ministry of Healing*, Norwich: Canterbury Press, 2004.

Charles W. Gusmer, *The Ministry of Healing in the Church of England: An Ecumenical-Liturgical Study*, Great Wakering: Mayhew-McCrimmon / Alcuin Club, 1974.

Robert Hannaford, *Penance and Absolution: Celebrating the Sacrament of Reconciliation* (*Derek Allen Lecture*), Colchester: Centre for Theology and Society in the University of Essex, 2001.

Carolyn Headley, *The Laying on of Hands and Anointing in Ministry for Wholeness and Healing* (Grove Worship Series 172), Cambridge: Grove Books, 2002.

John Leach, *Developing Prayer Ministry: A New Introduction for Churches* (Grove Renewal Series 1), Cambridge: Grove Books, 2000.

Trevor Lloyd and Phillip Tovey (eds), *Celebrating Forgiveness: An Original Text Drafted by Michael Vasey* (Alcuin/GROW Joint Liturgical Studies 58), Cambridge: Grove Books, 2004.

Francis MacNutt, *Healing*, Notre Dame, IN: Ave Maria Press, 1974.

Morris Maddocks, *The Christian Healing Ministry*, London: SPCK, 3rd ed. 1995.

Methodist Church, *The Church and the Ministry of Healing: A Statement Adopted by the Methodist Conference of 1977*, London: Methodist Conference Office, 1977.

Methodist Church, *Guidelines for Good Practice for Those Involved in the Christian Healing Ministry, Including a Code of Conduct*, Peterborough: Methodist Publishing House, 1997.

Bruce T. Morrill, *Divine Worship and Human Healing: Liturgical Theology at the Margins of Life and Death*, Collegeville, MN: Liturgical Press, 2009.

Mark Morton, *Personal Confession Reconsidered: Making Forgiveness Real* (Grove Spirituality Series 50), Nottingham: Grove Books, 1994.

Amanda Porterfield, *Healing in the History of Christianity*, Oxford: Oxford University Press, 2005.

Elizabeth Stuart, 'The Sacrament of Unction', in Jonathan Baxter (ed.), *Wounds that Heal: Theology, Imagination and Health*, London: SPCK, 2007.

Max Thurian, *Confession*, London: SCM Press, 1958.

Phillip Tovey, David Kennedy and Andrew Atherstone, *Common Worship Reconciliation and Restoration: A Commentary* (Grove Worship Series 187), Cambridge: Grove Books, 2006.

Funerals

Jan Brind and Tessa Wilkinson, *Creative Ideas for Pastoral Liturgy: Funeral, Memorial and Thanksgiving Services*, Norwich: Canterbury Press, 2008.

Churches' Funerals Group, *Funeral Services of the Christian Churches in England*, Norwich: Canterbury Press, 4th ed. 2009.

Christopher Cocksworth, *Prayer and the Departed* (Grove Worship Series 142), Cambridge: Grove Books, 1997.

J. Douglas Davies, *Cremation Today and Tomorrow* (Alcuin/GROW Joint Liturgical Studies 16), Nottingham: Grove Books, 1990.

Douglas Davies, *Death, Ritual and Belief: The Rhetoric of Funeral Rites*, London: Continuum, 2nd ed. 2002.

Douglas Davies, *The Theology of Death*, London: T&T Clark, 2008.

Donald Gray, *Memorial Services* (Alcuin Liturgy Guides 1), London: SPCK, 2002.

R. Anne Horton, *Using Common Worship: Funerals*, London: Church House Publishing, 2000.

Hugh James, *A Fitting End: Making the Most of a Funeral*, Norwich: Canterbury Press, 2004.

Peter C. Jupp, *From Dust to Ashes: Cremation and the British Way of Death*, Basingstoke: Palgrave Macmillan, 2006.

Peter C. Jupp (ed.), *Death our Future: Christian Theology and Pastoral Practice in Funeral Ministry*, London: Epworth, 2008.

Peter C. Jupp and Tony Rogers (eds), *Interpreting Death: Christian Theology and Pastoral Practice*, London: Cassell, 1997.

Trevor Lloyd, *Dying and Death Step by Step: A Funerals Flowchart* (Grove Worship Series 160), Cambridge: Grove Books, 2000.

Thomas G. Long, *Accompany Them with Singing: The Christian Funeral*, Louisville, KY: Westminster John Knox, 2009.

Jean Mayland ed., *Beyond our Tears: Resources for Times of Remembrance*, London: CTBI, 2004.

Michael Perham, *The Communion of Saints: The Place of the Christian Dead in the Belief, Worship and Calendars of the Church* (Alcuin Club Collections 62), London: SPCK, 1980.

Roman Catholic Church, *Order of Christian Funerals*, London: Geoffrey Chapman, 1990.

D. G. Rowell, *The Liturgy of Christian Burial*, London: SPCK, 1977.

Richard Rutherford, *The Death of a Christian: The Rite of Funerals*, New York: Pueblo, 1980.

Paul Sheppy, *Death Liturgy and Ritual. Volume 1: A Pastoral and Liturgical Theology*, Aldershot: Ashgate, 2003.

Paul Sheppy, *Death Liturgy and Ritual. Volume 2: A Commentary on Liturgical Texts*, Aldershot: Ashgate, 2004.

Paul Sheppy, *In Sure and Certain Hope: Liturgies, Prayers and Readings for Funerals and Memorials*, Norwich: Canterbury Press, 2003.

Tony Walter, *Funerals and How to Improve Them*, London: Hodder & Stoughton, 1990.

N. T. Wright, *For All the Saints? – Remembering the Christian Departed*, London: SPCK, 2003.

Moving on and out

Ann Morisy, *Beyond the Good Samaritan: Community Ministry and Mission*, London: Mowbray, 1997.

Ann Morisy, *Journeying Out: A New Approach to Christian Mission*, London: Morehouse, 2004.

Ann Morisy and Ann Jeffries, 'Apt Liturgy: To lift eyes above the horizon', in Tim Stratford (ed.), *Worship, Window of the Urban Church*, London: SPCK, 2006.

Copyright Acknowledgements

Index